THE

APOSTLE

ALSO BY JOHN POLLOCK

Biography

The Master: A Life of Jesus

The Cambridge Seven

Way to Glory (Havelock of Lucknow)

Hudson Taylor and Maria

D. L. Moody: Moody without Sankey

Billy Graham: The Authorized Biography (1966)

Billy Graham: Evangelist to the World (1979)

The Billy Graham Story (1985, 2003)

A Foreign Devil in China (L. Nelson Bell)

George Whitefield

Wilberforce

The Siberian Seven

Amazing Grace: John Newton's Story

Shaftesbury: The Poor Man's Earl

Fear No Foe: A Brother's Story

Gordon of Khartoum

Kitchener

History and Travel

A Cambridge Movement

Shadows Fall Apart

The Good Seed

Earth's Remotest End

The Keswick Story

The Faith of the Russian Evangelicals

THE
APOSTLE

A Life of Paul

JOHN POLLOCK

DAVID C COOK
transforming lives together

THE APOSTLE
Published by David C Cook
4050 Lee Vance Drive
Colorado Springs, CO 80918 U.S.A.

Integrity Music Limited, a Division of David C Cook
Brighton, East Sussex BN1 2RE, England

The graphic circle C logo is a registered trademark of David C Cook.

Library of Congress Control Number 2011938162
ISBN 978-0-7814-0573-7
eISBN 978-1-4347-0324-8

© 1969, 2012 John Pollock
First edition published by Hodder & Stoughton (British edition)
and Doubleday (US edition) in 1969 © John Pollock.

The Team: Richard Herkes, Amy Konyndyk, Jack Campbell, Karen Athen
Cover Design: Nick Lee
Cover Photo: Shutterstock

Printed in the United States of America
Third Edition 2012

11 12 13 14 15 16 17 18 16 17

122121

CONTENTS

PART THREE: LEAST OF THE APOSTLES
Map: Paul's Second Missionary Journey

PART FOUR: TO CAESAR YOU WILL GO
Map: Paul's Third Journey and His Journey to Rome

PREFACE

One of the most frequently mentioned figures in history, whose writings are read by millions every day, is little known to this generation as a person. The name of Saint Paul the Apostle is familiar to all Christians, to most Jews and Muslims; he is quoted, argued about, attacked, and defended. Yet even those who read his words and adventures with unfailing regularity have scant idea of what he was like—as I found for myself when my publisher suggested I write a life of Paul.

Many recall only one book about him: H. V. Morton's deservedly famous *In the Steps of St. Paul*. But that was a travelogue, not a biography, and written in the very different conditions of the mid-1930s. So the man or woman of today, whether Bible reader or not, misses the fascination of knowing Paul as Luke or Timothy or the objectionable Elymas knew him.

I felt therefore that it would not be impertinent to approach Paul as I did my previous biographies. As a biographer who has enjoyed the intense satisfaction of getting closer to his subjects, I decided to accept the New Testament as I had accepted the boxes of letters and papers that had formed the source material of my other subjects, use it in the same way, and see what happened. A biographer develops a nose, a sort of instinct, and it was not long before I was struck inescapably by the credibility, the genuineness of the person who was emerging from the Acts of the Apostles and the Epistles taken as a whole. A convincing character, with a completely credible if astonishingly unusual story, was taking hold of me, until I found more and more excitement in getting nearer the heart of the man. I have been familiar with the Bible since childhood, but now I was seeing Paul as if for the first time: his motives, aims, and priorities; what mattered to him and what he was indifferent to; his attitude toward his mistakes when he recognized them. And what he was willing to die for.

I began to learn his contemporaries' view of him. There have been plenty of opinions ever since. Nietzsche called him "one of the most ambitious of men, whose superstition was only equaled by his cunning; a much tortured, much to be pitied man, an exceedingly unpleasant person both to himself and to others." Farrar, the Victorian dean, portrayed him as loftily superior, disdaining mortal weaknesses above ordinary passions, a saint in cold marble. Basil Matthews made him a muscular Christian, a boy's hero. None of these Pauls resembled the man I was getting to know, neither as I studied the New Testament and many other writings nor as I drove my Volkswagen along the roads he had walked two thousand years before.

As any writer on Paul must, I have dug into the enormous and ever-growing mass of scholarship about him and his background, but since I write for the general reader I have not burdened the narrative with the arguments that led to my conclusions. In regard to the gaps in Paul's life, I have sought to introduce nothing that cannot be deduced from the evidence and have aimed at inference rather than conjecture. There is a world of difference between inference and conjecture, and imagination must not roam at the cost of authenticity.

Paul lived about sixty-seven generations back—just twice as long ago as the Norman Conquest of Britain, or five times the European colonization of the Americas. He has more than ever a contemporary interest. Recent radical thinkers have attracted the popular press because they are exciting; Paul is far more exciting and radical. I have tried to make him and his amazing story freshly alive to those for whom he is nothing except the man who wrote the chapter on charity and to those who read him frequently, whether Protestant, Catholic, Orthodox, or the Jews for whom he had such unbreakable love.

When I had finished writing, I felt rather as when nearing the summit of a high mountain. You recognize other routes up; you realize how little you know of the terrain. Yet you get a grand view—of the mountain and of the world around.

But I have not reached the top. There are some unattainable crags just below the summit.

ACKNOWLEDGMENTS

I am extremely grateful to the late Dr. F. F. Bruce, Rylands Professor of Biblical Criticism and Exegesis at the University of Manchester, who encouraged me from the start, shared his great knowledge of Paul and his background, and later read my typescript, making valuable corrections and suggestions.

My thanks also go to the following, who likewise read the typescript to my great benefit:

The late Dr. Frank E. Gaebelein, headmaster of Stony Brook School; the late Dr. L. Nelson Bell, surgeon and medical missionary in China and later moderator of the Presbyterian Church of the United States; and the late Sir Richard Barrett-Lennard, Bt., OBE, KStJ, my father-in-law, vice president of the Norwich Union insurance society.

I would also like to thank my nephew, Mr. Hugh Priestley, who sifted out phrases and allusions that were suitable at the time of first publication, but no longer.

My warm thanks to all who aided us on our travels in the Holy Land and other Middle East countries, and in Turkey, Greece, and Italy; especially Dr. Wilhelm Alzinger of the Austrian Archaeological Institute, director of research at Ephesus; the Rt. Rev. Abbot Brookes, OSB, of Rome; Mr. Courtenay Edwards, motoring correspondent of the *Sunday Telegraph*, London; Mr. F. J. Parkhouse and Mr. J. Wilcox of Exeter; and Miss Louise A. Shier, curator of the Kelsey Museum of Archaeology, University of Michigan.

And finally, a warm thank-you to the Rt. Revd. Timothy Dudley-Smith for his encouragement all through.

John Pollock

PART ONE

THE PURSUER
PURSUED

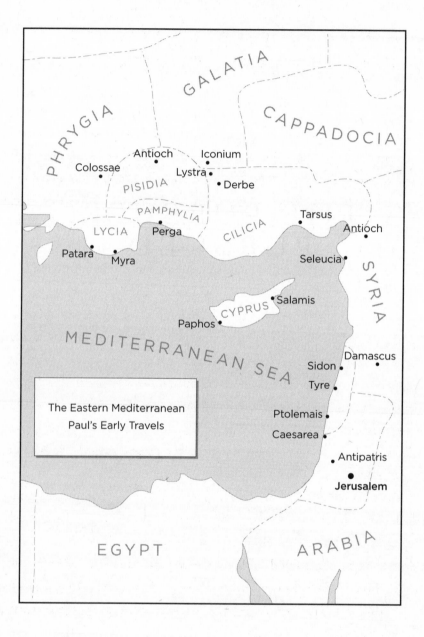

The Eastern Mediterranean
Paul's Early Travels

ONE

FROM THE LAND OF BLACK TENTS

The judges leaped from their places in fury. The Hall of Polished Stones, scene of grave debates and historic trials, reverberated to the baying of a lynch crowd that rushed at the young defendant and manhandled him down the steps into the strong sunlight of the Court of the Priests. Across this wide, open space, down more steps, through court after court, Stephen was swept by judges, bystanders, worshippers, and traders, until they had him out of the sacred temple precincts and into the streets of the Holy City.

No sentence of death had been passed, nor could be executed unless confirmed by the Roman authorities after a solemn ritual to ensure justice to the last. But judges and mob cared nothing for that. When the northern gate was behind them and they reached the Rock of Execution, "twice the height of a man," they should have solemnly stripped him and thrown him cleanly over to break his neck, or at least to stun him, so that death by stoning would not be too unmerciful. But they did not. Instead they pushed Stephen down as he was, his tangled clothes breaking the fall, and he staggered to his feet fully conscious.

The mob was shocked into reverting to forms of law. In a judicial stoning the first stones must be aimed by those who had brought the charges. These witnesses therefore elbowed their way to the front, threw off their outer clothes, and looked around for someone to guard them. A young lawyer, panting from the race through the streets, stepped forward. They recognized the Pharisee from Cilicia in Asia Minor, known as Saul among the Jews and Paul among Greeks and Romans.

Paul watched approvingly as each witness picked up a heavy, jagged stone, raised it above his head, and threw it to gash and maim the man below.

Then Paul heard Stephen's voice. Pained but clear, he spoke as if to someone invisible yet close: "Lord Jesus, receive my spirit."

Stones showered as the mob scrambled to complete what the witnesses had begun. Stephen mastered his pain while blood gushed from cuts and bruises. He knelt down in an attitude of prayer. Paul could not miss the words that came with surprising volume for a dying man: "Lord, do not hold this sin against them."

The next stone knocked Stephen flat. He lost consciousness. The mob continued stoning until the body became obscene.

Paul was born in a city between the mountains and the sea. The year was probably AD 1, but all early details are shadowy except his clear claim: "I am a Jew of Tarsus, a citizen of no mean city, of the people of Israel, of the tribe of Benjamin, a Hebrew born of Hebrews."

Tarsus was the principal city of the lush plain of Cilicia in the southwest corner of Asia Minor. The sea lay out of sight a dozen miles south. The Taurus mountains curved in a great arc some twenty-five miles inland, coming nearly to the sea on the west and marked to the north by gorges and cliffs that stood like rock fortresses before the snows; a magnificent background for childhood, especially in winter when the snow showed smooth on cloudless peaks.

The river Cydnus, narrow and swift, and usually brilliantly clear, ran through the city. It flowed into the artificial harbor, an engineering masterpiece of the ancient world, where Cleopatra had stepped ashore some forty years before Paul's birth to meet Antony, while all Tarsus marveled at silver oars, a poop deck of beaten gold, and purple sails "so perfumed that the winds were lovesick with them." Here, each spring when navigation resumed and the mountain pass thawed, slaves unloaded goods of the Orient. The city grew full of noise, smell, and prosperous bustle. Caravans set off due north up the Roman road and crossed the mountains by the Cilician Gates, a crevice that had been chiseled wide enough for a wagon—another feat of ancient Tarsian engineering.

Tarsus was a fusion of civilizations at peace under the rule of Rome: indigenous Cilicians; Hittites whose ancestors had once ruled Asia Minor; light-skinned Greeks; Assyrians and Persians; and Macedonians who had come with Alexander the Great on his march to India. After the carve-up of Alexander's empire, when Tarsus became part of the kingdom of the Seleucids who ruled from Syria, King Antiochus IV settled a colony of Jews about 170 BC. They had rights and privileges, and a determination never to marry into those outside their faith and blood, whom collectively they called Gentiles (meaning "nations" or "Greeks"). Paul's ancestors probably were among them. They may have sprung from an obscure town called Gischala in Galilee.

His father most likely was a master tentmaker, whose craftsmen worked in leather and in *cilicium*, a cloth woven from the hair of the large long-haired black goats that grazed (as they still do) on the slopes of the Taurus. The black tents of Tarsus were used by caravans, nomads, and armies all over Asia Minor and Syria. Of Paul's mother nothing is known; he never mentions her. Perhaps she died in his infancy or became alienated in some way, but he may simply have had no particular occasion to do so. He had at least one sister. His father must have been a citizen or burgess of Tarsus and obviously wealthy, for in a reform fifteen years earlier the rank of citizen had been removed from all householders without considerable fortune or property. Moreover, the family held the coveted title Citizens of Rome. At that period the *civis Romanus* was seldom granted except for services rendered or for a fat fee. Whether Paul's grandfather aided Pompey or Cicero when Rome first governed Cilicia, or whether his father paid money, the Roman citizenship conferred local distinction and hereditary privileges, which each member could claim wherever he traveled throughout the empire.

Roman citizenship also meant that Paul had a full Latin name, which would have been threefold (like Gaius Julius Caesar). The first two names were common to all the family (in Caesar's case Gaius Julius), but in Paul's

case these are lost because his Greek colleague first wrote his life story and no
Greek could understand Latin names. The third, the personal *cognomen*, was
Paullus. He was given also a Jewish name at the rite of circumcision on the
eighth day after birth: "Saul," chosen either for its meaning, "asked for," or in
honor of the most famous Benjamite in history, King Saul.

Saul was the name used at home and emphasized that the Jewish
inheritance meant the most in early years. Gentiles were all around, and
the columns of pagan temples dominated the marketplace. Nineveh of the
Assyrians, Babylon, Athens, and Rome had combined to create Tarsus, and
Paul was unconsciously the child of his Oriental-Hellenic world. In his youth
it seemed remote, for although many Jews throughout the Mediterranean
had been influenced by the Greek view of life, Paul's parents were Pharisees,
members of the party most fervent in Jewish nationalism and strict in obedience to the Law of Moses. They sought to guard their offspring against
contamination. Friendships with Gentile children were discouraged. Greek
ideas were despised. Though Paul from infancy could speak Greek, the *lingua
franca*, and had a working knowledge of Latin, his family at home spoke
Aramaic, a derivative of Hebrew, the language of Judea.

They looked to Jerusalem as Islam looks to Mecca. Their privileges as
freemen of Tarsus and Roman citizens were nothing to the high honor of
being Israelites, the people of promise, to whom alone the living God had
revealed His glory and His plans.

The school attached to the Tarsus synagogue taught nothing but the
Hebrew text of the sacred Law. Each boy repeated its phrases in chorus after
the *hazzan*, or synagogue keeper, until vowels, accent, and rhythm were
precisely correct. Paul learned to write the Hebrew characters accurately on
papyrus, thus gradually forming his own rolls of the Scriptures. His father
would have presented him with another set of rolls, on vellum: the Greek
translation of the Old Testament known as the Septuagint, from which the
set readings were taken in synagogue each Sabbath. By his thirteenth birthday
Paul had mastered Jewish history, the poetry of the psalms, and the majestic

literature of the prophets. His ear had been trained to the very pitch of accuracy, and a swift brain like his could retain what he heard as instantly and faithfully as a modern "photographic mind" retains a printed page. He was ready for higher education.

Tarsus had its own university, famous for local students such as Athenodorus, the tutor and confidant of the emperor Augustus, and the equally eminent Nestor, both of whom had returned in old age to be the most distinguished citizens in Paul's boyhood. But a strict Pharisee would not embroil his son in pagan moral philosophy. (Such studies would have to come later.) So, probably in the year that Augustus died, AD 14, the adolescent Paul was sent by sea to Palestine and climbed the hills to Jerusalem.

During the next five or six years, he sat at the feet of Gamaliel, grandson of Hillel, the supreme teacher who a few years earlier had died at the age of more than a hundred. Under the fragile, gentle Gamaliel, a contrast with the leaders of the rival School of Shammai, Paul learned to dissect a text until scores of possible meanings were disclosed according to the considered opinion of generations of rabbis. These had obscured the original sense by layers of tradition to protect an Israelite from the least possible infringement of the Law and, illogically, to help him avoid its inconveniences. Paul learned to debate in the question-and-answer style known to the ancient world as the diatribe, and to expound, for a rabbi was not only part preacher but also part lawyer, ready to prosecute or defend those accused of breaking the sacred Law.

Paul outstripped his contemporaries. He had a powerful mind, which could have led to a seat on the Sanhedrin in the Hall of Polished Stones and made him a "ruler of the Jews." The state was a theocracy, in which religious and national leaders were identical, so that the seventy-one members of the Sanhedrin were equally judges, senators, and spiritual masters. The court was supreme in all religious decisions and in what little self-government the Romans allowed. Some of its members were drawn from the hereditary priesthood. Others were lawyers and rabbis.

Before Paul could hope to be a master in Israel, he had to master a trade, for every Jew was bred to a trade, and in theory no rabbi took fees but rather supported himself. Paul therefore left Jerusalem in his early twenties. Had he been there during the ministry of Jesus of Nazareth, he would surely mention having argued against Him like other Pharisees did; in later years he spoke often of the death of Jesus by crucifixion but never as an eyewitness. Paul probably returned to Tarsus to work in the family tentmaking business and resumed the old routine: winter and spring in Tarsus until the plain grew steamy and malarial, then the summer city in the Taurus foothills. Winter or summer he would have taught in synagogue.

A hint in one of his letters suggests he was strongly missionary-minded. Wherever Jews worshipped, Gentile sympathizers were admitted as "God-fearers." Pharisees like Paul urged God-fearers to become proselytes, full Jews: to submit to the simple but painful rite of circumcision, and thereafter to honor the ceremonial and personal demands of the Law in all its rigor. The burden might be heavy but the reward would be great, as they earned the favor of God. Paul's father could take full and justified delight in this son who had followed in his steps as a Pharisee and had the intellectual force to reach the highest office in Israel.

Soon after his thirtieth birthday, Paul returned to Jerusalem—with or without a wife. He almost certainly had been married. Jews rarely remained celibate, and parenthood was a qualification required of candidates for the Sanhedrin. Yet Paul's wife is never mentioned in his writings. He may have suffered bereavement, losing not only his wife but an only child, for in later years, though he seemed impatient with women as a sex, he displayed gentleness toward individuals and an understanding of marriage, which belie his being a misogamist or misogynist; and he virtually adopted the young man Timothy as if to replace a son.

More likely his wife and family returned with Paul. In Jerusalem they could discharge the Law's more complicated and praiseworthy obligations and display zeal where it would be noticed.

There Paul could also combat the movement launched by Jesus of Nazareth. Tarsus must have heard echoes of the teaching and claims of the new prophet. And strange reports of miracles. Even a tale that He had risen from the dead.

TWO

STEPHEN

Compared with the marble and gold terraces of the temple, the synagogue in Jerusalem for Jews from Cilicia was small and austere, and cool despite the summer sun. The men sat on stone benches along the walls, beneath columns that supported the women's galleries. The elders faced the congregation. Near them stood a small platform and beside it the seven-branched candlestick and the veiled chest or "ark" for the Scrolls of the Law. Here the Law was read aloud and expounded by any whom the elders might invite. Paul accepted such an invitation as his due.

In Jerusalem there was no lack of candidates; he had to listen more than he spoke, and so he happened to hear a disciple of Jesus named Stephen.

Stephen and Paul were probably much the same age—the Greek word translated "young man," with which the historian Luke introduces Paul, denotes a male between youth and forty. Stephen's birthplace is unknown, for Jews from Egypt and elsewhere used the same synagogue as Cilicians, but he spoke Greek as fluently as Aramaic. Both men were quick thinkers, powerful minds, able controversialists. No tradition remains of Stephen's physique. Paul is believed to have been short, though he held himself well enough to stand out in a crowd. His face was rather oval with beetling eyebrows and fleshy from good living. He had a black beard, since Jews scorned the Roman taste for shaving, and his blue-fringed robe and the amulet strapped to a turban-like headdress displayed his pride in being a Pharisee. As he strode about the temple courts, he wore the arrogance of a man whose ancestors and actions made him feel important. He carried out the unending cycle of ritual cleansings of platters and cups as well as his own person. He kept the weekly fasts—between sunrise and sunset— and said the daily prayers in exact progression and number. He knew what was due to him: respectful greetings, high precedence, a prominent seat in the synagogue.

His days were consumed by his legal career and grooming himself for heaven. No time was left for the poor, the lame, and the outcast. Deep down in his character lay a vein of compassion, but he believed that a good man should keep away from bad men: Paul would have approved the Pharisee who, on seeing Jesus allow a prostitute to wash His feet with her tears and rub them with ointment, concluded that the man could be no prophet. Jesus' immortal picture of the Pharisee and the tax collector who went up to the temple to pray would have fitted Paul. Like that Pharisee, Paul was sure he deserved God's favor, despised others, and could have prayed, "God, I thank Thee I am not like other men, extortioners, unjust, adulterers, or even like this tax collector. I fast twice a week; I give tithes of all I get."

Stephen, on the other hand, spent much of his time in giving food and necessities to widows.

In the two years since the execution of Jesus, the Holy City had become pervaded with those who believed that He had risen from the dead. Most were nondescript and poor. Many lived in communal groups, and all of them shared their resources. When Greek-speaking disciples complained that widows were being neglected, Stephen and six others were chosen to undertake routine daily distribution of food.

Paul was disturbed that a man of Stephen's academic caliber should demean himself in social concerns and go around bringing happiness. Men respected Paul but feared him; they respected Stephen and loved him.

When Stephen preached, Paul could not fail to discern the gulf between them: Stephen always turned the Scriptures in the direction of Jesus of Nazareth as the Deliverer or Messiah (or "Christ," when he used Greek), whom every Jew awaited; and Stephen proved his point by citing the evidence of eyewitnesses who reported that, incredibly, a corpse had come to life again and climbed out of the grave. He claimed they had talked with Jesus in different places during the six weeks following His execution. Stephen himself was not an eyewitness, but he was sure Jesus was alive, and he claimed to know Him.

Paul considered Stephen's arguments nonsense. The Christ had not come yet. And the way to God was fixed forever: A man must belong to God's chosen people the Jews, and try to obey the Law's every detail. When he sinned, forgiveness depended on the ritual slaughter of animals day after day, year after year in the temple. Paul could not stomach Stephen's idea that the dying of one young man, by a common if degrading and revolting form of punishment, could blot out sins. As for the alleged resurrection, he pitied those who narrowed their lives to the following of a dead Messiah.

Paul felt no personal concern, knowing his own goodness, but he recognized Stephen's contentions as dangerous. Gamaliel had advised toleration; Simon Peter and other disciples of Jesus worshipped at the temple and continued to obey the Law. But Paul saw, as Stephen saw, that the old and the new were incompatible; man was saved either by the temple sacrifices and obedience to the Law, or by faith in Jesus. The old must destroy the new, or be destroyed.

Paul dedicated himself to demolishing Stephen's argument by the time-honored method of public debate. The synagogue benches were filled; the elders listened gravely.

Paul and his supporters argued from the Law that since Jesus had been nailed to a tree He must have lain under God's curse and could not possibly be the Christ. Paul disposed of the resurrection by the accepted explanation: The disciples stole the body. The alternative, that "the resurrection" was an imaginative symbolism or myth by which believers expressed the spiritual survival and triumph of Jesus, was not open to him. The tomb was empty. He knew that if the Jewish authorities had known that Jesus' body lay moldering in the grave, they would have exhumed it and thus exposed a fraud.

Stephen in reply showed that Moses and the prophets, David and the psalms, foreshadowed how the Christ would not strut as a conqueror when He came but allow Himself to be jeered at, hurt, and murdered. And He would rise from the dead. Stephen retold the story of that Passover two years before when

Jesus died and once again capped his case by quoting eyewitness evidence that Jesus had been seen alive after death.

Stephen won. The congregation voted him the honors, and some asked how to become believers in Jesus. It must have been then that Paul and his friends first had the sensation that they did not fight only Stephen but also a force they could not fathom. Luke stated, "They could not stand up against his wisdom or the Spirit by which he spoke."

Paul's reaction to defeat, to judge by scattered reminiscences in his letters, was the very opposite of the advice he would give in old age: "The Lord's servant must not be quarrelsome but kindly to everyone, correcting his opponents with gentleness." Instead, Paul pursued Stephen vindictively, stirring enmity, dissension, and jealousy, insulting and deriding Jesus and restraining neither hot temper nor sarcasm, both of which were strong components in Paul's character. Stephen did not retaliate. The qualities people recalled in Stephen were strength and charm; any indignation and scorn he kept for more positive use.

Paul's party had a stronger weapon than insult. If they could twist Stephen's words to sound blasphemous, they could silence him forever by due process of law. They set about it in a way from which Paul himself would often suffer in later years—the tortuous and indirect. They did not call at the high priest's house to lodge a formal complaint. Instead, there was much coming and going in the narrower lanes of the lower city. Soon afterward, apparently spontaneous incidents blew the activities of Stephen into the public eye. His meetings were disrupted by violence, until scribes and elders who had found no time for hearing him discovered that his suppression was urgent.

They had temple guards arrest him, and they arraigned him summarily before the Sanhedrin, while Paul and his fellow Cilicians remained in the background.

The seventy-one judges sat on great benches that curved on either side of the president's place in the Hall of Polished Stones. At each wing a secretary wrote on papyrus, trying to keep pace with Stephen's speech. Facing the judges and behind the prisoner were court servants, lawyers, teachers, and candidates for the Sanhedrin.

Paul sat among them, riveted to his opponent's words. Stephen held the court spellbound—from the president in his high priest's robe and jeweled breastplate to the youngest lawyer. They appeared gripped by the expression on his face, a blend of serenity and authority unusual in a man on trial for his life, and by his grasp of Jewish history as he delivered, *ex tempore*, a masterly analysis in answer to the charges. Paul never forgot the theme of that speech and would use it himself in very different circumstances in a faraway land; one phrase, "The Most High does not live in houses made by man," so engraved itself on his memory that it emerged even later when he was speaking below the Parthenon at Athens.

As Stephen continued, the atmosphere changed. Admiration gave way to annoyance. Uncomfortable memories obtruded of another trial in the same hall two years before and of that executed body that could not be found. Suddenly Stephen seemed to sense that his judges would not hear him out. Throwing caution to the winds, he asserted to their faces that they were obstinate hypocrites, who had betrayed and murdered their Messiah.

The learned judges snarled. The prisoner's reaction was astounding. He ignored their rage. He lifted his head in a gaze above and beyond them, and they could hardly believe their ears when this young enthusiast, whom they sought to condemn for blasphemy, called out that he saw God and that in the place of honor at God's side stood "the Son of Man"—by which, as everyone knew, he meant the late Jesus of Nazareth.

Thus began the mad rush that ended with a smashed corpse in a pool of blood below the Rock of Execution. It was no accident that the witnesses threw their clothes "at the feet of a young man named Saul"; they knew his responsibility. But Paul did not throw a stone. He watched and approved— and heard Stephen call out, "Lord Jesus, receive my spirit. Lord, do not hold this sin against them." And Paul's sharp mind saw, and repudiated, the essence of the prayer. "Lord, do not hold this sin against them" meant, in Stephen's teaching, "Lord, You took their sin on Yourself. May they believe in You, know You, love You."

During the rest of the summer when Stephen died (probably AD 31) and throughout the following winter, the Jewish authorities, with Paul as their chief agent, embarked on systematic suppression of Jesus' followers.

Paul charged like an animal tearing its prey. This was not the sad efficiency of an officer obeying distasteful orders; the heart was engaged, and the mind too, with the thoroughness of an inquisitor unmasking treason, until Paul's operations had reduced a vigorous citywide community to apparent impotence. Its leaders fled or went into hiding. Paul went from house to house, then held formal inquiries at the synagogues when the congregation assembled. Every suspect, man or woman, had to stand before the elders, while Paul, as the high priest's representative, put to them the demand that they should curse Jesus. On refusal, they were formally accused but had the right to employ the time-honored formula: "I have something to argue in favor of my acquittal."

Thus Paul heard the stories and beliefs of a cross-section of those who called Jesus "Lord." Many had met Him in Jerusalem or had traveled to Galilee to find Him, and these would repeat His words. Again and again the same phrases, the same parables would come up in the synagogue court. Nor was Paul surprised, since every rabbi insisted that his disciples should grasp his sayings word-perfect, reproducing the very tones of his voice. And the sayings, whether Paul wished or not, were at once stored in the expanding library of his retentive brain.

Some of the Nazarenes defended their devotion by recounting the influence of Jesus on their physical health, like the man with congenital blindness that Jesus had cured, who would have retorted to Paul as saucily as he had answered the indignant Pharisees after the miracle. Some had seen Jesus stumbling toward Golgotha or had watched Him die. Several insisted that they had seen Him alive after He was dead, not a wraith but vigorous—despite the scourge that had stripped the skin and laid the muscles of His back bare, and the shock, exhaustion, and exposure of a Roman crucifixion with its unavoidable finish by suffocation if death had not come already. Most of the accused, however, did not claim to be eyewitnesses themselves, but converts of those who were, particularly of Simon called Peter or "The Rock."

Again and again a nondescript disciple—poorly educated, uncouth, timid—would be hustled in front of the tribunal. After a few shy sentences, the man would be transformed: clear words, unashamed convictions, it was almost as if he were prompted. A few such prisoners would assert that they certainly were being told what to say. Oblivious of Paul's rage, they drew apt quotations from the countless sayings of Jesus committed to memory:

"When they bring you before the synagogues and the rulers and the authorities, do not be anxious how or what you are to answer or what you are to say; for the Holy Spirit will teach you in that very hour what you ought to say."

"This will be a time for you to bear testimony.... I will give you a mouth and wisdom, which none of your adversaries will be able to withstand or contradict."

Paul could laugh at that.

He helped throw many of these prisoners into dungeons. One or two may have been stoned: Paul seemed to suggest this ("When they were put to death I gave my vote against them"), but Jewish rights of capital punishment were strictly limited by the Romans. The majority were punished by public flogging, the "forty stripes save one," which was no sight for the squeamish. The courage of a few collapsed. About to be lashed, or after a few strokes, or when forced to watch a wife's or husband's torture, they screamed a curse on Jesus as Paul required.

He remained unmoved as men—and women—staggered away with backs a mass of weals and blood. He was equally unmoved by the refusal of grown men to be humiliated by a beating in front of neighbors. It was said that Jews beaten in synagogue would almost die of shame, but these seemed to be glad, and some called out that they were praying for those who despitefully used them and persecuted them.

Toward the end of winter, news came that followers of Jesus who had fled Jerusalem were not cowed but propagating their doctrines wherever they went—in Samaria, with outstanding success, and northward to Damascus; to the Phoenician country beyond the Lebanon range; and even overseas. Paul went in a rage to the high priest. "Still breathing threats and murder," as his first biographer described, he asked for official letters to the synagogues, authorizing him to arrest men or women who followed "the Way" and to bring them, roped or chained, for punishment in Jerusalem.

He suggested Damascus as the first objective. Though the Sanhedrin's discipline extended to Jews everywhere, the Romans disliked disturbances. But Damascus, though Roman, had two large communities with a wide measure of self-government: the Arabs, who owed allegiance to the Nabatean king in his rock capital at Petra, and the Jews. Paul probably intended to pursue and punish in Phoenicia next and then in Antioch, the great Roman capital of Syria. Surely he had a lifetime ahead.

As soon as traveling began in spring, Paul left at first light—not the sleepy dawn of northern latitudes but the strong luminosity of the Judean hills. He rode a donkey, or possibly a horse as Michelangelo imagined, and the small party may have led a baggage camel. They would have passed close to the place of Stephen's murder. If they took the direct route through Samaria, they traveled through stony hills carpeted with variegated spring flowers, and early on the second day had a brief glimpse of the distant snows of Mount Hermon, which dominates the road into Damascus. On the fourth or fifth day, they came to the Lake of Galilee, and there the very stones on the hillsides cried out. The place was alive with memories of Jesus, and no man could pass that way untouched. Paul would have met more people there than in Jerusalem who swore they had seen Jesus alive again, the scars still on His hands and feet.

Paul crossed the upper Jordan by the Roman bridge and climbed the bare heights, where, centuries later, the Syrian guns would bombard Jewish *kibbutzim* until swept away in the Six-Day War of 1967. He had knowledge now of what Jesus had done and said, even to the tones of His voice, of what He was like in appearance and character, this Man who had been only a few years older than himself.

Paul never suggested that, as his little caravan came in full sight of Mount Hermon, he was weighing up factors for or against Jesus. Jesus had been a blasphemous impostor and was dead.

THREE

DAMASCUS ROAD

On the last day of the journey, the caravan passed near Mount Hermon. Its peaks, still under snow, rose from brown foothills white with wild flowers, but the mountain no longer looked particularly high because they were too close under it to see the summit, and the Damascus plain itself is over two thousand feet. Far ahead, below a bare craggy hill, lay the green of the oasis, encouraging them to plod on to journey's end rather than make their normal daily stop before noon.

Paul and his party walked ahead, while one man led their donkeys roped together a little way to the rear. The road had emptied of country people making for market. Now and again they saw sheep or goats guarded by a small boy swinging his sling, or an occasional patch of cultivation where a man walked behind a rough plow, guiding his ox by a long goad or iron-tipped wand.

The sky was clear blue. Paul's memory is emphatic that there was no thunderstorm or violent wind, as some suggest who seek a natural explanation for what happened. He was not near a nervous breakdown or about to suffer an epileptic fit. He wasn't even in a hurry.

"Suddenly about midday a great light flashed from the sky all around me … a light more brilliant than the sun, shining all around me and my traveling companions."

Paul and the others fell to the ground. They were appalled by this phenomenon, not just a flash but sustained light, terrifying and inexplicable. The companions seemed to have stumbled to their feet. Paul remained prostrate. For him alone the light grew in intensity.

He heard a voice, at once calm and authoritative, say in Aramaic, "Saul, Saul, why do you persecute Me?"

He looked up. Within the center of light, which blinded him from his surroundings, he faced a Man of about his own age. Paul could not believe what he heard and saw. All his convictions, intellect, and training, his reputation, his self-respect, demanded that Jesus should not be alive again. He played for time and replied, "Who are You, Lord?" He was using a mode of address that might mean simply "Your honor."

"I am Jesus, whom you are persecuting. It is hard for you, this kicking against the goad."

Then Paul knew. In a second that seemed an eternity he saw the wounds in Jesus' hands and feet, saw the face, and knew he had seen the Lord, that He was alive, as Stephen and the others had said, and that He loved not only those whom Paul persecuted but also *Paul* himself: "It is hard for *you* to kick against the goad." Not one word of reproach.

Paul had never admitted to himself that he had felt pricks of a goad as he raged against Stephen and his disciples. But now, instantaneously, he was shatteringly aware that he had been fighting Jesus—and fighting himself, his conscience, his powerlessness, the darkness and chaos in his own soul. God hovered over this chaos and brought him to the moment of new creation. It wanted only his "Yes."

Paul broke.

He was trembling and in no state to weigh the pros and cons of changing sides. He only knew that he had heard a voice and had seen the Lord and that nothing mattered but to find and obey His will.

"What shall I do, Lord?"

He used the same ascription as before, but all the obedience and worship and love in heaven and earth went into that one word, "Lord." At that moment he knew he was utterly forgiven, utterly loved. In his own words: "God who said, 'Let light shine out of darkness,' has shined in our hearts to give the light of the knowledge of the glory of God in the face of Jesus Christ."

"Rise to your feet," he heard, "and stand upright and go into Damascus, and you will be told there what you are to do." He had trusted. Now he had to obey—and it was a humbling, almost trivial first order.

When at last he stood, he was blind. He put out his hand and groped until he was led by his frightened companions, who were all the more alarmed now that they could hear him speaking to no one. The riding and baggage animals had caught up, and now the little caravan walked toward Damascus in awed silence.

Paul moved blindly into the unknown, yet he was not in darkness but in light: "I could not see because of the brightness of that light." Though blue sky and the road's yellow dust and the green of the nearing oasis were all snuffed out, he did not miss them. Light suffused his blinded eyes, his mind. And as he walked, obeying that first command from his new Master, he made the first great discovery: Jesus remained beside him—not the form of a crucified, risen body, but someone invisible yet there.

They passed the stench of the caravansary, quiet in the early afternoon, and went under the city gate into the broad, colonnaded Via Recta, the Street called Straight, which bisected the city. This too was comparatively still, for the shops and booths had not opened after the midday sleep, and private homes were shuttered against the sun. They reached the house of a Damascene named Judas, probably a substantial Jewish merchant, a suitable host for a representative of the Sanhedrin. The synagogue elders must have been expecting Paul, for even the Nazarenes knew he was on his way to persecute.

Both sides lost sight of him. The escort delivered him and disappeared. He made no request of Judas but to be taken to the guest chamber—refusing even a meal—and was left alone.

Time became meaningless. Paul heard the evening trumpet, the cock's crow the next morning, the rumble of carts on the paving, shopkeepers shouting their wares, the distant murmur of bargainers, and the occasional bray of an ass. Then the stillness of midday. He lay on his bed, wide awake except for an hour or two of sleep, or knelt long at the bedside and then lay down again. He did not want human company, only to be alone with the Lord Jesus, as he now called Him. He soon forgot hunger and thirst. His entire personality was in mutation. He was being turned inside out as he let Jesus light the recesses of his soul.

"Saul, Saul, why do you persecute Me?" He would reply now in the words of David's psalm: "Have mercy upon me, O God, according to Thy loving-kindness: according to the multitude of Thy tender mercies, blot out my transgressions.... Against Thee, Thee only, have I sinned."

Paul felt defiled and loathsome. If they had been available he could have used the words in Augustine's *Confessions*: "You set me there before my face that I might see how vile I was, how twisted and unclean and spotted and ulcerous. I saw myself and was horrified." By the gauge of man's inhumanity to man—the Roman suppression of the two Jewish rebellions or Nero's massacre of Christians after the Fire of Rome or Hitler's "final solution"—Paul's persecution was trifling. But murder is always absolute to the awakened conscience of the murderer. Nor was it only murder and cruelty. He had blasphemed and insulted and persecuted the Lord, whose response had been to seek him out and show him a love that surpassed anything he had known. The more he bathed himself in this love as the hours flew by in blindness, the more he was broken down by the enormity of what he had done.

He had imagined that he served God. He had supposed himself climbing into God's favor. He had set up his standards of goodness and compared himself with others and seen that he was good. But now, in contrast with Jesus, whose Spirit had invaded him, he knew his purity was a counterfeit of the inexpressibly Pure, his good deeds a parody of Goodness. He had been mentally and spiritually hostile to God, though honoring Him by mouth; he had been busy in evil, though punctilious in religious rites; he had been altogether estranged, fit for nothing but to crawl away as far as he could from the blinding light that was God.

Yet Jesus had grasped hold of him. Paul would afterward cite this among the cast-iron proofs of the resurrection, however much men might scoff or call him a liar. God, incredibly, had raised the shattered body of Jesus from the grave; He was alive and had confronted Paul, not to crush and destroy, not to avenge the blood of the persecuted, but to rescue the persecutor and overwhelm him with love and forgiveness. Paul knew from the bottom of his heart that Jesus was the Messiah, the Christ, the Savior of the world. This was not a conclusion of cold logic, though that must come. It went beyond intellect. He knew, because he knew Jesus.

And in knowing Jesus, he understood what had happened on the cross.

Paul in his pride and wisdom had rejected Jesus because no man could be hanged on a tree unless cursed. As he now faced his sin, he saw by irresistible intuition that Jesus indeed had carried a curse on the cross, but not His own; it was Paul's and everyone's. Each hour that passed in blindness at the house of Judas, each day for the rest of his life, would unfold a little more of the breadth and length and height and depth, but the heart of the Good News was sure, now and forever: the love of Christ, "the Son of God who loved me and gave Himself for me." Paul could instantly be treated as a man who had never sinned, be welcomed with love and trust. The more he looked with blinded eyes at the brightness of the light, the more distinct grew the fact disclosed in that instant of time on the Damascus Road: Forgiveness was a gift, entire and whole and perfect, because forgiveness was Christ Himself. It could not be earned; no human merit could outweigh human sin, but in having Christ, Paul had all.

He could have shouted aloud in the house of Judas what he would write in the unknown years ahead:

"God has sent the Spirit of His Son into our hearts!"

"The mystery hidden for ages and generations but now made manifest is: Christ in you!"

"For to me to live is Christ!"

Already he had an urge to pray: not just the formal prayers of the glorious Jewish liturgy, but the conversation of a son with his Father: In talking with Jesus he talked with the Father; in worshipping the Father he conversed with the Son. He told the Lord all that was in his heart. Urgently he interceded for those he had persecuted, especially those he had forced to recant and blaspheme, for the Damascus Nazarenes who awaited him in fear, for his Jewish friends and superiors.

With prayer came hunger—for the words of Jesus. Like a newborn lamb that before it can stand searches instinctively for its mother's teats, Paul hungered for knowledge of all Jesus had said and done. Until his conversion he had been indifferent to the words of Jesus. But from the moment he had said, "What must I do, Lord?" he accepted Jesus' authority, and now it was of paramount importance to know what He had commanded and promised and warned and foretold, to know His attitude toward those who hated Him and those who loved Him, all He taught about the Father and about Himself, His verdicts on every matter of human behavior and destiny.

Paul had yet another urge: to broadcast his great discovery. Yet he had to wait. The Master's command had been "Go into Damascus and you will be told there what you are to do." Waiting, he heard the evening trumpet and the cock's crow and the country carts and then again the evening trumpet.

At last, as he prayed, he was shown what would happen next.

FOUR

A MAN SURPRISED

In a bedroom of a small house off the Street called Straight, a middle-aged Jew lay between sleep and waking.

Ananias was an honored member of the Jewish community in Damascus. He was also a follower of Jesus Christ, and he showed no surprise or hesitation when he heard a voice call: "Ananias."

"Here I am, Lord."

"Get up, and go to the Street called Straight and ask at the house of Judas for a Tarsian named Saul. He is praying! And he sees a man named Ananias coming in and laying hands on him so that he may recover his sight."

Ananias was aghast. His Lord must have made a mistake. Ananias probably had attended little meetings of Nazarenes, who at the news of Saul the Persecutor's approach had prayed that the Lord should rescue them … without, apparently, expecting their prayer to be answered.

"Lord," replied Ananias, "I have heard all about this man from many people, and the harm he has done to Your saints in Jerusalem. And he has the authority here to arrest everyone who calls on Your name!"

The voice said, "Go, because he is My chosen instrument." The Lord then confirmed and amplified His command.

At that, Ananias threw off the bedclothes and dressed.

As he hurried down the narrow lane past watercarriers already returning from the river, while the sunrise tipped the northern crags, he almost shouted, "Hallelujah!" So the Lord's hand was not shortened. He had stretched it out to heal, and the wolf would lie down with the lamb as in the ancient prophecy. And he, Ananias the obscure (never heard of before or since), had been chosen to baptize Saul.

This was to be the first example of a historical pattern that great ambassadors for Christ, however much prepared in other ways, would be brought to their vocation by unimportant agents: Augustine hears a child's voice repeat, "Take up and read!"; John Wesley listens to an anonymous Moravian reading Luther; D. L. Moody, wrapping up shoes in a store, pauses for a few words from his Sunday school teacher; Charles Haddon Spurgeon, sheltering from a snowstorm, hears a working man in a snowbound minister's pulpit.

Ananias was at once admitted and soon stood by Paul's bedside.

He looked at a face that had passed through deep suffering into peace. The skin sagged where Pharisaic good living had been drained away by fast; lines grooved by ruthlessness were still traceable, the beard straggled, the eyes stared. Yet it was a face relaxed, as if Paul had looked at the worst and no longer feared it, and looked at the best and knew he was being remade in its mold.

Ananias laid his hands on Paul's head.

"Saul, brother," he began (and if he had to gulp a little at calling the murderer of his friends "brother," the gulp was swallowed by joy), "the Lord has sent me—Jesus who appeared to you on your way here—so that you may recover your sight and be filled with the Holy Spirit."

At that instant it was as though a film were peeled away from Paul's eyes. He saw Ananias. And saw him clearly. George Matheson, the blind Scottish preacher and hymn writer (1842–1906), liked to think of Paul as semiblind for the rest of his life, the effect of those three days never quite leaving him. But there are recorded instances of Paul fixing an opponent with his eye, or compelling an audience's attention by a look, in a manner impossible to the half-blind. Paul recovered sight instantly and completely.

Ananias discharged the rest of his orders: "The God of our fathers has chosen you to know His will and see the Righteous One, to hear words from His own lips, and you are to be a witness to all men of what you have seen and heard." Paul would hear more, he said, direct from the Lord Jesus, who would give him a glimpse of what would be involved in pain and hardship as they adventured together, not to Israel only but to the Gentiles, small and great, slaves and kings—to "all men" whom previously as a Pharisee Paul had despised and rejected.

Then Ananias spoke more words, delivered as from Jesus Himself: "I send you to open their eyes! To turn them from darkness to light, and from the rule of Satan to God, so that, by trust in Me, they may have forgiveness of sins and a place with those whom God has made His own."

The scope and implication of this commission left Paul speechless.

Ananias said, "What are you waiting for? Get up, and be baptized and wash away your sins as you call on His name."

Ananias helped him off the bed. Normally, the followers of the Way baptized by immersion in a river or stream, like John the Baptist did, but Paul was weak after his long fast. They probably moved slowly out to the atrium, the garden court of Judas's house where there would have been a fountain. But then again Paul, with his iron will, may have insisted that he walk, leaning on Ananias, the half mile to the Abana River, which flowed outside the city's northern wall.

Never had trees looked fresher than these Damascus apricots and peaches, or water so clear as the Abana. The cream-colored stone of the city wall and gates threw back the sunshine, and the sky was blue. Paul had been promised storms enough, but at this time he could echo the nineteenth psalm: "The heavens declare the glory of God.... The sun like a strong man runs its course with joy."

Paul felt a physical well-being, all tension relaxed, his perception acute, his mind at peace. As he walked down the Street called Straight, which like all eastern streets was a medley of color and noise and movement, or turned into the spice bazaar or the metal workers' lane, he was in love with all mankind. Damascus, being a frontier city, drew a variety of people: Arabs and Jews, Parthians in their conical hats, the clank of Roman soldiers; Paul knew he was sent to them all—and to his own people, the Jews, for even they had barely a glimmer of what God was like ... except those who had seen Jesus.

That evening, with Ananias, Paul met the little knot of Nazarenes. Almost certainly a few who had fled from Jerusalem would have been among them, and we can imagine the heightened emotion when those who had received floggings at Paul's orders gave him the kiss of peace and when they shared bread and wine in token of their union with each other and the Lord.

An even more extraordinary incident occurred the next Sabbath at the most important of the numerous Damascus synagogues. The elders and congregation had no idea of Paul's conversion. He had not disclosed it even to Judas. They merely supposed he had recovered from indisposition and was ready for the work they had gossiped about since the announcement of his coming. The stricter members, as they took their seats, expressed pious satisfaction that heresy would be erased; the cruel had a pleasurable anticipation of possible bloodletting. The Nazarenes, however, who knew the affair would develop differently, were praying for him when the overseer, the *hazzan*, escorted him to the dais, still dressed like any Pharisee in blue-fringed robe with leather amulet on his turban, and handed him the scroll of the Law.

He read aloud the allotted passage, each inflection correct, and returned the scroll. In the moment's pause before he began to preach, he marveled at the divine strategy by which, during the past centuries, synagogues had arisen in countless Gentile cities—ready for the day when under his leadership they should be the spearheads of a great crusade for Jesus Christ! If he had seen the truth, surely they would too. He and they had been set apart to spread the Good News of Jesus Christ among the Gentiles. And they would begin in Damascus.

Then and there he proclaimed, "Jesus is the Son of God." Paul charged in with the same vehemence and abandon that he had charged into his persecution. Words tumbled out as he told how the Lord had met him, that the Lord was alive again and loved them.

The reaction was not at all as he had expected. The worshippers were stunned and aghast. Far from being convinced, they were angry. This turn-coat received as the high priest's representative had now declared himself the representative of Jesus.

Paul was taken aback. In the days that followed, he felt rather as Moses, who "thought his fellow countrymen would understand that God was offering them deliverance through him, but they did not understand." What is more, Paul grew impatient with the Nazarenes. He joined them each evening, but few had memories of Jesus. They had a stock of His sayings, which had been repeated by those who had known Him, but this could not satisfy Paul. He hungered for first-hand evidence. Yet he could not return to Jerusalem. Even if the apostles, who had known Jesus better than any, gave their confidence immediately, Paul must not risk the clutch of an enraged high priest, who would ensure Paul's disappearance by strangling or lifelong incarceration.

Each night at the house of Judas, or perhaps now at the house of Ananias, he tossed on his bed frustrated, the glory from those days of blindness already slipping away. At length he told the Lord he would leave it in His hands. Peace flowed back. No voice or light disclosed the next move, only a growing conviction that he must get away by himself, taking nothing but his scrolls of the Scriptures. Right now it was not the apostles Paul needed, but Jesus alone: not a city but the wilderness.

The next move was simple. Damascus was the terminus of one of the great spice routes from the myrrh and frankincense country in southern Arabia and the Horn of Africa. The camel caravans returned with coins and goods of the Roman world. The son of an important trading house had no difficulty in obtaining passage.

FIVE

ARABIA AND AFTER

Somewhere in Arabia lived Paul's first convert, probably a young Bedouin in the wilderness of cliffs and wadis between Sinai and the great sand desert. It is inconceivable that Paul could suppress his discovery of God's love for the world; rather, he shared his day's meditation each night by some campfire, learning to simplify for rough illiterate camel men.

Preaching was incidental to his primary purpose. He went to Arabia to learn—from the risen Jesus. Just as he claimed to have seen the Lord on the Damascus Road, so he always claimed to have been taught by Him directly: "The mystery was made known to me by revelation"; and he never ceased to wonder that God should have chosen for this an ex-persecutor, less than the least of all saints. It was not merely a matter of listening to a voice, whether speaking to his ears or his heart, but intense application of the mind. Christ had captured his will and emotions on the Damascus Road; in Arabia, Paul's thoughts were captured too.

Months drifted into years: winter storms, the spring when the desert was scented with flowers, the furnace of high summer. Paul was now lean and hard physically, his face burned dark by the sun.

In the third year after his conversion, he was ready.

The sequence is obscure, the most likely being that he walked into the Nabatean Arab capital, Petra, through the narrow gorge familiar to twenty-first-century tourists and took the earliest opportunity of preaching Christ in the synagogue of the Jewish colony. The uproar led King Aretas, who hated Jews, to order the arrest of the troublemaker. Paul fled Petra with a price on his head, his signal to leave Arabia. He must return to the mainstream, as Moses emerged from the desert to confront Pharaoh with God's demands, as the Lord Himself came out of the wilderness and entered the synagogues with the message: "The time has come; the kingdom of God is upon you; repent and believe the Gospel."

Paul, now in his mid-thirties, set out north to assume leadership of the great crusade in which the Jewish synagogues should become the spearheads of Christ. Jerusalem was still barred to him, for he could not expect the confidence of the apostles until he had proved himself, nor was he sure they yet realized that Gentiles, no less than Jews, were to be offered Christ. He therefore rejoined the caravan route and traveled northward with the spice and gold. Days before he came in sight of Damascus, Mount Hermon beckoned him across the barren plateau toward the place where Jesus had appeared to him on the road.

In Damascus, Paul's conversion could hardly have been forgotten, though many must have dismissed it as transient because he had blazed across the sky like a comet, to disappear as suddenly as he had appeared, while Ananias had resumed his gentle, slightly nervous policy of peaceful coexistence. Paul was welcomed immediately by the disciples and on the next Sabbath entered a synagogue to exercise his right to expound Scripture. And like Stephen, he reduced the Jews to confusion by proofs that Jesus was Christ. Those who remembered his earlier visit were amazed at his growth in understanding and conviction.

Luke said he grew more and more forceful. He did not attack the unbelieving Jews, nor display the bitterness of a renegade toward former friends who refused to be converted, yet there may have been one element lacking in this early preaching: "If I speak in the tongues of men and of angels, but have not love, I am a noisy gong or a clanging cymbal. And if I have prophetic powers, and understand all mysteries and all knowledge, and if I have all faith, so as to remove mountains, but have not love, I am nothing." Do these words of twenty years later contain an autobiographical echo?

Nevertheless he made disciples. And it was they who came to his rescue when Jews plotted to murder him.

The plot was hatched with slyness, the more necessary in that the local elders risked crucifixion should they attempt a killing inside the city. When a traveler from Petra mentioned the warrant out for Paul's arrest, they decided on a solution. The ethnarch appointed by King Aretas under his treaty with the Romans to protect and punish Damascus Arabs would not extradite a wanted man except on a capital charge, nor arrest him within the walls for an offense committed across the border. Rather, his troopers patrolled outside the gates to keep an eye on the Arab king's subjects as they entered and left. In return for a bribe, he gave orders to seize Paul, carry him off, and slit his throat.

Paul got wind of it, whether from a Jewish or Arab sympathizer or because no secret was safe in Damascus. His disciples took him at night to a friendly family who lived on the city walls in one of the private houses with windows jutting some eight or ten feet above the ground. They found a fish basket, a large shapeless sack that folded round his body so no casual observer would notice in the darkness that it hid a man. In the small hours they lowered him to the ground.

As Paul picked his way through vegetable gardens and fruit trees to strike the road out of sight of the troopers at the gates, his humiliation was complete. The crusade on which he had embarked so gloriously had come to a summary stop; the appointed leader was a fugitive already. Soon he became inwardly aware that he was not alone. He had been promised sufferings and rebuffs. Now they had begun and he had escaped lightly. He had been promised the unfailing presence of Jesus too. A phrase that, like a theme in a symphony, would sound again and again through his life, sounded over Paul's story that night: "Persecuted, but not forsaken."

As his spirits revived, the irony was not lost on him that the mighty Paul, who had originally approached Damascus with all the panoply of the high priest's representative, should make his last exit in a fish basket, helped by the very people he had come to hurt.

Paul decided to fulfill his ambition to make friends with Peter and learn all he could about Jesus. He retraced his earlier journey through Syria, Galilee, and Judea until once more he looked down from Mount Scopus and entered Jerusalem.

With a humility in contrast to his former attitudes in Jerusalem, and not always so evident in the future, he did not immediately accost the apostles but sought out a gathering of Christ's disciples. And he was appalled to find himself cold-shouldered. "They were all afraid of him," wrote Luke, "for they did not believe that he was a disciple." Some of them had suffered horribly from him, and though these had (or should have) forgiven him, his unannounced arrival was unnerving. The report of his conversion had been followed by long silence. His recent activities in Damascus were too brief for news to trickle to Jerusalem, and he had left in such a hurry that he carried no letter of commendation. He might have been a spy.

For a few hours or days it seemed he was rejected by both former friends and former enemies; a castaway, lonely, with nothing but Christ's promises and spiritual presence.

He was rescued by the man who later would become, for a time, his closest companion. Joseph Barnabas was a Cypriot. Being from a wealthy background, though of different tribes, the two may have had previous acquaintance. Barnabas was generous and much loved, a man of commanding presence with a gentle manner. His gifts lay in counseling rather than preaching, and he was skilled at discerning genuine faith and strengthening it: hence the Aramaic nickname the apostles had given him, "Son of encouragement." Barnabas took Paul aside, drew from him the whole story and knew it rang true.

Barnabas was an uncle or cousin of the young John Mark, who stood in special relationship with Simon Peter as a spiritual apprentice or assistant; through Mark and Mark's mother, Mary, and because of his own qualities, he had the ear of Peter. Nor did Peter hesitate to act on what Barnabas told him. In his impulsive, warm way, he and his wife asked Paul to stay in their home and at once opened their hearts and memories to him. Peter was Paul's age but a contrast in background and character. A bluff fisherman with a strong

Galilean rustic accent, he lacked higher education or the mental brilliance of Paul, though he was literate, as were most Jewish peasants of the day, and after three years with Jesus was well versed in the Old Testament Scriptures.

If Paul had persecuted Christ in His disciples, Peter had denied Him, and felt no superiority, though he bore already the scars of a beating for Christ's sake, while Paul, as far as we know, was unscathed. The risen Christ had transformed both men, and this was the link that would withstand the stresses of dissimilarity and, in the years far ahead, of dispute.

Paul spent much of the next fifteen days listening to Peter and questioning him. His attitude may be deduced from the attitude, in the next century, of the young Irenaeus, the future theologian, sitting at the feet of the aged Polycarp, who had actually known the apostle John. Polycarp, wrote Irenaeus, "would describe his conversation with John and with the rest who had seen the Lord, and he would relate their words. And whatsoever things he had heard from them about the Lord, and about His miracles, and about His teaching, Polycarp, as having received them from eyewitnesses of the Life of the Word, would relate altogether in accordance with the Scriptures. To these discourses I used to listen at the time with attention by God's mercy which was bestowed upon me, noting them down, not on paper, but in my heart; and by the grace of God I constantly ruminate upon them faithfully."

As Irenaeus implied, the early church had a strict test of teaching in the name of Jesus Christ: It must derive accurately from "eyewitnesses of the Life of the Word," those who had known Jesus personally, and it must be "altogether in accordance with the Scriptures," which to Paul and Peter meant the Old Testament. Paul himself refers to this test when he commented to the Corinthians, "I delivered to you as of first importance what I also received, that Christ died for our sins in accordance with the Scriptures, that He was buried, that He was raised on the third day in accordance with the Scriptures, and that He appeared to Cephas (Peter), then to the Twelve.... Then to more than five hundred brethren at one time, most of whom are still alive.... Then to James.... Last of all He appeared also to me."

Paul had dug deep into the Scriptures in Arabia, and he claimed since the Damascus Road that he was an eyewitness of the resurrection and thus had authority as an apostle; but these fifteen days with Peter provided the essential foundation of knowledge of "the Life of the Word." Peter had been convinced by the character, actions, and speech of Jesus over a long period before he realized who He was. Paul wanted evidence that Jesus really had lived sinless and to hear how love and purity had been demonstrated in this human life, which he believed to be the one complete revelation of God Himself. And he wanted as much as he could get of Jesus' sayings.

That the early church possessed an enormous fund of Christ's words and actions, far more than Paul could absorb in a fortnight, is reflected in the closing words of Saint John's gospel: "There are also many other things which Jesus did; were every one of them to be written, I suppose that the world itself could not contain the books that would be written." Moreover Paul could rely on the exact accuracy of all Peter had retailed, for the Jews had a rigid attitude to the sacredness of an actual quotation, a horror of tampering with tradition. A disciple could not blend his own ideas with those that he passed on as his master's.

What Paul received whenever he questioned those who had known the Lord, he would transmit. He spent many hours teaching in Antioch, Corinth, Ephesus—wherever he traveled. The fact that his letters seldom quote Christ's words directly is not an indication of ignorance. He needed all the limited space of a papyrus roll to deal with the specific situations that provoked the letter, and his readers knew Christ's words already from the oral teaching, to which Paul makes several allusions.

Just as his writing must have awakened echoes of this talking, so the Epistles awake echoes of the Gospels. Apart from the basic facts of the life, death, and resurrection of the Lord, Paul probably told converts the parables, such as the Good Seed (echoed in his words about God's husbandry to the Corinthians) and the House Built on a Rock. He came very near repeating in an epistle the Lord's statement about defilement and the evil things that come from the heart of man.[1] When he wrote that the Philippian Christians shone "as lights in the world, holding forth the word of life," they would have remembered the Lord's words, "You are the light of the world.... Let your light so shine."[2] Paul repeated Christ on loving your neighbor; he told of faithful stewards and how the laborer deserves his hire; he spoke of the new birth; and of the meekness, gentleness, graciousness, and humility of Christ.

All this would have been drawn in large measure from his conversations with Peter, which thus became a vital factor of preparation. Years later, when Paul preached with dogmatic certainty that the gospel had an urgent claim upon every human being to the end of time, a hearer might have cried, "Paul, how can you be so *sure?*" He would have answered by referring not only to the Damascus Road and the revelations in Arabia, to the Old Testament and to the believer's own private proof—the Holy Spirit guarding his heart—but also to the career and character of Jesus. Be imitators of the Lord, he would plead. Let the same mind be in you, walk worthy of Him; walk, like Christ, in love.

By his own recollection of this visit, Paul did not meet any of the other apostles "except James the Lord's brother," who, though not one of the Twelve and slow to believe in Jesus, had risen to leadership of the Jerusalem church. He did not seem to have told Peter and James of his special commission to preach to Gentiles everywhere whether or not they worshipped at a synagogue. Peter had not yet even half-understood Jesus' order to make disciples of all nations, for the vision on the housetop of Joppa lay in the future, when he argued with the Lord but afterward baptized the proselyte Italian centurion. James was firmly wedded to the Mosaic Law alongside his faith in Jesus Christ; Paul may have suspected the seeds of strife between himself and James and was wary. Or perhaps he thought it unnecessary for the present to raise awkward questions, since at this time he intended to work through the synagogues overseas, to stir congregations for Christ until they preached Him to the Gentiles. Besides, he had come to Jerusalem to listen, not to teach those who "were in Christ before me."

Paul spent long hours secluded with Peter in the cool of his home, or walking together deep in talk on the Mount of Olives or in the Courts of the Temple. Here Peter could quote Jesus' sermons and describe miracles in the places where they had happened. Even so, Paul never was a man to be happy unless active. Fully accepted now by the disciples, he "went in and out among them at Jerusalem, preaching boldly in the name of the Lord." He had no opportunity to travel around the Judean countryside, meeting disciples in outlying towns, but "they heard it said, 'Our former persecutor is preaching the Good News of the faith which once he tried to destroy,' and they praised God for me."

Paul did not limit his preaching to circles where he had no compromising past. He went to the synagogues of the Greek-speaking Jews, his old haunts, and took up where Stephen had left off, using the very methods by which Stephen had infuriated him four years before, all the time aware that another "Saul the persecutor" might be listening. He talked. He debated. And once again he provoked dissension: The man who longed to be the agent of reconciliation seemed to cause violent arguments wherever he went.

The dissension may have upset the disciples, for between the departure of Saul breathing threats and slaughter, and the return of Paul preaching boldly in the name of the Lord, they had recovered peace and numerical strength. When Jerusalem became too hot to hold him, they were almost relieved.

Once again there was a murder plot. Immediately after it leaked out, Paul was hurried out of danger. This time friends took him to the coast and sent him off to Tarsus.

Damascus … Jerusalem … his crusade had once again come to a halt. But he left Jerusalem assured that he would not be forgotten. Barnabas knew all about Paul's dedication to evangelize the Gentiles. When the time was ripe, Barnabas would find him.[3]

SIX

HIDDEN YEARS

The best years of Paul's life were slipping away between the Taurus mountains and the sea. It was even harder to bear because he cared so deeply that all men everywhere should hear and believe, yet during his later thirties and into the early forties, when a man approaches his prime, Paul dropped out of history. The story of this last major gap in his life cannot be pieced together with certainty. Fragmentary evidence suggests the outline, but it must be qualified with a large "possibly" or "perhaps."

He rejoined his family in Tarsus. His parents had served God with a clear conscience in the only way they knew, by keeping the Law. He began to tell them about Jesus Christ, who had fulfilled the Law, and the advice was not well received. Tension between father and son, understandably high since Paul's return with a ruined career, tightened yet further when Paul ceased to dress as a Pharisee or to observe the ceremonial rules; the fundamental moral law enshrined in Scripture was more absolute than ever, but the Mosaic injunctions were not.

He did not seem to have flaunted this freedom. He established the principle, then conformed to the family and the neighbors' ways when this helped his supreme purpose: "To the Jews I became like a Jew to win Jews. As they are subject to the Law of Moses, I put myself under that law to win them, although I am not myself subject to it. To win Gentiles, who are outside the law, I made myself like one of them, although I am not outside God's law, being under the law of Christ." He became "all things to all men, that I might by all means save some. I do it all for the sake of the Gospel."

It was this determination to win Gentiles that angered his family most, not least because he broke out of their spiritual ghetto and explored Gentile ways.

In youth his mind had been closed, for every prejudice of upbringing was a disinfectant against pagan ideas. He now had an even more satisfying answer to the puzzles of human strivings and destiny. Paganism at its philosophical best would appear a guttering candle to a man who followed the Light of the World, and more usually it was idolatry, mixed with license; especially in Tarsus, where the homosexuality for which the city was notorious had ties with local religion. Certain twentieth-century scholars argued that Paul was heavily influenced by pagan ideas, especially the "mysteries" coming in from eastern Asia and the fertility cults of gods who, to make winter lead to spring, "died" and "rose again." But to make him appear to borrow, these scholars had to depend on descriptions that dated from after his day, while rejecting evidence that later paganism parodied Christian features. Paul's most highly educated audience, at Athens, would certainly have recognized any pagan parallel if it existed; yet when he spoke of a Man who really rose again, they laughed.

His advice to converts throughout his career was "Shun idolatry." Disgust at idols, however, strengthened his love for idolaters, and the man who once had kept Gentile neighbors at a distance now listened to their problems, fears, and temptations. He enjoyed watching their games. Too old to compete in athletics, he probably joined in the calisthenics down by the river, stripping naked in the normal way, possibly boxing to harden his body for the tasks he was sure lay ahead, and certainly striking up friendships. He studied Greek literature too, which in a strict Pharisee's household would be despised or abhorred. Though direct references in his epistles are scanty, he quoted Menander, Aratus, and the Cretan poet Epimenides. In the speech to the intellectuals at Athens, he used an apt allusion from Aeschylus's *Eumenides* and another from Plato's *Phaedo* and makes a tactful paraphrase from Plato's *Republic*.[4] Such examples, which a fuller preservation of Paul's oral teaching would have multiplied, suggest a well-read man.

This interest in Gentiles threw him into conflict with the elders of the Tarsus synagogue. Their particular accusations are not known. He could have been disciplined for entering Gentile houses. He could have been scourged for eating food forbidden to Jews, which he might have accepted when dining with friends; or for disobedience after a plain order from his religious superiors, the offense for which Peter and John were flogged in Jerusalem. Writing in AD 56, he mentioned being punished no less than five times by the Jewish "forty stripes save one," yet none of this is recorded in Acts. Thus it is probable that he was whipped more than once in the hidden years of Tarsus. Scourging was regarded as the correction of a brother, purging his offense that he might resume a place in the family of the synagogue. The alternative was excommunication, to be flung out of Israel—a fate that Paul would wish to avoid, eager as he was to use the synagogues as Christ's spearheads.

At a trial before the elders and brethren he could now claim Christ's promise, which he had ridiculed in his persecuting days: "Do not be anxious … the Holy Spirit will teach you in that very hour what you are to say." He turned the occasion to a testimony and awaited sentence, knowing that Christ had warned him personally, through Ananias, that he would suffer.

It was the duty of the judges to estimate how much corporal punishment, up to the prescribed thirty-nine lashes, the culprit could take. Paul's physique was such that he was awarded the lot.

Watched by the congregation, he was bent and bound between two pillars. The *hazzan*, possibly the same who had taught him as a boy, solemnly tore at his robe until his torso was bare. The *hazzan* picked up a heavy whip formed by a four-pronged strap of calf hide with two prongs of ass hide, long enough to reach the navel from behind and above. He stood on a stone and with one hand, using "all his might," brought it down over Paul's shoulder to curl round and cut his chest. Thirteen lashes were counted, while a reader intoned curses from the Law: "If thou wilt not observe to do all the words of this Law that are written in this book, that thou mayest fear this glorious and fearful name, The Lord Thy God, then the Lord will make thy plagues wonderful."

After the thirteenth on the chest, the whipping was transferred to the back, thirteen hard strokes across one shoulder, thirteen across the other, cutting across weals already bleeding. The pain may be gauged by a description of flogging in early Australia from the autobiographical novel *Ralph Rashleigh*, for whom the first dozen strokes were "like jagged wire tearing furrows in the flesh, and the second dozen seemed like the filling of the furrows with molten lead.... Sensations of intense and intolerable pain."

The synagogue elder in charge could stop the punishment if the prisoner collapsed or lost control of his bowels, but such mercy was exercised seldom, for the scourger was expressly indemnified if the victim died. Paul endured to the end, tasting not only the agony he had inflicted on others but also the sharing of his pain with Jesus.

As he lay recovering in the family home (for despite their shame they were obliged to treat him as a son) or went stiffly about the tentmaking business, no doubt he reconsidered whether his stand was necessary. Should he not conform, repudiate Gentile friendships, and stop teaching salvation through faith? His conclusion could have been expressed in the words he used a few years later when the issue had become more than personal: "Christ has set us free, to be free men. Stand firm then, and refuse to be tied to the yoke of slavery again."

The elders sought a fresh pretext to punish him, and this time may have invoked a vicious clause in synagogue law, that if a culprit breaks two prohibitions and is sentenced on each, "he must suffer the first, be healed again, and then be scourged a second time." Thus twice more, making three of the five scourgings he mentioned, Paul stood stripped at the pillars, each stroke driving home the truth of Christ's warning to His disciples: "You will be *hated* for My name's sake."

In an age when brutal punishments were normal, Paul would have escaped much psychological damage, especially as he accepted persecution as a small price for the prize of knowing and serving "Christ Jesus my Lord." Physically, however, he was marked for life. A curious piece of evidence strengthens the probability that he was badly beaten in Tarsus. The second-century document from Asia Minor called *The Acts of Paul and Thecla*, a story invented by a presbyter who tried to pass it off as genuine and was unfrocked for the fraud, includes a description of Paul that may preserve the traditional memory of his appearance on the first great missionary journey: moderate height, rather bald with a long nose and beetling brows, and *bowlegged*. The "young man named Saul" who ran through the streets before the stoning of Stephen and stood out in the crowd would hardly have been bowlegged, yet this is a deformity common among men who have been severely flogged.

Whether or not the elders had him scourged yet again, there is strong probability that he was excommunicated from the Tarsus synagogue and that the tension in the family snapped. "Fathers, provoke not your children to wrath," Paul's exhortation to the Ephesians, may carry the memory of a final quarrel, when his hot temper was roused beyond endurance to betray "the meekness and gentleness of Christ" within him. Whether after violent argument or by his father's implacable decision, he was expelled and disinherited, reduced to apostolic poverty.

And what of his wife, if he were not a widower? In his First Letter to the Corinthians, he says on his own authority ("not the Lord") that "if any brother has a wife who is an unbeliever, and she consents to live with him, he should not divorce her ... but if the unbelieving partner desires to separate, let it be so; in such a case the brother or sister is not bound. For God has called us to peace." No one can ever know whether these words arose from the memory of a loved wife who rejected Christ, refused to join her husband in Damascus, returned to Tarsus, and finally deserted him.

Every advantage that Paul had gained by birth, "I considered lost for Christ's sake. Yes, and I look upon everything as loss compared with the overwhelming gain of knowing Christ Jesus my Lord. For His sake I did in actual fact suffer the loss of everything, but I considered it useless rubbish compared with being able to win Christ."

Cast out of home, comforts, and position, Paul disappeared into the wild country of the Taurus foothills. And here, in AD 41 or 42, possibly in the cave that used to be shown as "Saint Paul's Cave," he had a "vision and revelation of the Lord" so sacred that he never referred to it for over fourteen years, and then only in guarded terms in the third person: "I know of a man in Christ who was caught up to the third heaven—whether in the body or out of the body I do not know, God knows."

Unlike Saint John on Patmos, who was expressly ordered to write down what he saw, Paul "heard things that cannot be told, which man may not utter." In the humiliations and pains of years to come, when he was discouraged or temporarily defeated, he had the undying memory of this glimpse of eternity. "Eye has not seen, nor ear heard," he could encourage his converts, "nor have entered into the heart of man the things which God has prepared for those who love Him." He was quoting these words from Isaiah, but he had perceived by his own senses that the prophet spoke the truth, and it put into proportion the worst that man or nature could do. "I reckon that the sufferings of this present time are not worthy to be compared with the glory that shall be revealed in us."

Nevertheless, his exuberance must not grow inordinate. "To keep me from being too elated by the abundance of revelations, a thorn was given me in the flesh, a messenger of Satan, to harass [or buffet] me, to keep me from being too elated. Three times I besought the Lord about this, that it should leave me; but He said to me, 'My grace is sufficient for you, for My power is made perfect in weakness.'"

The ingenuity of two thousand years has been exercised over Paul's thorn or (literally) "stake for the flesh." Some supposed it severe sexual temptation, but he would have scorned the idea: Christ's Spirit would certainly master the works of the flesh in that sense. Others decided that he referred to the violence of opposition. The more usual and likely view is "a sharp pain in my body," "a physical handicap," but its nature remains obscure. Those who dismiss Paul's views and visions as hallucinations have argued that he was an epileptic; others have sought a clue in illnesses that may be deduced from the record, especially malaria, with its splitting headaches and ophthalmia; or the trouble may have sprung from tissues and nerves torn by the beatings.

Whether intermittent or chronic, the thorn threw him more fully on Christ.

So, leaving his cave, this half-bald, bandy-legged man of about forty-one, weak but tough, alone and obscure, yet light of heart, set out to talk about Jesus the Christ.

PART TWO

TO THE GENTILES

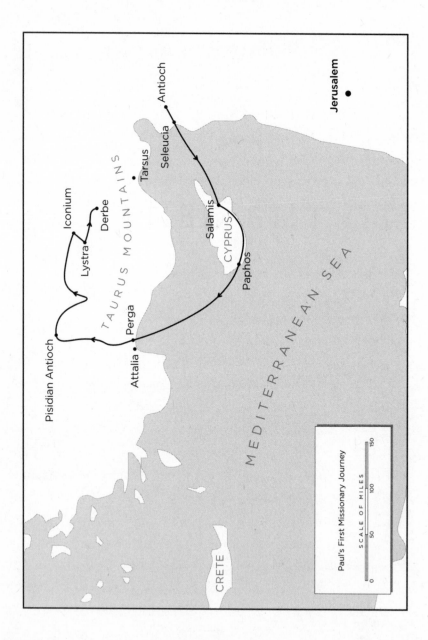

Jerusalem

Antioch

Seleucia

Tarsus

TAURUS MOUNTAINS

Iconium

Derbe

Lystra

Salamis

CYPRUS

Pisidian Antioch

Perga

Paphos

Attalia

MEDITERRANEAN SEA

CRETE

Paul's First Missionary Journey

SCALE OF MILES

0   50   100   150

SEVEN

THE NEW ERA

In mountain villages and isolated farms, walking the trails through forests of fir and ash and up the ridges leading toward the high snows of Taurus, Paul founded little groups of disciples that were still active when he returned years later. Probably also he took a ship along the coast where land routes were poor, for the hidden years must include the three shipwrecks he mentioned when writing in AD 56; after one of them, "I was adrift on the open sea for a night and a day."

In this traveling he was freelance. He always emphasized the importance of links between the churches of Jesus wherever they were, and of unity between itinerant evangelists and those who supported them, yet he was isolated from the apostles in Jerusalem and the main advances of the faith. He was lonely too. He worked best with one or more companions yet seemed to have had none from these country communities; and if there were converts in Tarsus, Acts never mentions them. As Christ had said, "A prophet is not without honor, except in his own country and among his own kin, and in his own house."

Then Paul heard that a man from Syria sought him, and at last they met. Luke implied that Barnabas had a considerable search: "Barnabas went forth to Tarsus to seek for Saul ..."

Barnabas brought important news. The faith had taken hold in Antioch, the capital of Syria. What is more, it had spread among pagans. Meanwhile Peter had undergone a remarkable experience with the household of an Italian centurion in Caesarea, a Jewish proselyte. Peter had entered rather gingerly after a direct order from the Lord, and the Holy Spirit came upon them as he preached. He told the brothers in Jerusalem who criticized him for entering a Gentile home: "If God gave the same gift to them as He gave to us when we believed in the Lord Jesus Christ, who was I that I could withstand God?" When, therefore, news reached the apostles that large numbers of non-Jews in Antioch had become believers, they selected Barnabas to investigate. He was delighted at what he found "and encouraged them all to hold fast to the Lord with resolute hearts."

Barnabas, who was unmarried, made his home in Antioch. Under his leadership, the church grew fast, and he wanted Paul to help him.

Antioch, the third greatest city of the Roman world, lay sixteen miles up the Orontes River, which flowed on through a barrier of hills to the sea. The city guarded the narrow plain that opened to the east toward the Syrian plateau and was guarded itself from the south by the crags of Mount Silpius, with the citadel on the summit and below it a huge rock carving of a faceless human head, popularly supposed to be of Charon who ferried dead souls to the underworld. The city was a magnificent example of town planning and architecture, a testimony to the supremacy of Greek civilization enhanced by the Roman peace. Like all capital cities of the time, it was an amalgam of splendor and poverty—broad, colonnaded thoroughfares, the palace of the imperial legate, temples, the hippodrome where the novel *Ben-Hur* places the chariot race, and mile upon square mile of overcrowded back streets.

Antiochenes had a rumbustious reputation, partly from their satirical wit and likely sense of the ridiculous but mainly because of a sex life that even ancient Rome rated excessive. Five miles south on the pass into the hills stood the extensive sacred Grove of Daphne, dominated by an enormous statue of the god Apollo, where hundreds of prostitutes gave their bodies to any man who cared to worship the goddess of love. Among the trees and temples lived also a human flotsam of escaped slaves, criminals, debtors, and others who had sought sanctuary.

Back streets and Daphne woods made fertile soil, and by the time Paul arrived, the Antioch church reflected the racial and social variety of this crossroads of the East. He could plunge right in, preaching and gossiping the gospel to pagans at the market, in homes, at the baths, in the dressing rooms of gymnasia and the hippodrome, knowing that there was already a warm, vigorous church life to welcome converts.

Believers used to meet (according to an early authority quoted in the sixth century) on Singon Street in the Epiphania district near the Pantheon, close under the carved head of Charon. They probably crowded into the house of a wealthy brother each Sunday, the day of the resurrection, which they called the Lord's Day, the Jews among them having already attended synagogue on the Saturday. Worship may have continued at all hours because slaves and the poor had to squeeze time from their labor. Antioch, which had scores of cults already, decided these people who had their own *ecclesia* or assembly and constantly talked about Jesus the Christ were not some new species of Jew, and so they coined the half-Greek, half-Latin term *Christiani*.

The church was rich in leadership. Besides Barnabas and Paul, there was Lucius of Cyrene, of whom nothing is known, and an elderly aristocrat named Manaen, a foster brother of Herod the Tetrarch who had executed John the Baptist and mocked the Lord Jesus and had lately lost his principality.

A leader named Simeon or Simon "Niger" was probably black. And the evidence leans toward his being "Simon of Cyrene, the father of Alexander and Rufus," the countryman coming into Jerusalem whom the Romans had conscripted to carry the cross of Jesus, and that he had fled to Antioch when Paul made havoc of the church. His son Rufus emigrated to Rome. Paul in his letter to Rome long after sent greetings to Rufus, "an outstanding follower of the Lord, and to his mother, whom I call mother too," which suggests that he found a home and affection in Antioch with those he had hurt in Jerusalem.

Thus Antioch gave Paul a home, friends, and work to heal the scars and strains of the lonely decade now ended. It brought him back to the mainstream of the Christian church. But it could not be more than a temporary stop. He was sure he was not called to serve a settled if rapidly growing Christian

community, but to be an apostle, sent out to proclaim the Good News where
the name of Christ was unknown.

The whole world waited. He itched to finish his slow apprenticeship and
start as a master builder.

A group from the Jerusalem church visited Antioch and were received with
delight, especially because they were prophets who, like the Old Testament
prophets, were recognized as able to reveal God's will about the present and
even the future. One of them, Agabus, stood up with the Spirit upon him
and gave solemn warning of a mass scarcity of wheat to come. The Antioch
Christians accepted this as a divine revelation and determined to hoard grain
while the market remained normal, ready to send relief to Jerusalem where
the unfertile hills would be hit hard by drought.

Most of the believers were poor. Each put into the famine fund what he
could, week by week, and men were appointed to travel around the lush lands
beside the great lake near Antioch, and up the Orontes, to buy grain wherever
they could find it stored. Organizing this was after Paul's heart, for though his
own work must be evangelizing and teaching, he would always show strong
social concern; he was eager to forge links between the Antioch church and
Jerusalem.

In due course the harvest failed. Tacitus, Suetonius, and Josephus, historians around this time, recorded food shortages during this period. The severity
of the famine in Judea was endorsed by Josephus's evidence that Queen
Helena, the Jewish mother of a pagan king beyond the empire, bought grain
in Egypt and figs in Cyprus to distribute relief in Jerusalem.

Barnabas and Paul were designated by the church to take the grain,
probably in August AD 46. For this considerable expedition, Paul chose as
an assistant the young convert of his own, Titus. The choice was deliberate.
Titus was a pure-blooded Greek and therefore uncircumcised. If Paul could
take him around in the heart of Judaism, he would have established the

principle that a Gentile can be a Christian without needing to become a Jew.

They would have carried the grain by sea to Joppa and up by mule train, and thus, in the eleventh year after his last visit and the fourteenth since his conversion, Paul could again echo the psalmist: "Our feet shall stand in thy gates, O Jerusalem." The gates, however, had changed, for the Romans had made Judea a kingdom once more under Herod Agrippa I, nephew of the Baptist's murderer, and he had begun new walls to the north; the sites of the crucifixion and Stephen's death were now within the city. This Herod had recently arrested Peter and James, John's brother. James had been executed. Peter escaped by a miracle in answer to prayer. Herod had died suddenly and miserably at Caesarea shortly before Barnabas and Paul reached Jerusalem.

They handed the supplies to the church elders, for the apostles maintained the rule they had established in Stephen's day of not entangling themselves in administration. The Antioch party was in no hurry to return and played a full part in the distribution of the grain to citizens of Jerusalem, not only to Jews who were Christians but to those who were not, though more and more were accepting Jesus as their Messiah.

But Paul had another, private task in Jerusalem.

He wanted to go over with Peter and other leaders "the Gospel that I preach among the Gentiles, lest somehow I should be running or had run in vain." If any detail in the revelations that had come to him, especially his conviction that pagan converts were not required to become Jews as well, conflicted with the words of Jesus and the attested narratives of the works of Jesus, then he was sure—as all early Christians would have been sure—that it was an aberration that could not have been taught him by the Spirit of God.

Taking Barnabas, he sought out Peter and arranged for a confidential discussion, together with John and the surviving James, the Lord's brother, who seemed the other foremost figures.

Paul was somewhat prickly about his status. He believed he qualified as an apostle as much as they, for like them he was an eyewitness of the risen Christ; he had been personally commissioned to tell what he had seen and to preach the gospel; and he had been directly instructed in Arabia as they had in Galilee and Judea. He was determined that no earthly leader should stand between himself and the Lord Jesus. He was relieved therefore to discover that these three appreciated his point and did not attempt to order him around. Indeed, they received him with utmost warmth and found nothing that jarred on their knowledge of the Lord's teaching and actions when He had lived among them until the day of His ascension. Paul's account of what God had done through him was plain evidence, they said, that he was assigned to the Gentiles just as Peter was assigned to the Jews. And they did not suggest that young Titus should submit to circumcision; Paul had needed already to be abrupt with a few Jewish Christians—he doubted the sincerity of their conversion and he hinted that they had spied on Titus when he was undressed—who grumbled that an uncircumcised Greek was only half a disciple of Jesus. But now even James stifled his reservations.

The conference ended with handclasps, goodwill, and a settled policy that Paul and Barnabas should go to Gentile territories while the others worked in Palestine. The three Jerusalem leaders' sole request was that Paul, Barnabas, and their Gentile friends should always remember the Jerusalem poor, "which very thing I was eager to do." Paul's apprenticeship was over. He was accepted as an apostle.

He left to pray in the temple. Here, the aged Simeon had seen the infant Jesus and offered his Nunc Dimittis, "for mine eyes have seen Thy salvation, which Thou has prepared before the face of all people; a light to lighten the Gentiles, and the glory of Thy people Israel." And now Paul had been chosen and acknowledged as an instrument in fulfilling the prophecy. His mind and soul were wrapped in praise and prayer. Though at forty-four he had little to show and might almost be counted a failure, the years ahead would be glorious, if arduous.

He still believed, as he had believed when he preached immediately after his conversion, that the worldwide church would be built on the foundation of the Jewish synagogues across the empire, each beaming Christ's light to city and countryside in the pagan lands around the Mediterranean. It seemed to him that the only way to begin was to inspire the Greek-speaking synagogues in Jerusalem. If he won these for Christ, the rest overseas would follow. At his early attempt in the previous decade, Jerusalem Jews had refused to listen because they considered him a turncoat. But the famine had opened their eyes and ears. Surely those who knew his past, how he had persecuted Christ's followers, knew now that he was an honorable, loving man who had brought his countrymen succor. Therefore they would see that the risen Jesus he had encountered, who had converted him, must be the Truth and the Way. Those in the synagogues would reverse their former verdict and accept what he told them about Jesus, and believe. The very fact that they knew he had persecuted the faith was his strongest claim to be heard.

Then, from Jerusalem, Paul would lead teams of Greek-speaking Jews and proselytes to the uttermost parts of the empire. They would be joined by pagan converts to carry the message of Christ yet farther. There would be one fold and one Shepherd.

As he mused and prayed, he lost all consciousness of the crowd of worshippers, of the din coming in from the outer courts, of money-changers and sellers of sacrificial pigeons and doves; he lost any sense of fatigue standing as the hours fled. He was conscious only of the Spirit of Jesus, the Lord Jesus, never absent, specially real whenever Paul's mind was uncluttered, and now more obviously present each passing minute. His heart was on fire. It was as if some atmosphere around him were thinning and the heat of God's love, of Christ's, burned in on his soul, unbelievable, precious.

And then it happened: "I saw Him."

As Paul recounted to a hostile audience years later almost at the self-same spot, "I saw Him there, speaking to me. 'Make haste,' He said, 'and leave Jerusalem without delay, for they will not accept your testimony about Me.'"

At that, Paul argued. As Ananias had argued, and Peter; arguing with the Son of God, who surely should see that Paul must remain in Jerusalem, that they would accept the word of a converted persecutor.

"Lord," he began, "they know that I imprisoned those who believe in You, and flogged them in every synagogue; and when the blood of Stephen, Your witness, was shed I stood by, approving, and I looked after the clothes of those who killed him—"

"Go! For I am sending you far away to the Gentiles."[5]

There was to be no argument.

EIGHT

APHRODITE'S ISLAND

All winter after Paul and his companions returned from Jerusalem, a sense of an imminent new beginning possessed the Antioch church. At length, at a time of worship and fasting there came a profound conviction of the Holy Spirit's will: "Set Barnabas and Saul apart for Me, to do the work to which I have called them." Then followed a solemn laying on of hands by the leaders in the sight of the church: The apostles would not be freelancers but representatives of the Antioch Christians; the lowliest slave, the newest convert would have a part in the enterprise, talking to the Lord about them, wondering how they prospered, lapping up scraps of news that might trickle back from travelers who crossed their paths.

Barnabas and Paul were formally released from their local ministry. They went by boat down the deep, winding valley of the Orontes the sixteen miles to the sea, and round the bluff to Antioch's port of Seleucia, sure that they had been commissioned by God Himself and that just as they were obeying the command of Jesus to spread His gospel, so they had His promise, "I am with you always."

They had His words in their memories—and very possibly on papyrus. For they were accompanied by Barnabas's relative John Mark, a young man with stumpy fingers and a terse way of speech, who had come back with them from his home in Jerusalem. He was their subordinate, yet an integral member of the team: Luke's term to describe his position was used in the Roman world for a document handler. Mark may have already written down, at Peter's behest, a collection of the authentic sayings and doings of Jesus, and he may have been sent by the Jerusalem church with the express intention of strengthening through public readings Barnabas and Paul in their ministry to the Gentiles. And he could add priceless eyewitness testimony of the sufferings of Jesus if, as is generally supposed, he was the young man who had followed Him in the Garden of Gethsemane and fled naked at the arrest.

The three missionaries shipped from Seleucia in the first days of the sailing season early in March AD 47 for the easy run to Cyprus, an obvious preliminary choice in that Barnabas was a Cypriot and the island had a substantial Jewish minority (large enough to raise a dangerous rebellion some fifty years later). There was also a big population of pagan slaves extracting the copper that gave Cyprus its wealth. The apostles landed at Salamis, the commercial center of the eastern half (near modern Famagusta), where they "proclaimed the Word of God in the synagogues of the Jews."

They next worked their way round the southern shore of the island, staying a short time at each town. If Paul thought that this method would not prove the best, he gave no sign or else deferred to the preference of Barnabas, the acknowledged leader. For Paul, Cyprus could be no more than a prelude; the Christian message had been known there since the arrival of refugees from his own persecution fifteen years before, whereas he was determined to go "where Christ was not named." He was confident that the Lord would unfold a strategy. He had the strongest awareness, as his actions showed, that the entire operation was in the hands of the Lord Jesus, who was no passive spectator but the invisible commander, ready to seize opportunities, recover from reverses, and deploy His forces as they gathered under His banner.

Barnabas possibly doubted whether the pagans would receive the Word; Antioch might have been a special case. Paul had no such doubts. Both awaited a sign.

They crossed low wooded hills, skirted the bay where, in Homer, Aphrodite the goddess of love emerged full grown from the foam. They avoided her famous temple at which, as in Daphne, prostitution counted for religious devotion, and came down to the Roman city of New Paphos, the capital and the best harbor on the southwest coast. Soon, surprisingly, they received a summons to lecture before the august presence of the proconsul of Cyprus, Sergius Paullus.

The palace of the proconsul stood a little above the city. As Barnabas and Paul walked up the processional way on a late spring day, the sun gleamed on gilded gods above the granite palace gate and touched the helmets of the legionnaires, who raised spears in salute to honored guests.

Sergius Paullus had been curator of the Tiber River before leaving Rome, and Luke was meticulously accurate in describing him as proconsul, since by constitutional theory Cyprus belonged to the senate and not the emperor, whose provincial governors were termed legates.[6] Sergius Paullus had a scientific mind: Pliny the Elder in his *Natural History* cited him as an authority. He had a taste for speculation and superstition too, as Barnabas and Paul realized when they saw among his entourage a notorious renegade Jew with the incongruous name of Bar-Jesus or "son of a savior," who purported to be a prophet of the living God but also an astrologer, a wise man of the East (or *magus*) who dabbled in the occult and could boast of the alternative name of Elymas, "Skillful" or "Sage."

Sergius Paullus was sitting on his proconsular throne in the spacious audience hall. A breeze gently blew through the marble pillars, which gave glimpses of the deep-blue bay and the white town below. He asked to hear what the apostles taught. Soon, according to a phrase in the very early though slightly expanded "Western Text" of Acts, the proconsul was "listening with much pleasure to them."

They were in full course, each adding to the other, when abruptly, in defiance of protocol, Elymas interrupted. He launched a venomous attack on them and their news, "trying to turn the Proconsul from the faith" with all the vigor of a man who sees his influence about to be overturned.

Paul stood it a few minutes, indignant, praying inwardly, struggling to master himself. Then he became aware of peace filling his mind, and fire, and knew for a certainty that the Holy Spirit had taken control.

Paul had a low flash point, a temper that could burst at times of extreme exasperation; but these next moments he was calm, his words the more terrible in owing nothing to temper. He saw right into Elymas, exactly what he was;

Paul saw too the urgency of the situation, the struggle for Sergius Paullus's soul. The Roman officers of the entourage could not care how many gods a man worshipped and had stifled a yawn or two before the sudden tension expelled indifference, but to Paul it mattered more than anything that Sergius Paullus should believe in Jesus; there was one truth, and if Elymas-Bar-Jesus perverted it, he must be judged. Paul cared nothing that he was about to risk his skin by exposing in the hearing of the quack's powerful protector this "son of a savior."

Paul fixed him with his eye. "You son of the devil," he began. "You enemy of all goodness, full of all deceit and every cunning, is it not high time you stopped making crooked the ways of the Lord?"

Elymas quailed. And Paul, totally in tune with the Lord of the universe, knew exactly what was about to happen. He could speak as a prophet, foretelling the immediate future. It was not Paul who was about to punish, but God.

"Look now! The hand of the Lord strikes you: you shall be blind, and for a time you shall not see sunlight!"

At once sight faded, then failed. Like Paul on the Damascus Road, Elymas groped for someone to lead him by the hand.

Insofar as medical reason may be adduced, he had probably suffered a blockage of a central vein. If the Lord could open the eyes of the blind, He could touch a central vein; intervention to frustrate an opponent of His messengers is scarcely ever recorded, but this was for Elymas's ultimate good, as was suggested by Luke's precision of terms: "Instantly a *mist* and *darkness* came over him." Luke never used words loosely, and he said plainly that Elymas did not go stone blind in a second: Light faded before total darkness supervened. This detail could only have been provided by Elymas himself, presumably recovered and, at the very least, friendly to a Christian historian.

As for Sergius Paullus, he was astounded. An educated Roman used to authority, he was convinced that what he heard was unique truth and power, not idle speculation. When he "saw what happened, he became a believer, deeply impressed by what he learned about the Lord." He passes out of the story, for Luke was not writing a detailed history of the expansion of Christianity. But in the year 1912, the archaeologist Sir William Ramsay unearthed an inscription in Anatolia that, to his expert knowledge, demonstrated that Sergius Paullus influenced his daughter to become a Christian; whereas his son, the governor of Galatia in the next generation, who probably was being educated in Rome at the time of his father's proconsulship of Cyprus, remained pagan.

For Paul and Barnabas, the incident was a sign that God would open a door to the Gentiles. And Barnabas joyfully conceded the leadership. He recognized that the Holy Spirit had fashioned Paul by background and training to lead them on, into the unknown.

NINE

INTO GALATIA

They set sail again, Paul and his company, for another short run, northwest to the coast of Pamphylia on the mainland of Asia Minor. And now at last they were truly pioneers. Pamphylia lay far west of any territory that Paul may have touched in the hidden years, nor had Christians made it that far.

Thus, in his late forties, an age when men settle to comforts and seek a firm base, Paul began his roughest travels. The task was immense. Against him stood the contemporary climate of thought, the great philosophies, the leading religions of the world. His ally was the age-old, unending human search for truth and security. In the first century as in the twenty-first, some were devout, some superstitious, others were frankly materialistic, even though in that age they paid lip service to the gods. Others, contemptuous of religion, believed only in mankind. But at heart, when disguises were torn away and defenses broken, lay the same anxieties and hopes.

The ship sailed into the Gulf of Attalia. Leaving on the port side a great mountain, and the harbor of Attalia below cliffs where streams fell by waterfalls to the sea, she worked her way a few miles up the Cestrus River to the lesser harbor near the walled city of Perga, a steamy, inland center nestled beneath its acropolis. Paul had no intention of stopping. His urge was to press on; the work lay in the hinterland, beyond a barrier of mountains that faced them across the narrow plain, steeper and fiercer than the eastern Taurus near Tarsus and more terrible than any hills known to the Cypriot Barnabas or the Judean John Mark.

Here Mark returned to Jerusalem.

Paul saw it as rank desertion. Mark's excuse has been variously guessed. Some think Paul had fallen ill of malaria and made for the mountains to seek cooler air rather than from deliberate intent, and Mark was frightened. But he would hardly have left a relative in a strange land with an invalid. Another guess, that he considered they were exceeding their commission by going to the Gentiles, does not square with the undisputed fact that his gospel was written primarily for Romans. He may have resented Barnabas's surrender of the leadership; he may have been a coward, or homesick, even lovesick. Whatever the cause, Mark's withdrawal left a wound in Paul that took years to heal.

Paul and Barnabas set off across the plain, where the dust rose in stifling clouds from the Roman road, and the next day, into the mountains by steep gorges where the heat hit back from the gray rock. Chariots and carts were not expected on these gradients; the modern road uses hairpin turns, but the Romans had laid theirs sheer up the pass, and the perspiration poured off walkers young and old. They entered a forbidding landscape of boulders and stunted pines. In Paul's era, between the peace of Augustus and the troubles of Nero, Roman roads were safer than at any time before or afterward for a thousand years, but he was entering one of the few regions within the empire not fully tamed. Brigands and wild tribesmen made short work of lone travelers; the apostles must join a caravan.

Each night a huge fire would be kept alive and they all slept round it, their feet toward the heat. Paul would take his turn on watch, probably wrapped in a sheepskin. Before dawn they would break camp, eat olives and goat cheese and, if cold, could drink mulled wine (tea was not known yet out of China, and Arabs had not discovered coffee). They started before sunrise to use the cool of the day. The pace was a steady plod, and they walked with occasional halts until noon, expecting to cover about fifteen miles.[7] Then they cooked their meal, slept in the shade, oiled themselves in preference to washing, and did nothing in particular.

The journey was slow. Passing day after day on indifferent food in a high altitude did not encourage foot travelers to quicken the pace or lengthen the stages or to do another stint in the evening as horsemen would. The heat, the sudden drenching storms that flooded the gullies, the cold at night when limbs were stiff and old scars hurt, the danger of sudden attack—this first journey was one of the toughest. It must have been in Paul's mind when he recalled his hardships in the Second Letter to the Corinthians, and the sonorous English of the *Authorized Version*, like his original Greek, seems to echo the rhythm of the march: "In perils of waters, in perils of robbers … in weariness and painfulness, in watchings often, in hunger and thirst, in fastings often, in cold and nakedness."

Paul would say in old age, "I have *learned* in whatever state I am, to be content.… In any and all circumstances, I have *learned* the secret of facing plenty and hunger, abundance and want. I can do all things in Him who strengthens me" (*or*, "I am ready for anything through the strength of the One who lives within me"). This secret was not learned at once. There may have been times when his endurance wore thin on this journey, or when, later, he found it difficult to control his temper toward rapacious innkeepers.

But with the equable Barnabas by his side, he quickly became a good traveler, encouraging the weak or fearful in the company, laughing at difficulties. The Victorian biographer J. S. Howson thought Paul lacked a sense of humor. First-century Jews had little natural humor, yet a man who wrote so much about cheerfulness—"rejoice in the Lord always," "love, joy, peace," "make melody in your heart," "God, who gives us richly all things to enjoy"—could hardly have been morose. Joy was a release of Paul's conversion, not the hearty backslapping practical-joking humor of the Victorians, nor the cynical satire or the flippancy of twenty-first-century mass media, just the gift of not taking himself or adversities too seriously.

Paul had his times of depression, even perhaps an inbuilt tendency toward melancholy, but he got a lot of fun out of life.

By now they were high up in the mountains and had crossed into the great province of Galatia, which stretched over much of central Anatolia. They filed down into more settled highland country, the caravans dispersed, and Paul and Barnabas continued by themselves. And so they came to one of the most beautiful lakes in the world, called Limnai in their day and Lake

Egirdir now. Hills all about them, a snowcapped mountain on their left and another, Mount Olympus, far ahead, made a perfect setting for the extraordinary turquoise of the water.

For three days they walked on the path beside the lake. Wherever the hills stood back, each promontory and bay had a scattering of farms and cottages thatched from the reeds that grew offshore. The apostles easily found lodging, and they probably talked about their mission; they would not stop to tell it to passing wayfarers, for Paul liked to make for a definite field rather than scatter seed by the wayside, though the friendliness and spiritual hunger of their hosts, whether slaves or small tenant farmers, must have offered a hint of the astonishing developments to come.

At last they joined a branch of the great road from the far-distant west coast and turned the corner of the lake until it was lost behind the hills. Pressing on to reach their destination before Sabbath, they crossed a final low pass and saw, dwarfed by another mountain range yet proud in its temples and gates, the city and colony of Caesarea Antiochea, commonly called Pisidian Antioch.

Pisidian Antioch had been refounded by the emperor Augustus as a Roman colony to keep the peace in the hills. It still had a frontier air and a touch, as it were, of Peshawar on the northwest frontier in the days of British India. Antioch, however, was better protected by nature than Peshawar, for below the southeastern wall, which would bear the brunt of tribal attacks, lay the deep, sheer gorge of the Anthios River.

Few remained of the tough old soldiers planted here by Augustus, but their descendants, together with the administrators of southern Galatia, were the aristocracy, holding Roman citizenship, and the native Phrygians did the hard labor. Pisidian Antioch, despite its name, lay in the district of Phrygia; Phrygians were considered as those with brawn but no brain. They were exported as slaves all over the empire, so that "Phrygian" was almost synonymous with "slave." Paul and Barnabas, exploring the city, climbed the steps through magnificent arches that commemorated the victories of Augustus on sea and land. They walked in the square named in his honor, dominated by the white marble temple where the late emperor was worshipped along with the local god. They could feel the arrogance of Rome and the bitterness of proud tribes conquered less than a generation before.

Antioch had its Jews, whose wealth and industry had earned Roman tolerance for their disrupting of the economy by stopping work one day in seven. On Sabbath morning Paul and Barnabas entered the synagogue and sat down in the seats for visiting rabbis. After the prayers and readings, the synagogue rulers sent the *hazzan* with a courteous message: "Brothers, if you have any word of exhortation for the people, say it."

Paul stood up. He noticed at once that the congregation included not only a considerable number of local converts to Judaism but also interested pagans, or "God-fearers." With a gesture that stilled the murmur of anticipation, he caught the attention of everybody by an unusual opening: Instead of following custom by ignoring the existence of God-fearers, he included them in his opening words: "Men of Israel and you God-fearers, listen!"

He began with a historical sketch closely modeled on Stephen's unforgettable defense. But whereas Stephen got no further than King David before the atmosphere grew so hostile that he broke off to accuse his judges, Paul was heard with complete attention.

From David's descendants, he said, "God has brought to Israel a Savior, Jesus, as He promised." Still they listened. For the first recorded time in a synagogue, Paul had a sympathetic audience. He went on:

"Men and brothers, sons of the race of Abraham, and all among you who fear God, it is to us that this message of salvation has now been sent. For the people of Jerusalem and their rulers refused to recognize Him and to understand the voice of the prophets which are read every Sabbath day. Even though they found no cause for putting Him to death, they begged Pilate to have Him executed."

He let the enormity of what had been done sink into their minds.

Then, in ringing tones, Paul proclaimed his amazing good news: *"But God raised Him from the dead!"*

He talked about the resurrection of Jesus, its witnesses, how it had been foretold. Reaching his climax, he swept away the barrier between Jew and Gentile to include every person present in God's offer of free forgiveness: "Know therefore, *brothers*"—pagan God-fearers had never been called "brothers" before—"that through this Man forgiveness of sins is proclaimed to you, and by Him everyone who believes is freed from everything, from which you could not be freed by the Law of Moses."

All over the synagogue Paul could see light dawning on faces, here a pagan, there a trueborn Jew, here a proselyte. He urged the need for personal repentance and faith in Jesus, and ended, "Beware, therefore, lest there come upon you what is said in the prophets: 'Behold, you scoffers, and wonder, and perish; for I do a deed in your days, a deed you will never believe, if one declares it to you.'"

As they went out, the congregation crowded round and begged for more the next Sabbath. The synagogue doors were shut behind them, perhaps a little pointedly. Jews and proselytes followed Paul and Barnabas toward their lodgings. All that day and during the week the apostles were busy with individuals and groups as they "urged them to hold fast to the grace of God."

The pagan God-fearers had scattered to their homes, scarcely daring to believe that faith in Jesus could bring immediate forgiveness and happiness without the necessity of circumcision and the rigors of the Jewish Law. They spread the news like wildfire. In the market, in the law courts, in the slave barracks of the tribune's mansion, the word went round that these traveling preachers had a message that made sense of life.

When on the next Sabbath Paul and Barnabas reached the synagogue, they found an enormous crowd, Gentiles outnumbering Jews. Every seat was filled. Veterans and their families, Greek shopmen, Phrygian slaves, all stood pressed about the door and down the narrow street and into the Square of Augustus. Priests of the pagan temples looked on amazed at the size, quietness, and earnestness of the crowd. This crowd ignored them, clearly interested solely in hearing, if they could, what the two Christians wanted to say. Only the higher aristocracy and their womenfolk held aloof.

In the synagogue the service never began.

Instead of warmly welcoming the largest congregation of their time, the rabbi, elders, and leading Jews were furious. They resented the response to Paul's message. What last week they had received respectfully they now repudiated root and branch, and the people who had flocked to learn about the power and love of Jesus heard His claims dismissed, His character slandered, His messengers covered with abuse.

Paul was not surprised. After all, they only said what He had once said.

He did not mind being spattered with verbal filth. He could stomach even the blasphemies hurled at his Lord. But he was not going to be muzzled. Gentiles and Jews wanted to hear the message, and no blind, self-satisfied Jewish elder was going to get in the way. The two missionaries stood up boldly (they risked being whipped for opposing lawful authority) and answered back: "It was necessary that the Word of God should be declared to you first. But since you reject it, and thus condemn yourselves as unworthy of eternal life, we now turn to the Gentiles. For these are our instructions from the Lord." Paul quoted the prophecy of Isaiah, which Simeon had used in the Nunc Dimittis: "'I have set you to be a light for the Gentiles, that you may bring salvation to the uttermost parts of the earth.'"

The apostles strode out of the synagogue, followed by all the Gentiles, who were patently delighted, and by many of the Jews. The crowds at the door made way for them, and they walked to the square and stood on the plinth of a statue. And there, to this great concourse of Galatians, Paul preached.

When he wrote his letter to the Galatians, he would remind them that, before their very eyes, Jesus Christ the crucified had been publicly declared.

TEN

PROGRESS AND PERSECUTION

Shortly afterward, Paul fell ill, or so it seems. In his letter to the Galatians,[8] he wrote, "As you know, it was bodily illness that originally led to my bringing you the Gospel, and you showed neither scorn nor disgust at the trial my poor body was enduring; you welcomed me as if I were an angel of God, as you might have welcomed Christ Jesus Himself." Paul could not be referring to that first sermon in the synagogue, for the elders would never have allowed him to preach in a repulsive physical condition; they rated illness a divine judgment. On the other hand, Paul could not have meant he came to Antioch because he fell ill at Perga, for he was not an object of scorn or disgust by the time he arrived—the grueling march would have killed or cured. He probably therefore meant that he stayed much longer in the area than he had originally intended, and that most of them heard the gospel because of this.

Until then, his strategy had been essentially mobile. In Cyprus he and Barnabas had preached in many places, staying briefly before moving on. At Pisidian Antioch he was forced to stop. Several weeks of high summer passed while he lay sick; lack of mention in Acts is not conclusive, since Luke's immediate purpose in writing was to commend the gospel to Romans, and he saw no cause to introduce subsidiary matters like illness, which would have offended a Roman reader anyway. The Galatians, however, were not offended. New converts displayed a most un-Roman concern for the sick man. They showered him with love and care, wished they could pluck out their own eyes to replace his streaming, rheumy, and pain-filled ones. And all the time the gospel spread.

Of the crowd that had heard Paul preach in the Square of Augustus, many believed. They showed an immediate desire to share their discovery, so that faith in Christ leaped from person to person like some divine epidemic, not of disease but of spiritual health. Barnabas had a hard time keeping abreast of it. By the time Paul recovered enough for action, the openings throughout the district were far too many to permit him to abandon Antioch. Therefore, for the first time, he adopted the strategy by which he would evangelize from then on: Settle in a center to reach a region, and reach it by the converts.

Even before he was well enough to walk, converts brought their friends to his bedside, and his Epistle to the Galatians gives retrospective glimpses of what he said. His entire message centered on Jesus Christ. Words used about Spurgeon by a contemporary could also apply to Paul: "The Lord Jesus was to him such an intense, living reality, he believed so in His nearness and presence and the wonderful love with which He loves us, that the hearer felt that he spoke out of living experience of what he had seen and heard." Paul could convey to a high degree the wonder and certainty of that recent event in history—the crucifixion of Christ for the sins of everyone—and the astonishing fact that *"God raised Him from the dead,"* the phrase in Paul's synagogue sermon that probably he used again and again, coming as it does in the letter as if already familiar to Galatians.

And they heard and believed because, as Paul reminded them, the Spirit drove his words to their hearts. Pagans turned from the grip of the gods, "which are no gods," and Jews turned from the grip of the Law and the pursuit of self-righteousness. It did not matter who they were, Gentiles or Jews, "for in Christ," Paul urged, the matter was "not circumcision or uncircumcision but the power of new birth."

The cost to Paul was immense. These were his spiritual children and the agony of childbirth (in a world without anesthetics) was the analogy he used to describe his concern and prayer and mental effort.

As soon as signs of a newborn personality appeared in young or old, he was prepared to let him be baptized, just as he himself had been baptized by Ananias a mere three days after conversion. Paul had strong views on changed character being the proof of genuine conversion. If the Spirit of Christ had come to a man, the "fruit of the Spirit" would appear: "love, joy, peace, patience, kindness, goodness, faithfulness, gentleness, self-control"; such things had been little known in Antioch, except stoical self-control among the upper classes. For a slave to be taught that he should no longer lie and cheat was revolutionary; more astonishing still was the slave's discovery that he did not now want to lie or cheat and that he now loved the owner whom he had once resented and feared.

Paul knew well enough that each convert had a conflict, that the new nature did not eradicate the old, and he warned them, as his letter would recall, against "the kind of behavior that belongs to the lower nature: fornication, impurity, and indecency; idolatry and sorcery; quarrels, a contentious temper, envy, fits of rage, selfish ambitions … drinking bouts, orgies and the like." Such behavior was all around them, waiting to suck them back into the mud, but "if you are guided by the Spirit, you will not fulfill the desires of the lower nature."

And so he worked hard to build them up in Christ. Their wish to pray was as natural as the cry of a newborn baby; he showed them how to pray. Their hunger for knowledge about the Lord Jesus was as sharp as in the newly converted Paul; he told them all he knew and taught them, whether ex-pagans or Jews, to treat the Scriptures of the Jews as the Word of God explained through Christ.

None of this was in isolation. They had been born into a family, and—a radical doctrine to Paul's hearers—each member had equal worth.

The ancient world was shot through with hatred or contempt of one class for another. A man's color, race, or religion (except for Jews) mattered less than his current position; a black or a Scythian from the steppes could attain wealth, power, and Roman citizenship; but a conquered king's son, white-skinned, delicately reared, when taken into slavery, became a disposable chattel; his owner might crack his skull in rage or have him whipped raw, for all the State or neighbors cared.

In contrast Paul taught, and the Spirit proved it true to their experience, "There is neither Jew nor Greek, slave nor freeman, male nor female; for you are all one in Christ Jesus." And so, as Barnabas and the convalescent Paul moved from one group to another, now in a rich Jew's home in the city, now in a Roman veteran's country estate, now in a Phrygian farmhouse, they would see master and slave, grandmother and youth, shopkeeper and soldier, share the cup of blessing and break the bread.

In years ahead the Galatians would have their failures and falls; they would nearly break Paul's heart. But in these first days as Christians they had a tremendous sense of Christ's reality, His action and presence working in and through them. Each had a passionate concern to serve his neighbor and his Savior by bringing the one to the other, being sure that trust in the Lord Jesus was the only entrance to the full life that began at once and came to fullness at death. Therefore, while still learning from the two apostles, the converts fanned out until, as Luke recorded, "the Word of the Lord spread throughout all the region."

Paul encouraged them. He expected the Spirit to turn "disciples," those who are passive and learning, into "apostles," active and proclaiming the message. He seems mentally to have upgraded true converts to the status of colleagues remarkably swiftly, and thus suffered almost exaggerated sorrow and deflation when any failed him.

Converts who were not tied by servitude pushed into the hills, and over to the great lake where the thatched cottages dotted the bays, and up into the high mountain range that divided the Antioch countryside from the central plateau. They preached the grace of God, and they knew that Jesus worked with them, for now and again they saw light dawn on a listening face. In a matter of weeks a flourishing, expanding church sprang up. Since families often joined as one, there could be shallow faith mixed with deep, the tares among the wheat, but even so these days were like a springtime of spirit.

Two goatherds watching the kids would talk freely about Jesus. Among the fishing boats on Limnai, returning early with their catch, a crew would be seen dropping their oars to bow their heads in prayer. A woman meeting an acquaintance at market would discover that she too was a believer. A field slave on a great estate would find the last, worst hour before sunset more bearable and shorter because Christ was with him. The soldier on the wall at night about the gorge had a new song to hum.

Paul and Barnabas wished to stay until they were sure that the church could stand on its own. But after about two months in the city, when Antioch was frizzling in August heat and the dust irritated man and beast, a storm broke about their heads.

All this time the Jews who refused to believe in Christ had stayed passive. They could not attack directly because the apostles had withdrawn from the synagogue, nor would the city-colony magistrates hear complaints against law-abiding strangers. Yet the Christian influence widened, and these Jews could bear it no longer. They therefore worked on two or three aristocratic women proselytes until their anxiety about the likely spread of disaffection among the lower orders grew as intense as their repugnance at Paul's teaching. In Antioch, as in all Asia Minor, pagan devotion to the Mother Goddess under her various names had left women a marked influence in the community. The proselytes' husbands, typical Romans whose religion was loyalty to the divine emperor, listened with respect to their wives and decided that the new preachers were indeed nothing but vagrants up to mischief.

What happened next may be deduced from the brief guarded phrase of Luke and a reference by Paul in a letter written in old age.

Leading men of the city lodged an accusation, not with the provincial administrators, whose writ did not run in the local affairs of a Roman colony, but with the magistrates. The aim was to expel Paul and Barnabas, but expulsion always involved summary punishment: When the two were thrown into jail, they knew what lay ahead. Paul, however, was a Roman citizen; he may actually have carried a diptych on which his citizenship was recorded. He could certainly make the claim, "I am a Roman citizen," and though expelled, would escape a beating or indignities to his person. Barnabas, however, was not a citizen and would receive the full force of the law.

But Paul had no intention of escaping what Barnabas must endure, and he said nothing about his citizenship.

The next morning with a harum-scarum knot of petty thieves and recaptured slaves, the apostles were herded into a pen in the town square. The magistrates took their seats on the raised platform called the *bema*. Behind them stood their broad-shouldered lictors, each holding his fasces, the bundle of rods strapped round an ax, symbol of the magistrate's authority in a Roman colony and the means of its execution.

The proceedings were public; many Christians watched sadly from the crowd. Paul and Barnabas, manacled, were pushed into the space below the magistrates. The case was soon heard and sentence given. A lictor stepped down. First Paul, then Barnabas, was pulled across to the waist-high whipping pillar. Their clothes were torn off them and thrown in a heap. Naked, they were bent over the pillar and tied. The lictor drew birch rods from his fasces. Then he inflicted punishment.

Afterward, the manacles were removed and the bleeding apostles were dressed in their torn clothes. Then, without opportunity to recover, they were escorted the mile or two to the colony boundary and thrown out. Christians followed, along with unbelieving Jews who gloated at the success of the ploy, and it was probably because of these that Paul and Barnabas drew themselves up and solemnly carried out the action ordered by the Lord Jesus in His instructions to His first messengers: "If any place will not receive you and they refuse to hear you, when you leave shake off the dust that is on your feet as a testimony against them."

ELEVEN

STONED

Among the Christian converts who witnessed the beating were an elderly Jewess named Lois, her daughter, Eunice, who had married a Greek, and Eunice's son Timothy. Lois had believed first, then her daughter. Timothy, seventeen or eighteen years old, was Paul's "own son in the faith," one of those for whom he had suffered "labor pains" bringing to new birth, a bond that never would be forgotten on either side. They were citizens of Lystra, the next Roman city-colony about 130 miles to the east. They evidently arranged to travel homeward at once with the apostles, who to Timothy seemed surprisingly cheerful in their pain.

Expulsion from Antioch did not affect freedom of movement beyond the immediate area. Paul and Barnabas may have lain up a day or two with Christians living beside the poplar-lined Augustan Way, which ran straight over the low hills on the east of the city, to recover from the worst of the beating and to give final instructions. They found, to their delight, that far from being discouraged or fearful, converts were rejoicing, sure that the Holy Spirit would not forsake them, though His messengers must leave, and confident that if Paul's punishment were the prelude to their own persecution, they would endure. With the Lord on their side, they would not fear what man might do.

So the little party set off on the Augustan Way, Eunice and Lois fussing a little about the half-healed wounds and Timothy carrying their necessaries. Once they had covered two days' journey and were well into the broken country below the northern range, they had to stay at inns, which in the Roman Empire were usually brothels too. Paul could only look to the day when Galatia and all Asia Minor—and the world—should be dotted with Christian homes eager to put up Christian travelers.

On the seventh day's walk their road forked, after rising from a narrow fertile plain beside another lake backed by the Taurus. Whether the women continued along the military road direct to Lystra or not, Timothy stayed with the apostles, who took the left fork through a pass and down to the ancient city of Iconium on the edge of the central plateau. The two apostles entered unheralded and unnoticed, but Paul took the first opportunity of preaching in the synagogue, and as at Antioch the effect was phenomenal. A large number of Jews and Greeks believed, so that from its first hours this second Galatian church was to Paul what a church should be: a union of races—whether born Jews or Gentiles, they were all one in Christ Jesus.

Jews who refused to believe that their promised Messiah could be Jesus counterattacked immediately: "They stirred up the Gentiles and poisoned their minds against the Christians." While the converted were experiencing the new dimension that Paul called "eternal life," the unconverted were busily propagating tales that made the uncommitted shudder. Thus Iconium, with its dust and winds and the strange little twin peaks that stick up like pyramids, became the first place in the world to see on any large scale a pattern that would be repeated through history: If men and women begin to live like Jesus Christ, their enemies blacken their names, "hated for their secret crimes … convicted of hatred for the human race … men of the worst character and deserving of the severest punishment." The phrases come from Tacitus's near-contemporary account of Christians in Nero's reign, though they would equally apply in twentieth-century Soviet propaganda.

And as in Rome and Russia, so in Iconium: The air of contention proved healthy for the gospel of peace. Day after day, week after week, Paul and Barnabas "stayed on and spoke boldly and openly in reliance on the Lord, and He confirmed the message of His grace by causing signs and miracles to be worked at their hands."

Western theologians have sometimes dismissed that phrase "signs and miracles" or "signs and wonders" as a later gloss, or as evidence that Luke believed old wives' tales, but it does not baffle Christians in the less-developed world outside of the industrialized nations. Nor will any spiritually sensitive Westerner who has slept unknowingly near the altar to the spirits in a tribal house, or has confronted a witch doctor, be disposed to doubt Luke's normal accuracy. The powers of evil may prefer sophisticated forms in the West, but the rest of the world is wary of dismissing "evil spirits" or "demons" as figments of the imagination. And the "signs and miracles" at Iconium were probably instances of men and women finding, through Christ, sudden release from mental suffering, nervous illness, or conscious slavery to evil spirits. Luke was writing another chapter in the story that had begun in Galilee: "He healed many who were sick of various diseases, and cast out many demons."

Tension rose. The city split between those who followed or sympathized with the apostles and those who hated them. Paul was frequently mishandled in the streets, yet he planned to winter in Iconium. Then, one day in late autumn, he heard that unfriendly Jews and Gentiles had won the ear of the district administrators, who were prepared to turn a blind eye to mob violence. He and Barnabas were to be stoned, not by judicial process but like dogs.

They decided to flee. A stoning could be lethal. And public assault condoned by the authorities might provoke widespread persecution of converts. Though the apostles' flight would leave these to fend by themselves, Antioch had shown that a young church was ready to stand alone in Christ's strength sooner than its founders might expect. Therefore, with Timothy as guide, they obeyed the Lord's instruction: "When they persecute you in one city, flee to another."

Early next morning, as soon as the gates were opened, they slipped out and headed south. It was obvious where to go—to Lystra, the city-colony that lay out of Phrygia and in the neighboring Galatian district, Lycaonia, where Iconium magistrates had no jurisdiction. Lystra was Timothy's home. "You have observed," Paul would remind him long after, when they had trod many trails together, "my teaching, my conduct, my aim in life, my faith, my patience, my love, my persecutions, my sufferings, what befell me at Antioch, at Iconium, at Lystra, what persecutions I endured, yet from them all the Lord rescued me." By a forced march across the plain, with the distant abrupt lump of Black Mountain always on their left until they moved into the foothills of the Taurus, they covered twenty-five miles in the day. At last they saw the city of Lystra standing out above a shallow valley.

In front of the city, clear in the evening light, stood the Temple of Zeus, soon to be the cause of one of the most terrifying episodes in Paul's career.

Paul and Barnabas had not in the least lost ebullience or zeal through the troubles at Antioch and Iconium, and soon converts were out again two by two, taking the gospel to little settlements that hugged the pools tucked here and there in the folds of the hills, and across the plain toward Derbe. These converts were mostly Gentiles. If a Jewish synagogue existed, no trace of it remains in literature or ruin (though Lystra has never been properly excavated), and the Romans, who spoke Latin here more than those in the colony of Antioch, were little interested. Lycaonians listened, for the harvest was in, and they knew Greek as their language of trade.

Few, however, believed, until an extraordinary incident occurred in the sunshine of a winter's day. Close to Paul's favorite preaching spot in the forum was the squatting place of a congenital cripple, a well-known local character who had never been able to walk because he had no strength in his feet. Each day friends would carry him to the colonnade. Paul was speaking of the Almighty God who raised Christ from the dead. His gaze ranged over the audience, some idly indifferent, others puzzled, attentive, or hopeful. Suddenly he noticed the cripple's face. He stopped preaching. His eyes bore right in. He knew without doubt that the man had faith to be healed not only in spirit but also in body and that the Power who had told a cripple in Galilee to take up his bed and walk was present, waiting to honor faith—Paul's and the cripple's.

Paul shouted, "Stand up straight on your feet!"

Instantly, the man leaped up and walked. No hesitant, cautious prod of the toe but a leap into vigorous movement.

The effect on the crowd was electric. They began to jabber in Lycaonian—neither Paul nor Barnabas knew what, only that the entire audience buzzed with an intensely reverential excitement, and some of the young men had pushed out of the forum to run in the direction of the Temple of Zeus.

In Lystra's legendary past, as every child learned at his or her mother's knee, the supreme god, Zeus, and his messenger and herald, Hermes, had disguised themselves as poor travelers and sought shelter among Lycaonians rich and poor. They were repeatedly turned away until they knocked at the door of an old peasant couple, Philemon and Baucis, who sheltered and fed them. The gods disclosed themselves, turned the inhospitable into frogs and the cottage of Baucis into a gold and marble temple that had stood outside Lystra since long before the Romans. Lycaonians had always looked to the day when the two gods should return, this time to be treated with honor.

And now it all fitted. Of the two wonder workers who had come upon them, one was small and volatile and made many speeches—he was obviously Hermes (or Mercury in Latin). The other, tall, calm, speaking little in public but using his herald to convey his words, showed the marks of the supreme god, Zeus (or Jupiter).[9]

The chief priest of Zeus hurriedly brought sacrificial oxen from the temple pasture and garlanded them with olive branches and colored wools, seized his knife, and with blasts on a horn proceeded toward the city, where crowds were already collecting in the broad space just within the gates. In the forum chanting, dancing Lycaonians surrounded the puzzled Paul and Barnabas. A procession formed. With much reverence and bowing, they were invited to walk up the wide street toward the gate. Only then did the apostles realize, to their horror, what the chant proclaimed: "The gods have come down to us in human form" and that sacrifice was about to be offered.

Instinctively, they tore their clothes, the Jewish reaction to blasphemy, and rushed up the street to implore the priest to stop. Paul clambered onto the sacrificial stone. "Men, what is this that you are doing?" he cried, his torn robe flapping in the breeze. "We are only human beings, no less mortal than you. The Good News we bring tells you to turn from these follies to the Living God, who made heaven and earth and sea and everything in them. In past ages He allowed all nations to go their own way; and yet He has not left you without some clue to His nature, in the kindness He shows: He sends you rain from heaven and crops in their seasons, and gives you food and good cheer in plenty."

It was touch and go. The priest hesitated. The crowd wavered, murmuring, fearful lest they anger a divinity, either their own idol or this Living God Paul talked about.

Just then strangers came on the scene: Jews by their dress, recognizable to Paul as antagonists from Pisidian Antioch and Iconium, probably trading in Lystra.

These men harangued the crowd. The murmurs swelled. With that terrifying suddenness of volatile mobs, the mood changed from worship to fury. A youth picked up a stone, took aim, and with a vicious flick caught Paul full face. In a moment, before Barnabas or his friends could protect him, he was under a shower of stones, on his jaw, the pit of his stomach, his groin, his chest, his temple. He fell stark and stiff, blood streaming from nose and eyes. The crowd dragged the body out of the city and melted quickly away before the Roman guards at the gate could identify individual perpetrators.

Converts who had watched appalled at the sudden assault formed a ring round the body, shocked and uncertain.

Paul stirred. With every muscle and nerve seared, head throbbing, stomach retching, he forced himself to stand.

Sympathizers helped him slowly through streets now emptied of the mob for fear of civic action. They dressed his wounds, and the next day, when every bone in his body cried out to rest, he set off with Barnabas. Though Paul may have been lent a donkey, the journey could not be anything but torture as they followed the road eastward along the line of hills a short way, then into the great plain, into the teeth of winter winds and occasional snow flurries. Mile upon mile they made their way through featureless country, while volcanic Black Mountain stood like an island ahead, seeming little nearer with every painful hour.

Across the boundary line of the native kingdom of Commagene they were safe.

For years experts wondered how Paul could have found shelter in Derbe when Lystra became too hot to hold him, since both were cities of Galatian Lycaonia and reasonably close together. But no one could discover Derbe's exact site. Then in 1964 it was finally identified; not, as had been supposed, on the near side of Black Mountain to Lystra, but at Devri Sehri on the far, eastern side, and thus across the border of the native state. It had been part of Galatian Lycaonia, even honored by the reigning emperor Claudius, until ceded a year or two before Paul's visit, along with its more important neighbor, Laranda, to King Antiochus of Commagene, who ruled the territory between Galatia and Cilicia as a vassal of the Romans.

Here the battered Paul found welcome, response, and recovery. Indeed, it may have been the people of Derbe—who still considered themselves Galatians, since the transference of rule was merely an administrative convenience—that Paul had in mind when he wrote those words in his letter to all the widely scattered churches: "You resisted any temptation to show score or disgust at the poor state of my body; you welcomed me as if I were an angel of God…. You would have torn out your very eyes and given them to me."

The apostles made many disciples in Derbe that winter. While his iron constitution mended, Paul would not shelve his commission. The very scars on his body were a constant reminder of man's violence and sin. To him they were a symbol of the crucifixion too: He called them "the stigmata of the Lord Jesus," and the consciousness of man's need and God's love pressed on him almost to neurosis, one reason why he preferred to evangelize in a team. A colleague like Barnabas could comfort him in illness and keep him from overstrain when fit.

As the snow melted in the plains and foothills, and the winds dropped, the apostles left Derbe. They could have followed the trade route eastward to the Cilician Gates and reached Syria by Tarsus comparatively quickly. Instead, they turned back to retrace their route through the three cities that had despitefully used them. It is true that a new year meant new magistrates and the lapse of inhibitions imposed by the old order, but Paul and Barnabas were marked men. It required courage to face more potential stoning and beating.

On arrival at Lystra, they were enormously encouraged. The church had not dissolved or ceased to grow, despite problems and difficulties, persecution and hardships. The apostles did not hurry away but "strengthened the souls of the disciples, exhorting them to continue in the faith, and saying that through many tribulations we must enter the kingdom of God." All the time they watched closely to discern who among the converts should be entrusted with the oversight of the church. Paul had not yet defined the gifts of character required, but he and Barnabas believed they could tell whom the Spirit might be preparing, and they were determined that each local church should be locally led, even though no Galatian had long experience of Christ.

When the choice was made, the Christians set aside a day for prayer and fasting, closing with a solemn ordination, after which the apostles committed the new elders and their flock "to the Lord in whom they had put faith."

The two walked north. Plows turned up the brown earth in patches of cultivation; blossoms were on the trees. They came over the brow and saw Iconium's twin peaks and rejoiced. To their right, Black Mountain, topped with snow, reminded them that people were praying for them in Derbe.

After strengthening and ordaining in Iconium, they took the long march west. As they approached Pisidian Antioch, a plowman near the road might come running to greet them; soon men and women of different backgrounds jostled happily to assure Paul that what he had told them was true, in good days and bad. They had found for themselves that the Lord Jesus was all that

Paul had promised, and more. The apostles had the excitement, too, of meeting many who had joined the church after they had left.

They stayed on in Antioch two or three weeks and at last turned for home. Beside Lake Limnai, where they had walked as strangers the year before, they had almost a triumphal progress. Each day a Christian family would escort them to the next Christian home. Sometimes they would be put on donkeys with foals following or be rowed the next stage of their journey on the water. At evening all the Christians in the area would gather in the home, with their children, and there would be the deepest sense of the Lord Jesus among them as Paul and Barnabas gave words of encouragement and advice, always ordaining elders for the new community of faith.

The next morning they walked on, the lake so peaceful, the atmosphere so happy: "He leadeth me beside the still waters, He restoreth my soul." It was almost possible to believe that disappointments were at an end.

TWELVE

"I OPPOSED HIM TO HIS FACE"

It was AD 48. Christians of Antioch in Syria, as many as could, crowded into the open-air atrium of the large house on Singon Street, the owner of which was host to the church. Oblivious of the stench that arose from the city at the end of a hot day and of their own sweat as they sat shoulder to shoulder, Jew and Gentile, rich and poor, slaves and free had a single thought on this late summer evening: Paul and Barnabas were back.

They had arrived unannounced like all but the most exalted travelers in the ancient world, journeying by coaster of shallow enough draft to sail up the Orontes direct to Antioch. At once they had summoned their partners, the entire church. Their momentous report lasted far into the night, first one speaking, then the other, broken only by an occasional hymn of praise. They told the whole story from their arrival in Cyprus until finally they left Pisidian Antioch for home by walking back through the Taurus to Perga, where this time they had stayed to give their message. They had continued along the plain a brief distance, then down the cliff to the harbor of Attalia.[10] They may have been wrecked at sea, for Attalia to Antioch was Paul's longest recorded voyage before the date when he wrote "three times I have been shipwrecked."

They had covered over a thousand miles on foot—sixty days entirely consumed in land travel—and as for the brutalities they had endured, some of Paul's scars were only too evident and his gait more crooked than before. The emphasis, however, was not on sufferings and adventures but on "all that God had done with them." Above everything they stressed how He had "opened a door of faith to the Gentiles." Syrian Antioch had not been a special case: Southern Galatia had proved beyond doubt that Christ offered Himself to all men.

Then Paul and Barnabas took their place once more as preachers and teachers in the ordered life of the Antioch church. Paul's desire was to thrust out farther, to the provinces of Asia and Bithynia, eventually into Macedonia and beyond, but he was willing to wait, recovering full physical strength and deepening his spiritual roots.

He had to wait longer than he wished.

Peter came to Antioch. A few weeks later he was followed from Jerusalem by Jews who had remained Pharisees, even though they had become disciples of Christ. The subsequent controversy that devastated the Antioch church and brought Paul into conflict with Peter was of crucial importance to the development of Christianity. Like many disputes that in retrospect proved turning points of history, the subjects might seem trivial to later ages: invitations to dinner, and a nick on the male organ. The issues, however, were profound: first, whether Christianity should be merely a variety of Judaism; and second, whether a man may be forgiven simply and instantly by trusting Jesus Christ, or whether such forgiveness is incomplete and conditional until he can show that he has worked faithfully and obediently to his life's end to do what is right.

When Peter came to Antioch, which was the only place in the world where ex-pagans were living on terms of complete equality with Christian Jews, everybody watched what he would do. His courageous words and gifts of leadership had made him the central figure of the early church; his willingness to shock Jews by eating with the Roman Cornelius had opened the way to the winning of Gentiles. Yet at Jerusalem, where the disciples were primarily concerned to commend Jesus Christ to Jews, he had continued to observe Jewish laws, including the normal segregation when eating. If, in the mixed community that was the Antioch church, he went off and ate by himself, he would give the strongest support to those who still believed that, on becoming a Christian, a pagan must accept Jewish ways and Jewish law. And that would mean the new faith remained simply a liberal Jewish sect.

Peter, however, joined Paul and Barnabas in living like a Gentile, thereby ruining his status in the eyes of the orthodox Jews. He no longer observed the Mosaic fasts or taboos, nor refused to eat with Gentile converts at the common meal called *agapē*—the "love feast"—which preceded the Lord's Supper. He thereby made plain that he believed as Paul did: No Gentile Christian need live like a Jew.

Then the Christian Pharisees arrived. Their words and actions were repudiated afterward, but they claimed to be traveling with the authority of the recognized local leader of the mother church, James, the Lord's brother. They were shocked by the laxity of the Antioch church—and of Peter. They saw Jews eating with "sinners and Gentiles" (to Pharisees the words were synonymous), implying they were equal with Jews.

They discovered that every Gentile believer had been excused the necessity, binding on all proselytes, of submitting to the rite of circumcision. At once they began a campaign: "Except you are circumcised according to the custom of Moses," they told converts, "you cannot be saved." Everybody involved in the dispute knew what they meant: "Except, after believing in Jesus, you become a proselyte by undergoing the surgical operation, and thereafter observe all the ceremonies and do the good works required by the Mosaic Law, and keep ritually undefiled—all in addition to your trust in Jesus Christ—you cannot be saved; Jesus by Himself cannot fit a man for heaven." The implications of such an argument went far wider than the issue at Antioch, which remained in the context of Jewish obligations. Paul saw that the Christian Pharisees' contention was totally at variance with a truth he had understood since Damascus and would expound fully in his letters later on: that self-righteousness, however expressed, is the rival and not the complement of grace.

The matter came to a head over the issue of ritual defilement. The advocates of "circumcision" argued their case so hotly and cogently that Peter stopped eating with Gentiles. Paul was indignant. Peter may have been swayed by representations that his actions in Antioch must severely embarrass

his Jerusalem friends in their ministry to Jews, but Paul was sure Peter did
not honestly believe the Judaizers were right; he conformed from fear of their
tongues, or from a willingness to sacrifice principle for peace and unity. He
was dissembling. If any apostle was walking crooked here, it was not bandy-
legged Paul but Peter.

Next, most of the Jewish members of the congregation followed Peter's
example. Then Barnabas wavered—Barnabas, who had taken Paul's part
when the point had been discussed in Jerusalem during the famine visit, who
had seen overwhelming evidence in Galatia that God remade pagans into
full Christians. Paul resolved to speak out. This deep crack in the Christian
church must not be papered over in order to preserve a spurious unity. The
dispute was not about trivialities. The fundamental principle was whether
anyone might be justified by faith alone.

Paul could not oppose Peter privately. The damage was public; the opposition must be public if the faith were to be secured for all men everywhere.
The same instinctive courage that drove Paul to risk his skin by rebuking a
bad man, Elymas, in front of the proconsul drove him to risk his standing in
the church by correcting a good man, the greatly loved and honored Peter,
in front of them all. Paul did not care. Though he saw himself in God's sight
the least of all saints, he considered himself in man's sight the equal of any
apostle.

He chose an occasion before virtually the whole congregation. In the
most public manner, he criticized Peter to his face using words that not
only pilloried the inconsistency but emphasized the heart of the matter:
"If you," said Paul loudly for all to hear, "a Jew born and bred, live like
a Gentile, and not like a Jew, how can you insist that Gentiles must live
like Jews?"

It was a moment when the church might split into factions and destroy
itself. But the man who had wept when the Lord, at His trial, turned and
looked on the disciple who had denied Him with oaths, immediately accepted
the justice of Paul's rebuke. Peter repented, and when the issue was debated

again months later at Jerusalem, it was Peter's strong support of Paul's position that gained the day.

Peter returned to Jerusalem. That the question in dispute had been by no means trivial, nor fully settled, was shown by bad news that reached Antioch from Galatia.

Christian Pharisees—either those who had left Antioch defeated or, more likely, others who had hurried on through Cilicia—had been welcomed by the Galatians, had taught them "circumcision," and had met instant, wide-spread success. Paul's first missionary church, so promising and apparently healthy, had been swept into another gospel. Former pagans who had trusted Christ and rejoiced in being "new creations" were making their lives a misery by trying to keep the Jewish Law.

As Paul cross-questioned his informants, he could see what must have happened in Galatia. These false teachers had first undermined his credentials by pointing out that he had never been a personal disciple of Jesus; he was the emissary of ordinary men from whom he had picked up his ideas, which held no more authority than other human opinions. His teaching had been good but incomplete. They then propounded what Paul had left out: circumcision and the keeping of the Law. The Galatians fell into the trap.

When Paul was among them, they had leaped at the offer of grace that was totally free and gave them freedom. The old sinful life—whether of self-righteousness as Jews or of idolatry, lust, and fear as pagans—had been replaced by Christ within them, and all they wanted was to please Him by molding their lives in His pattern, by His strength. After Paul had gone, some of them fell back into grievous sin. They repented but found it difficult to take literally that they could be utterly forgiven, cleansed, and healed, that no repentant, trusting Christian could ever be in disgrace with God or need earn a return to favor. Their natural instinct was not to depend on Christ's cross alone but on Christ and their own effort. The very simplicity of the gospel was their stumbling block.

And now the new "apostles" who disparaged Paul taught that he was wrong and their natural instinct right; and by being circumcised and keeping the Law, they would have a bonus too in that they would no longer be persecuted by Jews.

Paul and Barnabas were appalled by the news from Galatia. Paul walked around Antioch in a confusion of emotions. He was indignant with the false brethren and astonished at the Galatians' speedy disloyalty to Christ. He was disappointed and hurt, for though he had grown a thick skin toward the malice of outsiders, Christian brothers who were false or converts who had failed bothered him.

Yet he had a yearning, a panting to help them, his little children, for whom he felt himself undergoing birth pains all over again. And because he loved them deeply, he determined to put them back on the right course. It was vital to them; it was vital to Christ. He could not bear the thought of Christ's agony on the cross being dismissed as secondary. He could not accept that an ill-defined or partial belief in Jesus was enough to make a man a Christian, even if that led to a more numerous, popular church. Nor could he tolerate teachers—whose spiritual descendants are much in evidence in the twenty-first century—who used the name of Christ as an accolade on their own ideas of the nature of God.

All these emotions and desires exploded in a letter.

THIRTEEN

DEAR IDIOTS OF GALATIA

Paul summoned the Antioch leaders so that his letter should carry the authority of the church that had sent the first missionaries to Galatia. He secured a roll of papyrus and a swift penman. With the leaders sitting around, he began dictating urgently, rapidly.

"Paul an apostle—not from men nor through man, but through Jesus Christ and God the Father, who raised Him from the dead—and all the brethren with me,

"To the churches of Galatia:

"Grace to you and peace from God the Father and our Lord Jesus Christ, who gave Himself for our sins to deliver us from the present evil age, according to the will of our God and Father; to whom be glory for ever and ever. Amen.

"I am *astonished* that you are so quickly deserting him who called you in the grace of Christ and turning to a different gospel—not that there is another gospel, but there are some who trouble you and want to pervert the Gospel of Christ. But even if we, or an angel from heaven, should preach to you a gospel contrary to that which we preached to you, let him be accursed. As we have said before, so now I say again. If anyone is preaching to you a gospel contrary to that which you received, *let him be accursed!*"

At this time Paul's character had a strong dash of controlled anger that could make him thoroughly alarming to wrongdoers, but righteous anger too easily leads to sin; in later years he grew to feel that fury was no weapon to be found in the armory of a Christian. When he wrote to the Galatians, however, the fire that burned within was allowed to scorch. This first letter sparked and flamed with no regard to sensitive feelings—or to literary polish.

Paul knew it would be read aloud and seem to the hearers almost as if he were there, so that the force of this writing would be doubled by the memory of his speaking—one reason why he always preferred to dictate.

What he was going to tell them he had previously taught them in person. This time he must make it even plainer. His passionate love for converts, his uncompromising devotion to truth, drove him to wrestle mentally until his words could resolve with crystal clarity the key issue of the Christian faith—whether a man is forgiven through his own merit or God's grace.

Paul's first task was to establish beyond question his credentials as a messenger direct from Christ. He referred again, briefly, to the persecuting zeal of his early life, and how after seeing the risen Christ he had gone, not to Jerusalem, but to Arabia. Truth had not been taught him by man but revealed by God, just as it had been to Peter. When Peter had blurted out to Jesus, "You are the Christ, the Son of the Living God," he was told, as Paul probably had recounted to the Galatians orally, "Flesh and blood has not revealed this to you, but My Father who is in heaven." In the same way Paul did not "confer with flesh and blood" but had received the message direct from God.

He continued the story up to the recent conflict with Peter and from there went straight to the crux: that a man is not justified (reckoned righteous) "by doing what the Law demands, but only through faith in Christ.... We have put our faith in Jesus Christ, in order that we might be justified through this faith, and not through deeds dictated by Law; for by such deeds, the Scripture says, no mortal man shall be justified." Paul, as he often did, illustrated the truth by his own case. The former Paul who had struggled to earn his way to heaven had died: "I have been crucified with Christ. It is no longer 'I' who live, but Christ who lives in me; and the life I now live in the flesh I live by the faith of the Son of God, who loved me and gave Himself for me. I will not nullify the grace of God; if righteousness comes by Law, then Christ died for nothing."

The order of words in Paul's original Greek makes him even more emphatic: "Christ I have been crucified with, but I live, no longer I, but lives in me Christ!" His testimony has echoed down the ages as one of the most decisive passages in the Bible, beloved of Luther and Bunyan, opening the eyes of Charles Wesley.

Paul's mind was on the Galatians. "O you dear idiots of Galatia, who saw Jesus Christ the crucified so plainly: Who has been casting a spell over you? I will ask you one simple question: Did you receive the Spirit of God by trying to keep the Law or by believing the message of the Gospel? Surely you can't be so idiotic as to think that a man begins his spiritual life in the Spirit and then completes it by reverting to outward observances? Has all your painful experience brought you nowhere? I simply cannot believe it of you! Does God, who gives you His Spirit and works miracles among you, do these things because you have obeyed the Law or because you have believed the Gospel? Ask yourselves that."

He developed his argument of the essential weakness of the Law: that a man who attempts to earn acceptance by keeping it must do so totally, or be rejected. In contrast, "Christ bought us freedom from the curse of the Law by becoming for our sake a cursed thing; for Scripture says, 'Cursed is everyone who is hanged on a tree.' ... If a law had been given which had power to bestow life, then indeed righteousness would have come from keeping the Law. But Scripture has declared the whole world to be prisoners in subjection to sin, so that faith in Jesus Christ may be the ground on which the promised blessing is given, and given to those who have such faith."

All the time he was expounding, Paul's puzzlement and dismay at the Galatians kept breaking in: "How can you turn back again? ... I am afraid I have labored over you in vain.... You were running well; who hindered you from obeying the truth?" His indignation at those who had corrupted his Galatians swelled into a thoroughly earthy expression: "I wish those who unsettle you would mutilate themselves!"—which his readers may have interpreted as a mute reference to the god Cybele's frenzied dancers whose climax was self-castration.

Paul realized that after all this the Galatians could be genuinely puzzled about the Law, since he himself had taught them to revere and learn from it. To explain its role, he selected analogies they would easily recognize.

The Law was like a tutor exercising strict discipline during schooldays: Galatians who lived in cities knew the *paidagógos*, the slave who looked after a boy and took him to and from school: Boys were not expected to remain under him all their lives but to be free. So, "the Law was a kind of tutor in charge of us until Christ should come, when we should be justified through faith; and now that faith has come, the tutor's charge is at an end."

And the Law was a guardian: Galatians in the countryside who were slaves or tenants on great estates knew that during an heir's minority his guardians kept entire control; he must obey them as if he were a slave, although owner of all. So, the Law was the guardian of the whole world's minority. "But when the term was completed, God sent His own Son, born of a woman, born under the Law, to purchase freedom for the subjects of the Law, in order that we might attain the status of sons. To prove that you are sons, God has sent into our hearts the Spirit of His Son, crying, '*Abba!* Father.' You are therefore no longer a slave but a son, and if a son, then also by God's own act an heir."

Paul could not bear the thought that these sons of God were slipping back into slavery, that they were chained to feasts and fasts, to rules and regulations. "Christ set us free, to be free men! Stand fast therefore, and do not submit again to a yoke of slavery." Over and over, he worked his argument, approaching it now from this angle, now from that, until the stupidest Galatian must see that submitting to circumcision as a religious duty, and trying to keep the Law, made nonsense of Christ's cross.

Only one law mattered for those in Christ Jesus: "Faith working through love." He emphasized the point. "You were called to freedom, brethren: only do not use your freedom as an opportunity for the flesh, but through love be servants of one another, for the whole Law is fulfilled in one word, 'You shall love your neighbor as yourself.'"

Paul's concern for the here and now, for man's behavior to man, glowed warm and strong, but he knew that the here and now turns sour unless behavior grows from the right root. He had warned the Galatians in person, and he warned them again, that the lower nature, the "flesh," behaves in a way that cannot inherit the kingdom of God: "sexual immorality, impurity of mind, sensuality, worship of false gods, witchcraft, hatred, quarreling, jealousy, bad temper, rivalry, factions, party-spirit, envy, drunkenness, orgies, and things like that. But the harvest of the Spirit"—and his mind may have flashed to the rich earth of the uplands being turned by the spring plow—"is love, joy, peace, patience, kindness, goodness, faithfulness, gentleness, self-control; against such there is no law. And those who belong to Christ have crucified the flesh with its passions and desires. If we live by the Spirit, let us also walk by the Spirit. Let us have no self-conceit, no provoking of one another, no envy of one another."

He was nearly done. One problem remained. He saw that those who had resisted the false teaching might feel smug toward those who had not.

"Brothers," dictated Paul, "if a man is caught in some offense, you, the spiritual ones, should put him right in a spirit of gentleness." (Did Paul feel he had been too harsh in the way he corrected Peter?) "Each of you think whether you yourself may be tempted. Bear one another's burdens and so fulfill the law of Christ."

With the addition of a few more words, the dictation was finished, a long morning of hard writing for the penman, hard thinking for Paul, close listening for Barnabas and the elders of Antioch. They may have broken off for a meal; then Paul made the penman read the entire letter. The penman reached again the very last words: "Let us not grow weary in well-doing, for in due season we shall reap if we do not lose heart. So then, as we have opportunity, let us do good to all men, and especially those who are of the household of faith."

Paul took the papyrus. There was still space on the roll. He seized a reed pen.

"Look at these huge letters I am making in writing these words to you with my own hand!" And in the silence of the room after the long dictation, he scrawled with the pen, unable to leave the Galatians and their troubles: "These men who are always urging you to be circumcised—what are they after? They want to present a pleasing front to the world, and they want to avoid being persecuted for the cross of Christ. For even those who have been circumcised do not themselves keep the Law. But they want you circumcised so that they may be able to boast about your submission to their ruling. Yet God forbid that I should boast about anything or anybody except the cross of our Lord Jesus Christ, which means that the world is a dead thing to me and I am a dead man to the world. For in Christ it is not circumcision or uncircumcision that counts but the power of new birth. To all who live by this principle, to the true Israel of God, may there be peace and mercy!

"Let no one interfere with me after this. I carry on my scarred body the marks of my Owner, the Lord Jesus.

"The grace of our Lord Jesus Christ be with your spirit, brothers."[11]

FOURTEEN

A FRESH START

Since controversy continued, the Antioch church sent Paul, Barnabas, and several others to Jerusalem to seek a common mind about "circumcision" and to finally settle the question.

They traveled by land, unhurriedly. In Phoenicia (modern Lebanon) and the hills of Samaria, where most of the local disciples were not pure-bred Jews and thus had been rated as only half-Christian, Paul and Barnabas brought joy by recounting all that had happened in Galatia. At Jerusalem the great welcome meeting contrasted strikingly with Paul's solitary first arrival, a convert cold-shouldered until rescued by Barnabas. Now the two friends, never closer, warmed to the atmosphere of love and encouragement as they told what God had done to create new Christians in a faraway land. But when the report ended, Christian Pharisees stepped forward. The old charge sounded again: "They must be circumcised and told to keep the Law of Moses."

The matter was adjourned for formal discussion. To resolve major disputes, the apostles with the elders, a considerable number, were accustomed to seek the will of God by studying the Old Testament and by recalling what Jesus had taught. On "circumcision," however, they had no clear word, the subject presumably being one on which Jesus could not instruct them until He had been crucified, had risen from the dead and left them, and the Holy Spirit had come. He had promised that His Spirit would lead them into all truth, and it was now their duty, as they met together, to find what He was saying. They seem to have followed the custom of the Sanhedrin by inviting junior members to give their opinions first, and the debate was long. Then Peter stood up. He had spoken no more than a few words when Paul's heart leaped.

"Brothers," said Peter, "you know that from the earliest days God chose me as the one from whose lips the Gentiles should hear the Word and should believe it. Moreover, God who knows men's inmost thoughts has plainly shown that this is so, for when He had cleansed their hearts through their faith He gave the Holy Spirit to the Gentiles exactly as He did to us. Why then must you now strain the patience of God by trying to put on the shoulders of these disciples a burden which neither our fathers nor we were able to bear? Surely the fact is that it is by the grace of the Lord Jesus that we are saved, through faith, just as they are!"

He stopped. Not a word broke the silence. Then Barnabas spoke. (Paul had dropped tactfully to second place in the city where his friend had been a leader when he himself was still an enemy of the church.) Barnabas began to recount in close detail the amazing happenings in Galatia. Eventually Paul took up the tale, and the hours fled as once more their epic narrative unfolded. Again no one argued.

At length, James, as president of the assembly, put into words what he conceived to be the general conclusion. James was a man of such devotion that long praying, so tradition says, had made his knees as hard as a camel's. And like Paul he had been converted by meeting, all alone, the risen Jesus, his half-brother, whose claims he had doubted. James loved the Law of Moses and was held in high respect by non-Christian Jews, but he wished to obey his risen Lord's will. He now saw that this will—if only they would all admit—had been made plain years before: when the Spirit had endorsed Simon Peter's action in entering the home of Cornelius. What Barnabas and Paul had since told, though it had swung the assembly, merely proved Peter's point. James rightly focused on Peter's speech, which, he emphasized with a long quotation, was in accord with prophecy.

"My judgment therefore," he said, "is that we should impose no irksome restrictions on those of the Gentiles who are turning to God." Lest, however, the new freedom prove needlessly offensive to nonbelieving Jews, Gentile Christians should not eat meat that had been consecrated to idols before being sold in market, should not indulge in a pagan sex life, nor eat the meat of strangled animals (a prohibition imposed long before the Law), nor drink blood.

The council's decisions were endorsed by the laity and elders of the entire Jerusalem church and embodied in a formal reply to Antioch and its daughter churches in the united Roman province of Syria and Cilicia, which disavowed those who had "unsettled your minds although we gave them no instructions." It paid generous tribute to "our beloved Barnabas and Paul, men who have hazarded their lives for the name of our Lord Jesus Christ."

Paul and Barnabas brought the letter to Antioch, and all the Christians rejoiced. Two outstanding Jerusalem preachers came too and stayed on. As Judas Barsabbas and Silvanus, informally known as Silas, unfolded fresh meaning from the Scriptures, the Antioch church went from strength to strength, and Paul and Barnabas sat at their feet. Paul never supposed that he had nothing to learn; even with young believers he expected encouragement to be mutual.

That winter, after Judas and Silas returned to Jerusalem, Paul's body remained in Antioch, but his heart and mind strayed more and more to Galatia. A desire swelled until it hurt, to know whether his urgent letter had solved their problems, whether they were progressing or failing. He spoke emphatically to Barnabas: "Let's definitely go back and visit our brothers in every city where we proclaimed the word of the Lord." Barnabas agreed, suggesting taking his relative John Mark again.

Paul demurred. He was not at all happy at having with them day by day the young man who had deserted them at Perga. Barnabas felt Paul was wrong. He should give the youth another chance; Mark had the stuff of an evangelist in him if properly encouraged. Paul declined the risk. Hardships, disappointments, opportunities lay ahead, for he had no intention of stopping short in Galatia—he would press onward into the unknown. His team must be close-knit, thoroughly reliable. He refused to accept Mark.

Feelings frayed. Luke did not hide the apostles' humanity any more than the Old Testament hides that gross human failing of King David's adultery. He described the sharp argument by a Greek word that denotes violent anger and is the root of the English word *paroxysm*. Whoever was right, they were both to blame for letting the dispute grow fierce. There must have been serious wrong in a situation that made lovable, even-tempered Barnabas use angry words, and Paul had far to go before he could write, "Love is patient and kind.... Love does not insist on its own way."

Both insisted. It became obvious that their partnership must end.

Thereupon, Barnabas recovered his characteristic love of conciliation: He removed himself, sailing away to Cyprus with Mark. Paul chose Silas to replace Barnabas. Silas would bring the expedition an advantage in that he was a Roman citizen; when next faced with the prospect of a beating with rods, they could both claim citizenship.

The only trouble was Silas had returned to Jerusalem. With the season of travel already upon them, and much to do on the way, Paul could not wait. He sent a message, never doubting Silas would respond, and set off alone: Luke was emphatic in saying, "*He* departed ... *he* went through Syria and Cilicia strengthening the churches." The "*they*" does not begin until after he reached Derbe.

Thus in the spring of AD 50, Paul walked alone into the mountains northwest of Antioch and came down by the "Syrian Gates" to the splendid bay of Alexandria (Iskenderun), where probably he found one of the churches he wished to strengthen. He walked on along the undulating coastal plain, close to the battlefield of Issus, where Alexander had defeated Darius the Mede three hundred years before. Paul was lonely, rather lost without a companion, and the quarrel had aged him; he was now about fifty years old, and the next letter he would write, to the church in Thessalonica later that year, reads like the letter of a man who had aged considerably. But as he walked, he could see the mountains of Cilicia ahead across the gulf where the Levant turns west to become southern Anatolia. He was coming home; though his family had repudiated him, the mountains were the mountains he had known as a boy.

Whether he stopped awhile at Tarsus or approached his family is not recorded. He spent time seeking out and encouraging congregations he had founded in his hidden years and then joined the busy road over the Taurus through the Cilician Gates, probably early in May, for the snow is gone by mid-April from the pass and the slightly higher plateau just to the north. From there he made for the native kingdom of Commagene. Across the wide plain with its volcanic outcrops, he followed the Roman road until at last he saw Black Mountain again and returned to his converts at Derbe.

Derbe was evidently the rendezvous for Silas, if he had traveled direct from Jerusalem. He would probably have journeyed by sea to Tarsus and then up the safe and frequented road. Together they delivered the Jerusalem decisions, completed the work of Paul's own letter in healing breaches left by the "circumcision" dispute, and saw that once again the congregation was growing every day in depth and in size.

Paul took Silas on to introduce him at Lystra. Here too the church had grown. And here, eager as ever, was Timothy.

Timothy was now about twenty-one. His faith and zeal were highly regarded by the Christians in Lystra and Iconium.

Paul invited him to leave his mother and grandmother and join the team, although he could not say when, if ever, Timothy would see home again. He thereby gained more than a substitute for Mark. He gained a dearly loved son, perhaps replacing the actual son who may have died in Paul's early married life or, if alive, had been irrevocably estranged with his mother by Paul's conversion.

Timothy was a complicated character. He had a weak stomach and looked very young. Nervous, a little afraid of hardship, though enduring it without flinching, he was tempted occasionally to be ashamed of Paul and the gospel. But he was no weakling. Warm-blooded—Paul had to warn him to flee youthful lusts—and equally virile spiritually, Timothy became an able preacher who soon could be trusted with important missions of his own. From his pagan Greek father, evidently a man of culture and substance but now dead, he had inherited intellectual interests and an inquiring mind; from his mother, Eunice, he had learned the Jewish Scriptures, and from Paul had discovered their key. His one desire was to serve Christ: Paul was afterward to say that of all his fellow workers, Timothy alone was totally without self-interest.

Eunice had brought Timothy up as a Jew before their Christian conversion, but he had not been circumcised; the father may have forbidden it to save the boy embarrassment in the gymnasium. Paul took him quietly to a surgeon and had the operation performed; or perhaps he did it himself, since many rabbis had the necessary surgical qualification.

This action was not inconsistent with the attack on "those who would compel you to be circumcised." The offspring of a Jewish mother and a Greek father was regarded by Jews as a Jew, but if uncircumcised as illegitimate. In the Galatian cities, which would be Timothy's first field, his parentage was known, and if Paul used an "illegitimate" Jew for an assistant, that would hinder the work. He never inveighed against circumcision as a rite for Jews, even though he held it unnecessary; had Timothy been a Gentile, like Titus, nothing would have induced Paul to "circumcise him because of the Jews that were in those places."

After Timothy had recovered from the operation, and before they left Lystra, a solemn ordination service attended by a numerous congregation set him apart, calling down the Spirit's gifts that his high vocation required. He confessed his faith publicly, boldly. A prophet, probably Silas, proclaimed in a memorable sermon that Timothy would fight gallantly, armed with faith and a good conscience.

The Galatian trouble had convinced Paul that he must change his strategy.

His aim remained twofold: to win individuals to Christ and to form churches that not only would endure without him but also send out missionaries themselves to repeat the process, until all the world was Christ's. The Galatians, however, had stumbled after Paul left. Therefore he should stay in a center longer, not move from place to place as he had been forced to do in southern Galatia, but find a city positioned to be the pivot of a widespread mission.

Ephesus, capital and principal port of the rich province of Asia, which included the entire Aegean coast of Asia Minor, was the obvious choice. It had a big population and was the focal point of roads and rivers giving access to the hinterland. Since all roads led to Rome, the main road from southern Galatia ran about 250 miles westward from Pisidian Antioch to Ephesus, where imperial messengers crossed to Greece and on to Rome. Paul, Silas, and Timothy would follow their route. When Ephesus and Asia were thoroughly evangelized, they could ship to Corinth and work all southern Greece. And from there to Rome.

Paul's attempt to reach Ephesus failed. They were very distinctly "forbidden by the Holy Spirit to preach the Word in Asia." It is possible that illness supervened, a fresh attack of Paul's "thorn in the flesh" accompanied by a conviction that he was not to evangelize Ephesus yet. Or he and his companions may have been turned back. They were sure that wherever God wanted them He would direct them, and if like a shepherd directing his flock to better pastures by throwing stones He hit them with setbacks, they would not complain. Adverse circumstances were often to be the means of guidance without Luke making a specific reference to the Spirit. Quite likely Paul and Silas were forbidden by a definite word of revelation delivered by a Galatian Christian whom they accepted as a "prophet," just as the Syrian Antioch congregation had accepted Agabus's warning about the famine.

They continued to strengthen the churches in Phrygian Galatia. Then they tried again.

The other remaining province of importance in Asia Minor was Bithynia, opposite Byzantium to the northeast—smaller than Asia but with two highly cultured Greek cities, Nicea and Nicomedia, and many Jews. They set off across the mountains above Pisidian Antioch and down into Asia, where the Spirit had not forbidden travel. The route led north mile by mile, day by day through midsummer, a tedious dusty road that had secondary status because it did not lead direct toward Rome, and wound from valley to valley against the lay of the land.

At Dorylaion on the Tembris River, or at another town near the Bithynian border, they met a check. Official action was again unlikely, since they were private travelers unknown in those parts, unless civil disturbance in Bithynia had closed the frontier to all strangers. Luke wrote that "the Spirit of *Jesus*"[12] would not allow them to enter Bithynia, which may suggest that Paul reported a vision of the Lord such as he had had in the temple and on the Damascus Road.

Disappointments soldered the missionaries together, as no easy success could have forged them, for a purpose not yet clear: The guidance showed only that they should not remain in Anatolia.

They turned west through Mysia, the northernmost district of the province of Asia. Their obvious course was to make for the coast, to the port of Alexandria Troas near the ruins of ancient Troy. From there it would be a short sea passage northwest to Macedonia, or longer and southwest to southern Greece, the province of Achaia.

Whichever way the Spirit would lead, they were ready.

FIFTEEN

ACROSS TO EUROPE

At Troas Luke slipped into the picture. In the best tradition of historians, he never thrust himself forward and thus left his origins wide open to speculation. It is known he was a doctor: Paul called him "the beloved physician," and he showed close attention to medical detail. He was plainly a Greek. Early tradition makes him a citizen of Antioch in Syria—the Western Text inserts a "we" into the description of the church in Antioch, while a further, if intriguingly circumstantial, piece of evidence is Luke's odd lack of reference to Titus of Antioch despite his importance to Paul. It has been suggested that Titus was Luke's brother, whom he did not wish to mention lest it seem family pride.

He must have met Paul, Silas, and Timothy at Troas by coincidence, for they had no prior intention of going there. He may have been traveling to or from the medical center of the ancient world at the Shrine of Aesculapius near Pergamum, not very far from Troas. Or perhaps he practiced at Troas, as an immigrant Antiochene, a Christian whose spiritual ambitions before he met Paul had not advanced beyond a little local church formed as a footnote to personal faith. Another view is that he was a Macedonian and a pagan whom Paul converted at Troas.

Whatever the truth, Luke, as he matured in Paul's companionship, grew to be a man of charm and compassion; quiet, unexcitable, watching the foibles of mankind with a shrewd, twinkling eye. His writings have delicious touches of humor. He cared especially about the downtrodden and despised. He was a friendly person, who used nicknames or diminutives when Paul retained formal names. Where Paul was the brilliant, original thinker, Luke was the careful scholar, investigating incidents and background with a physician's strict regard for accuracy. Paul's prose pours out like talk, in the language of the people. Luke's has literary grace and style, concise without being terse.

He had no doubt at all, after examining the case, that the man Jesus rose from the dead and was the Son of God and Savior of the world. Luke had a vivid sense of the continuing, direct work of God among men and saw the Spirit's hand where some might see only changes and chances.

Paul accepted Luke gratefully. Indifferent health, wrestling against a constitution whose iron was mainly a matter of indomitable will, cried out for a personal physician. It says much for Paul's unselfishness that he would shortly be prepared to lose him for the sake of an infant church.

Luke wrote, "They went down into Troas. And in the night a vision appeared to Paul; a man, a Macedonian, was standing and beseeching him and saying, 'Come into Macedonia and help us.' When he had seen the vision, immediately we sought to go on into Macedonia, being utterly convinced that God was calling us to proclaim the Good News to them." There was a pause while they sought a ship, but when they found one, probably in the last week of July 50, the very winds seemed to approve. A strong south wind blew them in two days a distance that on another occasion, in reverse, would have taken them five.

Luke loved the sea and remembered any incident whenever they sailed, but this was an unmemorable voyage, out by Tenedos, the island where in the Trojan War the Greeks built their wooden horse; past the opening of the Hellespont, or Dardanelles, with the Cape Helles peninsula shimmering in the afternoon heat haze across the deep blue of the sea. They rode out the night off the island of Samothrace, and the next morning could still run northwest before the wind, and through the strait between Thasos and the Macedonian shore.

They did not think of themselves as passing from the continent of Asia to Europe. The terms were in use, but the Aegean was Greek on either side. They had, instead, the excitement of approaching a new province, bringing them nearer Rome. They knew that beyond Macedonia they could reach Achaia and Italy, and the vast lands of Gaul, Spain, Germania, even the mist-bound island of Britain lately added to the empire: all save Rome untouched by the

Good News. They were not bringing force of arms or a political program: just four men—and Another, invisible, who had known these seas and shores before Achilles or Agamemnon or Ulysses; who could demolish empires and cities by the breath of His mouth, but who had chosen to humble Himself and come to Macedonia as quietly now as He had come, in the flesh, to Bethlehem half a century before.

They landed the second evening at Neapolis (now Kavála, the little tobacco port, where in 1967 King Constantine fled from the airfield), a new harbor tucked close under a ridge of the Pangaean range. This they climbed the next day with the broad Via Egnatia, one of the great roads to Rome. From the top of the pass they saw the city of Philippi. Beyond lay the narrow plain where the world's fate had been settled at the Battle of Philippi when Octavius (Augustus) defeated the murderers of Caesar. The city stood compact in granite glory on either side of the road, below an acropolis 1,020 feet high.

Philippi, named after Philip of Macedon, father of Alexander the Great, had become a Roman colony after the battle and was a bustling center of military activity, the leading city of eastern Macedonia, though not the seat of administration. It was self-governing, a "little Rome" that used Latin for all official business. It had a virile, brisk, no-nonsense air, the streets full of muscular young legionaries and hard-bitten veterans and their families, proud of the Roman eagle in forum and basilica. It was a place where Roman citizens were held in high honor.

Paul and his friends took lodgings. They saw idol temples but no synagogue, its absence showing that fewer than ten Jewish males lived in all Philippi. Paul's first stopping place in Europe therefore lacked his usual launching pad for the gospel, and if any Jews or proselytes existed, they would worship on the Sabbath in the open air—outside the walls near the river for the sake of ritual ablutions. Therefore, early on Sabbath morning, Paul, Silas, Luke, and Timothy threaded their way past wagons with peasants coming into market and out by the northwestern gate built in honor of Augustus.

They walked about a mile and a half under the shade of the finely arched trees down to the narrow Gangites River. A little way from the bridge, they found in a small grove some women preparing to offer praises and prayers, and there they sat down.

Very informally, they introduced themselves and made friends with the Philippians. One was a woman of substance, a Gentile God-fearer from Thyatira, a city in the district of Lydia in the province of Asia. She used the name Lydia and ran a business selling the rich purple-dyed cloth for which Thyatira was famous. Several of the other women were members of her household. At Sabbath worship, Paul told why they had come. He spoke of the Lord Jesus, how He had emptied Himself of His glory to be born as a mortal man, humbling Himself to die like a common criminal on a cross. He told of the resurrection of Jesus, and how to trust in Him. As Luke watched, he saw such understanding dawn on Lydia's face that he knew it was not through words alone. A miracle was taking place before his eyes: "The Lord opened her heart to respond to what Paul said."

This was clear to Paul too as soon as he talked with Lydia. He baptized her then and there in the river. Several of her household who were worshipping with her—the houseslaves and salespeople of a God-fearer would be given the Sabbath rest—were baptized too. Paul was content that they received Christ as best they knew; the One who had begun a good work in them would continue it.

Lydia said, "If you judge me to be a true believer in the Lord, then come to my house and stay."

Paul declined. He had a strong objection to their laying themselves open to the charge of being scroungers like the wandering philosophers of the day. It was true that the Lord had instructed His disciples to stay in the first house that invited them, for the laborer was worthy of his hire, but Paul preferred not to exercise the right. Lydia urged them until they agreed. Philippi was the only place where Paul accepted free board and lodging. It proved a good decision.

From the start the new church had a strong sense of partnership with the apostles. Young Timothy proved the genuineness of his vocation by the way he identified himself with the Philippians; Paul's own happiness, the aroma of peace about him, his delight in beauty of character and action, gave them an example they strove to follow as they shared the joy and the strength of God and worked together to pass on and defend the Good News. During the next days, several slaves and tough young soldiers were baptized. They found new perspectives that transformed the drudgery of slavery or the hardship of soldiering because now they were, in Paul's words, "God's dear children, blameless, sincere, and wholesome, living in a warped and diseased world, and shining there like lights in a dark place. For you hold in your hands the very word of life."

The Philippian church, which retained a very special place in Paul's affection, did not expand spectacularly, yet its influence even in this first short period may be gauged from the gossip that spread rapidly across Macedonia: Paul and his friends were turning the world upside down.

SIXTEEN

FLOGGED IN PHILIPPI

Here in Philippi, Paul thought he had found the city where they could stay for a time to dig deep foundations.

He went daily with the others to the riverside place of prayer. Being near the road, it could always attract an audience of wayfarers and citizens when Paul and Silas propounded and proved their Good News. One day, probably in August and about the twelfth day after their arrival, they were all walking down the Via Egnatia toward the river when they heard an eerie voice, oddly high-pitched, crying out behind them: "These men are slaves of the Supreme God and are announcing to you a way of salvation!"

Paul ignored the cry. Luke found that the girl was a slave, a "Pythoness" from Delphi, or Pytho, the world-famous shrine of Apollo on the southern slope of Mount Parnassus overlooking the Gulf of Corinth. The Delphic oracle was consulted by statesmen and ambassadors; a girl controlled by whatever strange force of evil lay at the back of it would be in much demand by men and women wanting to peer into the future. She was so valuable that she had been bought by a syndicate.

The next day the eerie voice cried again, "These men are slaves of the Supreme God and are announcing to you a way of salvation." Paul again took no notice, though he was now more irritated; he had no desire to be advertised by an evil spirit or demon, whether from Delphi or anywhere else. Jesus Himself had ordered demons to keep silent when they cried through the lips of those whom they controlled, "You are the Son of God!" Anyone who acknowledged Him at the word of an evil spirit would be a pseudo-disciple still under demon influence, and the last state of the man would be worse than the first.

Each day that the girl cried, Paul grew more worked up; there is no previous record in precise terms of Paul casting out an evil spirit, though the "signs and wonders" in Galatia would seem to imply this. The power of evil presented by Delphi was considerable. It is possible that Paul hesitated because he knew himself confronted by an enormity before which even he, who had seen the cripple of Lystra leap in the name of Jesus, was weak in faith.

On the third or fourth day, Paul and Silas were going to the place of prayer by themselves and had not reached the gate when again they heard the high-pitched cry, the same words: "These men are slaves of the Supreme God and are announcing to you a way of salvation." Now Paul's disgust at the shameless exploitation of an innocent girl, at the parody of evangelism coming from her lips, boiled over. He turned and said, "I command you in the name of Jesus Christ to come out of her!"

The girl suddenly relaxed, lost her wild look, and spoke in a normal voice.

Her owners were furious. They knew enough to see that she was no longer a medium. From a highly lucrative investment, she had been devalued into an ordinary slave girl good for nothing but scrubbing. As old soldiers they reacted to a tactical defeat by instant counterattack. They turned on Paul and Silas and shouted to the bystanders, and swung the crowd standing openmouthed at the miracle. Everyone began to yell and rush the apostles toward the center of the city.

In the forum, sitting on the bema, a judgment seat on the east side across from the gymnasium, with their lictors behind them, the elected magistrates of the colony had not completed the day's lawsuits and prosecutions when they were shocked to see a disturbance at the far end of the square: a yelling mob dragging two strangers who were thrust panting in front of them. As a threat to public order, this case, whatever it was, must be dealt with at once.

The slaveowners' case was weak: the law took no cognizance of a medium losing occult powers through the influence of a third party; it is even doubtful whether damages could be recovered in a civil suit. But the slaveowners wanted revenge, a revenge that could hurt.

"These men are causing a disturbance in our city—"

The magistrates could see it was so, as the crowd yelled and pummeled Paul.

"They are Jews in the first place—"

That was bad. Jews always caused trouble, and Claudius had lately expelled them from Rome. A "little Rome" should do the same.

"And they teach customs which it is not lawful for us to accept or practice, being Romans!"

That was worse. Magistrates were expected to suppress unauthorized religious practices lest they undermine public order, as these undoubtedly had. The case was clear. Every moment that the crowd continued yelling made immediate action more necessary; Roman discipline was collapsing and the magistrates would be held responsible.

Quite illegally, they never asked for a defense. The proceedings were in Latin. Paul knew Latin yet had no opportunity to cry that both were Roman citizens, or if he did, none heard him in the noise.

No formal sentence was uttered, merely a quick order to the lictors. The slaveowners looked on with grim satisfaction, the crowd quieted a little, as the lictors drew their rods. They stepped down, one to each missionary, and stripped him of all his clothes. When Paul's scarred, knotted back was exposed to the sun, nobody had further doubts. They were thrown at the flogging posts. It is doubtful whether in the hurry they were tied; plenty of strong arms could grip either if he struggled. The lictors began.

As the blood ran from the cuts, the crowd roared. When a savage blow caught a vertebra and even a tough apostle could not suppress a cry, the people loved it. Paul and Silas fought the pain with prayer. Urged on by the crowd, the lictors swung their rods with a will, until both backs were bloody. "The blows burnt like fire," wrote Pastor Richard Wurmbrand, who suffered rods frequently in Communist prisons. "It was as if your back were being grilled by a furnace, and the shock to the nervous system was great."[13]

The magistrates stopped it before either collapsed. They gave another order. The lictors half-pushed, half-carried the apostles up from the forum, across the Via Egnatia, to the prison built on and in the hillside below the acropolis, not far from the theater. The jailer, another veteran, was given strict instructions to guard them closely and assumed they were dangerous criminals who probably would be sent off to the provincial capital and end as galley slaves. He had them manhandled, still naked, across the main prison chamber where fettered thieves and small-time brigands awaited sentence and through a low opening into a windowless cave. Here was a contraption used both for security and torture. Rough bars of wood were so placed that a criminal's legs could be stretched wide, held tight, and his wrists and even his neck gripped in various positions depending on how much pain the jailer wished to inflict.

Because this was merely a security matter, he had Paul and Silas thrown to the ground and only their feet clamped in the bars, leaving the rest of their bodies free. Their clothes were thrown in after them.

Outside, the sun dropped and set beyond the Pangaean mountains. In Lydia's house, Timothy and Luke had probably gathered the others to pray. There is a possible allusion to these prayers in words that Paul wrote to the Philippians from a later imprisonment, that he *knew* he would be delivered through their prayers and the resources of the Spirit of Jesus Christ.

In the cave Paul and Silas lay side by side silent in a state of physical shock, the blood congealing, their muscles stiffening, unable to rest on their torn backs yet in acute discomfort when they sat upright. Their feet were numbed and the wooden bar pressed on their ankles. The clothes they had put round each other's backs could not stop the shivering, and they were forced to lie in their own excrement.

Sleep never came. Nor at first could they pray. When shock subsided and the pain eased, their minds sought an answer to the outrage, indignity, and injury that had engulfed them though Roman citizens in a Roman colony. There may have been depression, even a trace of resentment while each "*learned* in whatever state I am, to be content," until as night wore on, any trace of spiritual or mental misery was assuaged, then overwhelmed by knowledge that in all these things they could be more than conquerors through Him who loved them. His arms had been under them when conscious awareness was impossible, and He knew what suffering meant. They began to pray. As they prayed, prayers turned to praise.

Softly, a little brokenly at first, they started to sing. (Paul often wrote about music and singing and may have had a rich voice.) They were not singing to keep their spirits up; melody bubbled out of hearts for whom the Presence grew rapidly more real than aches, soreness, hunger, stench, and darkness:

> At the name of Jesus
> Every knee shall bow,
> In heaven, on earth, under the earth.

It is sometimes thought that Paul's great passage written to the Philippians from another prison, about the self-emptying of God the Son, His death and glory, was putting them in mind of a song they knew already. If so, it may have been improvised by Paul and Silas that night as their agony turned to joy, until the rousing climax rang out from the stocks:

> And every tongue confess
> That Jesus Christ is Lord,
> To the glory of God the Father.

In the main chamber of the prison, the other dozen or so who lay chained to the wall heard the sound, each from his private misery as he faced possible torture, hard labor, or death. They had seen the raw backs of the men who had been thrown into the cave, yet now those two poor wretches were singing, and singing for joy. An extraordinary, infectious happiness, peace, and hope flooded the prison.

The jailer, in his house a few feet up the hillside, lay fast asleep.

Paul and Silas sang more. The prisoners listened. Suddenly the whole prison shook in a split-second earthquake. Earth tremors were common in Macedonia in summer, but this was a shake strong enough to throw the stocks loose in the cave, dislodge the iron rings that anchored the other prisoners' chains, knock the bars off the inner and outer doors and leave them swinging. And wake the jailer.

His inevitable reaction was to jump out of bed, seize his short sword and run into the unlighted courtyard. He saw the doors were open right through to the street. His prisoners must be gone and he must be ruined; his life was forfeit for theirs. Appalled, but without a moment's hesitation, he chose suicide rather than public disgrace and execution. He drew his sword. The clink and the clatter as the scabbard fell to the ground sounded clear in the night. But then he heard a loud voice from the depths of the prison, "Don't injure yourself! We are all here."

He stopped. In the moonlight he could see that Philippi stood. The earth-quake had been entirely local under his patch of hillside. To a Macedonian, all earth tremors and quakes, small and great, were the touch of an angry god; this god had singled him out and the jailer was terrified. More amazing, the god had kept the prisoners from escaping, and now came that strong voice from the cave, "Don't injure yourself! We are all here." The chastised Jews cared more for their jailer than for escape. The whole thing was beyond him.

Trembling, he shouted to his wide-awake, gibbering slaves for lights; every second's delay while they fumbled with pitch-pine torches was agony lest the god strike again. The jailer must have heard a smattering about why the two Jews were in prison, that they were servants of a divinity and talked about salvation. He desperately needed to speak to them.

The torches flaming at last, he dashed into the prison chamber behind a slave and through to the cave. He saw Paul and Silas standing, filthy but serene. He threw himself at their feet. "Sirs, what must I do to be saved?"

"Put your trust in the Lord Jesus, and you will be saved, you and your household!"

By now his two or three slaves and the family had crowded into the prison chamber. The other prisoners, their loose chains clanking, pressed round the opening of the cave as eager as the jailer. And there Paul and Silas, with matted hair and backs stiff with dried blood, "spoke the word of the Lord to him and to everyone in his house."

The jailer then led them out. In the courtyard was a well or fountain where, helped by the women and slaves, he washed their wounds with his own hands. Immediately afterward, under the light of the torches, he was baptized, quickly followed by all his family and slaves.[14]

After the baptism, the jailer took the apostles up to his house for a much-needed meal, "and he rejoiced with all his household that he had believed in God." When dawn broke, they were still sitting with Paul and Silas, asking more about Jesus, sharing together the incredible happiness that had spilled over and welled up within them.

Shortly after sunrise the lictors arrived at the prison with an order from the magistrates that the two Jews were to be released. Beating and a night in jail were sufficient summary correction; the whipped, disgraced strangers would of course leave town. The lictors waited in the courtyard to conduct them to the city limits while the jailer, glad that the punishment was over, hastened into his house. It was nothing to the lictors where he kept prisoners, provided he produced them when required.

"The magistrates have sent to have you released. So now you can leave this place and go on your way in peace."

Paul would have none of it. To the jailer's surprise and alarm he replied, "They gave us a public flogging, though we are Roman citizens and have not been found guilty; they threw us into prison, and are they now to smuggle us out privately? I don't think so! Let them come in person and escort us out."

This was a serious matter. The jailer did not doubt their word that they were Romans. No man would fraudulently claim citizenship and risk a capital charge. When the lictors reported the words to the magistrates, their pomposity quickly subsided. By the *Lex Valeria*, the *Lex Porcia*, and more recently the *Lex Julia,* a Roman citizen could not be beaten except for refusal to obey a direct order of a magistrate, and then only after full trial and formal conviction. By beating Paul and Silas publicly and uncondemned, the magistrates had exposed themselves to complaint at Rome and to ruin. Worse, they would not know whether these outraged citizens intended to seek revenge or not. Safety lay only in abject servility.

The magistrates hurried across to the prison, entered the jailer's home, and offered humble apologies, to which Paul and Silas made no reply, knowing that the best protection for the young Philippian church was to keep the magistrates on tenterhooks. It was also a sure way of turning the other cheek and doing good to persecutors, for the magistrates and the lictors might pay attention to the teaching of a church founded by Romans.

With much public honor in front of the small crowd that would have followed the rush to the prison, the magistrates escorted the apostles out of jail and begged as a favor that they leave the city to avoid the risk of another breach of peace. Paul and Silas, perhaps with the jailer himself, went first to Lydia's house. Every Christian who could leave work ran there too and praised God together and took fresh courage from all that the apostles told. It was too soon to ordain elders and presbyters, but Luke, much as he might wish to accompany his battered friends and patients, agreed to remain behind; he could set up a medical practice while shepherding the church.

Then Paul and Silas, with Timothy, took sturdy sticks and set off northwest over the bridge and across the plain.

SEVENTEEN

THROWN OUT OF THESSALONICA

A Jew bearing the Greek name Aristarchus went as usual to the large syna-gogue of the powerful Jewish minority in Thessalonica, the free city at the head of the Gulf of Thermae, where the governor of Macedonia resided. On this mid-August Sabbath, the elders had invited a visiting rabbi to read and expound the Law. As Aristarchus listened in the sultry heat, little did he know that for this man's sake, in a few years' time, he would be manhandled by a mob, go two long journeys with him, be shipwrecked, and share imprison-ment at Rome.

He could see at once that the man was unusual. The poor fellow walked to the reading desk stiffly on rather bow legs and occasionally winced, which suggested recent severe physical pain. It had not soured him though. His face had a sparkle, an attractive friendliness unspoiled by the beetling brows, yet he showed traces of nervousness when he addressed his audience, as if half-expecting them to hurt him.

This was less surprising when Aristarchus heard the controversial nature of the sermon. The stranger started with the set passage, then drew scripture after scripture to prove that the expected Messiah should not, as they had supposed, immediately refound the kingdom in Jerusalem, but should suffer and die—and come alive again. To Aristarchus, the stranger's copious biblical references made his point. When he talked of a man named Jesus who had been crucified recently, and when, without polish or style but with curiously compelling force he told how this Jesus had risen from the dead, Aristarchus was sure, on the stranger's word, that it was so. "This Jesus whom I am proclaiming to you," the sermon ended, "*is* the Messiah!"

Afterward, the elders were polite, if unenthusiastic, and intimated that Paul should address them on the next Sabbath. Aristarchus and several others sought him out. Another member of the congregation named Jason invited him home with Silas and Timothy so that any who wished might meet them. There Paul and Silas told how they "had been treated abominably at Philippi, and we came on to you only because God gave us courage. We came to tell you the Good News, whatever the opposition might be." Their walk of about a hundred miles along the Via Egnatia through two other important cities, Amphipolis near the lagoon-like mouth of the Strymon River, guarded by its ancient stone lion, and Apollonia on the shores of a lake, had restored their health; but when they came over the hills and down into Thessalonica, a conscious effort had been required to face the risk of further hurt as they proclaimed the gospel. Paul therefore was all the more grateful that "when you received the Word of God which you heard from us, you accepted it, not as the word of men but as what it really is, the Word of God."

The first quality that impressed Aristarchus and the others at Jason's house was the genuineness of Paul and Silas, the integrity in their ways and in their words, which shrewd merchants could recognize and respect. They had a mental cleanness about them, an absence of the tricks strolling prophets often used. They showed no interest in money or goods, only a touching gratitude for the friendliness of their hearers.

Paul's character might attract, but it was his message that convinced—a message rooted in fact. Paul offered no nebulous fancies, nor asserted that only faith mattered irrespective of whether Jesus' life, death, and resurrection were facts or myth; his conviction of their truth was overwhelming. As Aristarchus listened, he again sensed something more than reason drawing him to believe and to commit himself to the Jesus whom Paul preached. Paul was not surprised. He said that this power was the Holy Spirit of God the Father—and of Jesus. When Aristarchus, Jason, and several others from the synagogue were converted, Paul refused any credit.

The courage and conviction of Paul and Silas bred further courage and conviction. Not only did converts assure fellow Jews that Jesus certainly was the Messiah, but they also broke out of their prejudices to tell pagan business acquaintances and the slaves who carried their goods from the docks that He was the Savior of everyone. Soon Jason's house, in a most un-Jewish way, became the center of a movement that spread like wildfire across the city. In a few astonishing days "the church of the Thessalonians in God the Father and the Lord Jesus Christ" had more Greeks than Jews, both men and influential aristocratic women.

Again Paul showed his integrity. He refused to flatter. When he spoke to inquirers, he made no attempt to disguise his belief that the very roots of their lives were twisted, that the little idols they worshipped in their homes and the classically beautiful idols that graced the temples were false gods, impotent, dead.

And because Paul dealt honestly with them, and because his gospel was grounded in the facts of history and came "not only in word but also in power and in the Holy Spirit and with much conviction," he could rejoice about "the welcome we had among you, and how you turned to God from idols to serve the living and true God."

Thessalonica stood at a strategic position. The city was near enough to Philippi for a sense of unity to develop between the churches; Paul was delighted when a messenger reached him with a gift of funds, for he had not stopped praying for his Philippians and was touched that they remembered him. Westward, when his work in Thessalonica was complete, the Via Egnatia could take him to the Adriatic and so to Rome. To the south, beyond the gulf, which from the harbor appeared nearly landlocked, he could see Mount Olympus, legendary home of the gods whom Christ had come to supplant. Few Greeks now believed that gods resided on Olympus, but their existence seemed real to those who worshipped them.

Beyond Olympus lay the plains of Thessaly and all Achaia (southern Greece); trading ships plied back and forth, so that from Thessalonica the gospel could soon "ring out," as Paul put it, wherever seafaring Christians went about their business—to Corinth and Piraeus, to the Aegean islands, to Ephesus on the Asian shore.

Once again Paul thought he had found the city in which to settle down. He and Silas accepted Jason's house as their home but refused to impose themselves on his hospitality or to take free meals in other parts. "We did not accept board and lodging from anyone without paying for it; we toiled and drudged, we worked for a living night and day, rather than be a burden to any of you—not because we have not the right to maintenance, but to set an example for you to imitate ... we laid down the rule; the man who will not work shall not eat."

Paul became a tentmaker again. Thessalonica is the first place in which he or Luke mentioned his earning a living. On the first missionary journey all wants may have been supplied by Barnabas, for though Barnabas had sold his land and donated the proceeds to the Jerusalem church, this could have been a deliberate evidence of repentance because he was a Levite, and Levites were not supposed to own land, though many did. It does not necessarily mean he had reduced himself to apostolic poverty. He may have drawn an income from copper mines or other family business in Cyprus on which he and Paul had lived until the breach. But now Paul was without such private means.

All waking hours that he, Silas, and Timothy were not out teaching they worked (the other men's trades are not specified), and as they worked, they talked with converts or inquirers. Or they prayed for fellow believers. Paul is scarcely ever described in Acts as praying alone. Only once does he withdraw by himself and then he is walking. Yet prayer is constantly mentioned in his epistles. It would seem that when traveling between cities, the apostles spent part of their time in intercession as they walked. When settled in a city and at the loom, they again took to prayer, together or with converts, or each alone, the steady rhythmic actions of tenting and its kindred leatherwork providing the element of slight distraction to keep the mind from wandering.

Each Sabbath Paul continued to preach, opening up the Scriptures, demonstrating their fulfillment in Jesus, debating after the liturgical service with those who disputed this conclusion. Always he rooted his argument in facts of history and experience, and always, when he preached, a few more Jews and God-fearers would put his allegations to the test, only to discover that they too could meet God.

All through the week Paul told Jews, proselytes, and pagans about Christ and strengthened the baptized. These would sit and listen, conscious of three loves blending in Paul: love for God, love for their neighbors, and especially love for them, his "brothers and sisters in Christ." Paul brought a new concept of love, though he would say that it was God teaching them beyond any words he might impart. Where eroticism was in the very air, even in a city such as theirs not dominated by the cults of Apollo or Aphrodite, Paul used the new word *agapē*, which Christians had coined to replace the debased word *eros*, and expounded a love that purified and transformed. Love at its highest and lowest was an urgent topic. Letters that Paul wrote back following his flight from Thessalonica disclose that the church included many young men and women. The men did not find it easy to allow Christ to control their sexual instincts. When they were pagans, they had thought nothing of seducing a friend's wife or fornicating with any girl who caught their fancy. Turning consciously from evil to faith did not always bring immediate awareness of how to please God in this matter.

Paul guided them precisely. "You know what instructions we gave you through the Lord Jesus," he would remind them in his first letter. "This is the will of God that you should be holy; you must abstain from fornication: each one of you must learn to gain mastery over his body, to hallow and honor it, not giving way to lust like the pagans who are ignorant of God."

Paul and his friends were not soothing an effete club of escapists but molding a high-spirited band who had lived all their days in a permissive society where sexual prowess was admired and its consequences could be exposed on hillsides. These men and women had now given their allegiance to Jesus as king, given it so fervently that rumor in the city spoke of Paul recruiting for a rival to Claudius Caesar. They wanted to obey this King Jesus; His words were now their chief authority. They wanted to be like Him, though the old appetites surged in their veins together with the new. Paul strengthened and directed the new by making the most of their conscious desire to obey and to imitate Jesus. He told them what Jesus had said and done.

Nor did Paul confine himself to matters of present conduct. He told them of the coming kingdom when Jesus would return to earth to reign over all people.

Again he based instruction carefully on the words of Jesus. The letters to the Thessalonians, echoing this teaching, contain close parallels to the sayings of Jesus recorded by Luke and give some substance to the tradition—not highly regarded by biblical scholars—that Luke in making his gospel wrote down what Paul preached. "Know this," Jesus had said, "that if the house-holder had known at what hour the thief was coming, he would have been awake…. You also must be ready, for the Son of man is coming at an hour you do not expect." Paul wrote, "You yourselves well know that the Day of the Lord will come like a thief in the night." Or again, "This we declare to you by the word of the Lord: … the Lord Himself will descend from heaven with a cry of command, with the archangel's call, and with the sound of the trumpet of God." Jesus had said, "They will see the Son of man coming in a cloud with power and great glory."[15]

Much of what Paul taught about the return of Christ was a puzzle to his hearers, just as the Lord's sayings puzzled His disciples at the time they were spoken. The misinterpretations that the Thessalonians put on Paul's words would soon force him to define his understanding more clearly. He was con-vinced by Old Testament prophecy and the words of Jesus that the Lord would suddenly end the present age, with its lust, oppression, and crime, by returning bodily in majesty and power, but the details were obscure. And

Paul's perspective was foreshortened. He looked for the Second Coming as a man reaching a mountain pass might look at the next snowcapped range: It seems only a few hours' march, though as he crosses the plain, the range grows no nearer while still beckoning him. So Paul walked on, forever expecting, hoping that his Lord might return at once, yet grateful for every new day that renewed the opportunity to tell men and women about the King who had come—and was returning.

Meanwhile, as Paul's letters also disclose, the three missionaries not only taught the Thessalonians in groups but took time and trouble with them "one by one, as a father deals with his children," encouraging and warning and sorting out the special problems of each. The three men gave themselves completely. And though it would have been easier to demand unquestioning obedience, they preferred to work gently, patiently, "like a devoted nurse among her babies," until Paul grew so personally involved in his converts that when the wrench came it was as if flesh were torn from his body.

It came unexpectedly.

By the fourth week he had ordained elders who were to encourage, admonish, and teach—and lead the church forward. In Paul's view a church should not merely survive in its unfriendly pagan environment, but advance. Christians should have nothing to do with a sad acceptance of harsh surroundings, bearing heavy crosses with uncomplaining gloom, cultivating an oppressive sense of sin. They were to be positive, doing good to one another and to unbelieving Jews and pagans regardless of abuse or injury. "Rejoice evermore, pray without ceasing, in everything give thanks." No matter how adverse the circumstances, their way of life should be a rebuke to foulness and a spur to their neighbors to seek for themselves this new, extraordinary existence; Christians must outlove, outjoy, outthink, and always welcome those who opposed them.

Thus, the infant Thessalonian church became a mighty movement. Men were remade, relationships sweetened between masters and slaves, husbands and wives. But families were divided too and neighborhoods split. The new faith was discussed, praised, maligned. Paul was loved and admired by some, hated by others. Few stayed indifferent.

The climax came when unbelieving Jews could no longer contain their jealousy. They "recruited some low fellows from the dregs of the populace," wrote Luke, "roused the rabble and had the city in an uproar. They mobbed Jason's house, with the intention of bringing Paul and Silas before the town assembly." Not finding them, the mob hustled Jason and some other Christians out of the house and forced them to the *politarchs*, the men responsible for law and order in a Macedonian city that was not a Roman colony.

The ringleaders shouted, "These men who have turned the world upside down have come here also, and Jason has received them. And they are all acting against the decrees of Caesar, saying that there is another king, Jesus."

The mob yelled for blood. The *politarchs*, however, showed a sanity very different from the hasty illegalities of the *strategoi* of Philippi. The charge disturbed them, for they must have known of the expulsion of Jews from Rome and its cause, which the early second-century historian Suetonius ascribed to their "indulging in constant riots at the instigation of one Chrestus," most likely a garbled reference to Jewish violence against Christ's earliest followers in Rome. But evidence of sedition in Thessalonica, of recruiting for a rival Caesar, proved scanty. Its alleged ringleaders were not even before the court.

The *politarchs* therefore adopted a cautious policy. They bound over Jason and his friends in a considerable sum. This would be forfeit, and they themselves arrested, if the strangers were seen again in the city.

Paul had to make a decision.

EIGHTEEN

THE FUGITIVE

Paul had no option but to flee with Silas at once. Not only did he have Jason to consider; if the prosecutors could contrive more incriminating evidence, soldiers might be sent out to bring him back.

When night fell, Christian brothers led Paul and Silas through the Arch of Augustus and on to the Egnatian Way. Timothy remained, though it is probable that a Thessalonian accompanied them as they walked quickly through the night to reach the broad river Axios by dawn. While they waited for the ferry, they kept an eye out for horsemen who might gallop up with orders to arrest them, but they passed over safely, walked on through the September morning as the haze enveloped the hills, then turned southwest off the Via Egnatia.

Had Paul stayed at Thessalonica as long as he wished, his probable next move would have been westward into the coastal province of Illyricum. Having evangelized there, he had hoped to cross the Adriatic to Rome. But Rome at present was closed to Jewish travelers; nor did he want to leave the Thessalonians to fend alone, for despite his own teaching about the ability of the Holy Spirit to look after them, he was agitated lest these spiritual babies should weaken under persecution. He therefore chose the little town of Berea in the foothills of Olympus, well-known as a summer resort and a refuge for exiles from Thessalonica yet near enough for a quick return should the ban be lifted once the falsity of the charges was exposed. Paul hoped to be back for winter when gales blew round Mount Athos and snow blocked the Macedonian passes.

They reached Berea on the third day, a peaceful city in majestic surroundings looking down with a narrow view to the sea and up to the gorge from which a river emerged from the mountain. They found a synagogue. Here at the first opportunity Paul and Silas preached.

Their reception was friendly. The local Jewish elders showed no prejudice. Paul considered them, as Luke wrote, much more noble than those at
Thessalonica in that "they received the message with great eagerness, studying
the Scriptures every day to see whether it was as they said. Many of them
therefore became believers, and so did a fair number of Greeks, women of
standing as well as men." There was no need to seek neutral ground for evangelizing and teaching; the synagogue itself became the center of Christian faith.
Unexpectedly, when Paul's heart was sore at expulsion from Thessalonica, this
little hill town of Berea provided what he had longed for—a synagogue that
became a spearhead for Christ.

Timothy arrived with the encouragement that despite persecution,
of which Paul had forewarned them, the Thessalonian converts kept their
faith. Yet Paul worried lest they lose heart if it grew fiercer, especially
when after about fifteen days in Berea all his plans were disrupted once
again. Jews from Thessalonica, maddened by the news that had traveled
swiftly back, arrived to make trouble. Seeing at once that the synagogue
leadership had no sympathy with their fury, they began rousing the
people to destroy Paul by riot or murder. The Christians of Berea sensed
that Paul's life hung by a thread, so before a riot could begin, they hurried
him secretly out of the town and down toward the coast, leaving Silas and
Timothy.

Paul longed to be in Thessalonica again and waited in the little port
below Olympus while a messenger went to the city to judge whether this
would be safe. He returned with bad news. As Paul wrote a few weeks later:
"Since we were bereft of you, brethren, for a short time, in person not in
heart, we endeavored the more eagerly and with great desire to see you face
to face; because we wanted to come to you—I Paul, again and again—but
Satan hindered us."

Winter was coming on. Paul could not wander around Macedonia
waiting. The Berean brothers persuaded him to let them take him by sea to
Athens. There he would be safe until his next steps became plain.

They took a ship[16] down the Aegean past mountains famous in Greek mythology: Olympus far back from the shore but clear in the morning light, then Ossa, which the giants had piled on its neighboring peak of Pelion in their attempt to reach heaven. For Paul, if his Berean friends pointed out Ossa and the forests of Pelion, the myth represented falsehood, which Christ had come to supplant, and Christ was conquering even if His servants must flee. The next day they were in the long, narrow gulf separating Euboea from the mainland, and the ship had no need to shelter when night fell, provided the winds were gentle. The following morning they rounded the point of Sounion. Dominated by the glorious marble temple of Poseidon, god of the sea, this was a center of worship and loyalty to which the sailors made prayer as they passed. Its white-robed priests were clearly visible in the strong light, which is peculiarly Grecian. The temple seemed to mock the weakness of the battered traveler who watched from the deck with a different prayer in his heart.

As they sailed deeper into the Saronic Bay toward the port of Piraeus, Paul had his first distant sight of Athens—the pagan beauties of the Acropolis and the Parthenon, the marble of its great columns reflecting clear despite the intervening distance, its cool arrogance disdaining Paul's audacity.

The Bereans took Paul up the busy road from Piraeus between the half-ruined fortified walls and through the double gate. They found lodgings for him, but he was restless. His heart remained in Macedonia. He fussed lest Christians had broken under the strain. He who had assured them so strongly that they would find Christ true and powerful whatever the malice of man was nervous that continuous and severe persecution should seem to disprove this and turn them against both Savior and servant. He had not yet reached the level of faith where he could leave the issue totally in God's hands.

"And so when we could bear it no longer, we decided to remain alone at Athens.… When I could bear it no longer I sent to find out about your faith, fearing that the tempter might have tempted you and my labor might be lost." He persuaded the Bereans to hurry back home and tell Timothy that he must visit Thessalonica and encourage them to stand firm and strong in the faith and not be "unsettled by the present troubles." Then Timothy and Silas were to come to Paul at Athens as fast as they could.

To be left alone in Athens, city of idolatry and pagan philosophy, where the Jewish synagogue gave little welcome, was pain almost sharper than the rods of Philippi's lictors. Paul craved company and sympathy, but the Thessalonians mattered more. For them, he was willing to endure an autumn of waiting.

Though worse was in store immediately, though the fiercest spiritual crisis lay several years ahead, the day when Paul waved farewell to the Bereans was one of the hardest in his life.

NINETEEN

LAUGHTER IN ATHENS

The immense granite cliff topped with the Western world's most famous temples held the eye of Paul or any visitor to Athens by purity of line and color against the cloudless blue of the late September sky.

Paul was not blind to beauty, but if he took note of the exquisite forms of the Propylea and the Temple of Athene, Giver of Victory, or the Parthenon itself, he would not climb the hill to enter these centers of rampant paganism. He knew that the gleaming statue of Athene was an object of worship, that the famous frieze, which would become the Elgin Marbles, represented religious rituals. Until Greek art should be stripped of religion its very loveliness strengthened Paul's repudiation.

He had not intended to evangelize Athens; he was without helpers and half hoped to return to the Thessalonians, and he needed rest. But as he saw the extraordinary number of idols on every side, he became more and more exasperated. Below the Acropolis, he walked in the busy agora, the marketplace flanked by the chaste Doric magnificence of the Theseion and other temples where worship took place daily; even the city hall had its sacred fire. In the open space and under the porticoes, wedged together with statues of illustrious Athenians and wealthy Romans, were idols and altars of every divinity known or unknown. Yet this was the intellectual center of the world, where rich youths from every land in the empire were sent to complete their education by selecting a philosophy to their taste. The blend of shallow piety with philosophies that scoffed at the supernatural had created a flippant attitude, which Luke described neatly: "All Athenians and the foreigners staying there spent their time in nothing else but telling and hearing whatever was new."

Paul's soul revolted at this misuse of human faculties, especially because, as his own words would show, he knew something of the long-ago intellectual

splendors of classical Athens and of its search for truth. But when he unbur-
dened himself in the synagogue, he met apathy; the Jews had written off their
Greek neighbors and were content to treat them as lucrative customers whose
moral and religious blindness were of no concern. He went therefore to work
in the agora, where with his customary adaptability he became an Athenian
to the Athenians by using the method of Socrates, engaging the strollers and
bystanders in question-and-answer discussion. Socrates had been content to
remain in one city, devoting himself to goodness as he saw it. Paul could not
restrict himself to one city. No man in previous history had traveled so far or
suffered so much to bring men truth; he could not stay still or silent while
others remained ignorant of the Word of Truth, and the Life. Every day he
told all about Jesus and His resurrection, undeterred by lack of response.

This little man with bandy legs and quite unfashionable earnestness
became sufficiently familiar to attract the attention of the two principal
schools of philosophy. Stoics taught that people should strive, unafraid and
proud, to accept the law of the universe however harsh and should work
toward a world state founded on reason. They believed that the soul survived
the body. Their rivals, the Epicureans, did not. These taught that happiness or
pleasure was the highest good, which should be pursued unaided by whatever
gods there be, but their idea had degenerated into: "Eat, drink, and be merry,
for tomorrow we die." By Paul's day the disciples of each philosophy had lost
much of their drive to make converts; a man's beliefs were his personal affair,
and philosophy had degenerated into an elaborate intellectual exercise.

Stoics and Epicureans listened to Paul, whom they took to be one of the
usual scum of foreigners seeking patrons in Athens, and were amused. First,
Paul kept emphasizing that he did not speak on his own authority, being
presumably an intellectual bankrupt. Then, instead of offering a rational philosophy, he sounded as if he were commending a divinity or two. The words
Jesous and *anastasis* (resurrection) were frequently on his lips. *Jesous* sounded
rather like the name of the Ionic goddess of health, especially as he linked
it with the *sōter* (savior), which to a Greek suggested a god who gave health

of body and mind. As for *anastasis*, they had myths of gods returning from the underworld, and this might be another. Yet Paul talked as if he referred to a real flesh-and-blood person who had been talked with, watched, and listened to, and then executed by crucifixion, which no one could survive. Paul seemed to be trying to persuade them this man had risen bodily from the grave.

"What *is* this gutter-sparrow trying to say?" they asked each other, using the typical slang word (literally a "seed-picker") for a rogue who picks up scraps from the gutter or hawks other men's ideas because he is too lazy or dull to have his own.

"He seems to be a herald for foreign gods," others said.

It all sounded rubbish. And possibly dangerous to the morals of such Athenians who troubled to listen; though speech was free in Athens, there were limits. They decided that he must expound his views before the venerable Court of the Areopagus, which had the right to expel unsuitable philosophers. They approached Paul good-humoredly and invited him to accompany them up the slope of the Acropolis and onto the small steep rock, the Hill of Ares, from which the court took its name.[17]

As Paul stood on the Areopagus, on the white Stone of Shame reserved for the defendant (whether of a thesis or against a criminal accusation), the immediate background was filled by the pink-white marble of the shrines that man's religious devotion and incomparable architecture had raised on the Acropolis crag. At eye level was the Boule Gate below the summit; above it the twin Propylea, that dignified entrance to the sacred area, flanked by two temples. He could not see the Parthenon, but over the Propylea the sunlight glinted on the shield, spear, and helmet of the colossal goddess Athene, a supreme example of human craftsmanship proclaiming the shape of the deity, while in the foreground, ready to listen, stood the heirs of Socrates, Plato, and Aristotle, of Zeno and Euripides.

The "prosecutor" stepped forward to the Stone of Pride, and with a grave courtesy that hid his amusement, addressed Paul: "May we know what this new teaching is which you present? For you bring some strange things to our ears; we wish to know therefore what these things mean."

A hint of menace hid in his words; Socrates had been sentenced to death for teaching strange doctrines, and although Paul was in no danger of hemlock, he might be expelled.

Paul was in his element. He was only too ready to talk about Jesus before so august an assembly. Sometimes when addressing country folk and city slaves, he may have had to humble his intellect, but here he could call up his knowledge of Greek thought and lead it higher. He was not in the least abashed. As a lawyer, he knew the resurrection to be a thoroughly attested fact of recent history, for which only the seas between Athens and Palestine prevented him calling witnesses. As a converted sinner, he knew the existence of the risen Christ to be self-evident. The Christian faith was not only more reasonable than any held by these philosophers, it was also truth. With utmost confidence he could adapt himself to his special audience, approach them by their reason, tell them of the resurrection, and lead them on from there.

He began tactfully and appropriately, using a rare word (translated "objects of worship") that would have awakened immediate echoes of the passage in the *Eumenides* of Aeschylus where Athene tells how the Court of Areopagus came to be instituted. Later he echoed Plato's reference, in the Tenth Book of the *Republic*, to the great Architect of the Universe who "makes everything which grows out of the ground and animates all living things." He also introduced direct quotations from the Cretan poet Epimenides and Aratus the Cilician, and a touch of Euripides. But the very way he used his Greek allusions showed that he rated their thought a feeble, pale reflection of the God of the Jews and in Jesus Christ. Paul was polite but most unsycophantic.

"Gentlemen of Athens," he began, "I see that in every way you are very religious, for as I passed along and looked at your objects of worship, I also found an altar with the inscription: 'To the Unknown God.' That which you worship without knowing—this I proclaim to you!

"The God who made the world and all that is in it, being Lord of heaven and earth, does not live in man-made shrines"—and Paul must have waved a hand toward the Acropolis while his mind flashed back to Stephen's use of that very phrase in his trial long ago—"nor is He served by man's hands as if He needed anything, for He Himself gives life and breath and all else. And He made from one stock every race of man to inhabit the surface of the earth, having determined and planned in advance the limits of their epochs and their boundaries. They were to seek God, if they might grope after Him and might find Him, though indeed He is not far from each of us, for in Him we 'live and move and have our being.' As some of your own poets have said, 'We are also His offspring.'

"As God's offspring, we ought not think that the divine is like an image in gold or silver or stone, a work of man's art and imagination"—and again his hand must have pointed toward the venerated colossus of Athene—"God overlooked these times of ignorance. But now He commands all men, everywhere, to repent"—("*all* men"? Several Areopagites would curl their lips at the idea of a philosopher, dedicated to the pursuit of truth, needing repentance. But Paul was warming to his theme)—"because He has fixed a day on which He will judge the whole inhabited world [the *oikoumene* that the Greeks talked so much about] in strict justice by a Man whom He has appointed.

"He has attested this to all by raising Him from the dead—"

A guffaw broke the decorum of the assembly. A hubbub of voices and laughter interrupted Paul. They had heard enough. If he really thought that a man could come to life again after he dies and the earth drinks up his blood, such folly proved him unworthy to be accredited a teacher among the wise of Athens. They said, "We will hear you on this subject some other time."

Paul knew that it was a dismissal. He withdrew, descending the rock with his back to the Acropolis. One Areopagite, Dionysius, followed him, determined to take literally the council's polite words of prevarication and to hear more; for instead of an irrevocable fate fixed by a hostile universe, instead of the horror of the shade after death, which men feared though none should show it, Paul had said that eternity depended on a Person who had conquered death.

Dionysius became a believer. There was also an aristocratic woman named Damaris, who may have been a God-fearer who heard Paul at the synagogue, and a few more. But none of them seemed to have been baptized, perhaps because of their civic positions or because their husbands kept them secret disciples. The first to be baptized in Achaia would be a household of Corinth.

Paul had to leave quickly. The council had refused him license to teach, yet he declined to be muzzled. He would move onward, relying on Silas and Timothy to catch up with him.

Athens had rejected him. He could not know that his speech would go down to posterity beside the Funeral Oration of Pericles and the Philippics of Demosthenes as one of the great speeches of Athens. He could not know that whole books would be written about it or that in a few hundred years the Parthenon would become a Christian church; and that nineteen centuries on, when Greece became once more a sovereign state, the national flag that flies beside the ruins of the Parthenon would be lowered to half-mast each Good Friday and raised on Easter Day in honor of Christ's resurrection.

PART THREE

LEAST OF THE APOSTLES

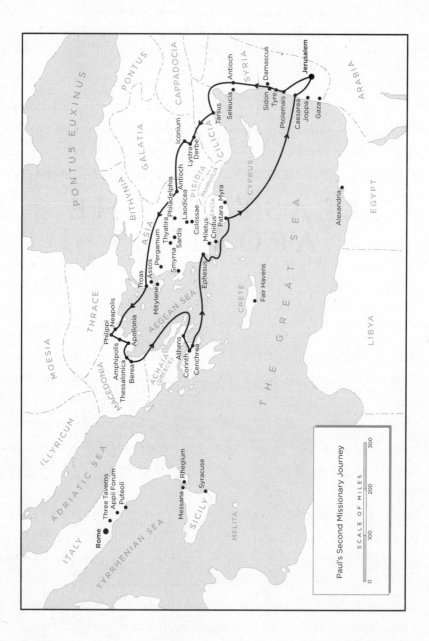

Paul's Second Missionary Journey

SCALE OF MILES

0   100   200   300

TWENTY

CITY OF UNBRIDLED LOVE

Across the Isthmus of Corinth, Paul passed slaves who portaged goods, and whole teams heaving and sweating under the overseer's lash to drag ships on rollers from one sea to the other. He walked through the port of Lechaion and up the slight incline to enter the walls of Corinth, the capital of Achaia.

"When I came to you," he told the Corinthians afterward, "I declared the attested truth of God without display of fine words or wisdom. I resolved that while I was with you I would think of nothing but Jesus Christ—Christ nailed to the cross. I came before you weak, as I was then, nervous and shaking with fear."

Encouragements came at once. While inquiring for a certain Christian tentmaker and his wife lately come from Rome, whom he had heard about from a mutual acquaintance or by letter, he met comments that convinced him that travelers from Thessalonica had already talked unashamedly about Christ. Then he discovered the tentmakers, probably in a typical open-fronted shop in a street near the Lechaion road, and was received with open arms and soon invited to make his home in their cramped quarters upstairs and ply his craft.

He had found two of the best friends he ever made. Aquila was a Jew born in Pontus province on the southern shore of the Euxine, or Black, Sea. Probably he was younger than Paul and became an early convert when the Christian faith reached Rome by means that have never been precisely determined. His wife's name, Prisca, suggests with other clues that she was a Latin and of a higher class than her husband. She might be known as the Lady Prisca, but her unaffected simplicity and hospitable ways made it more usual to call her by the familiar "Priscilla." When Claudius expelled Jews from Rome because of "Chrestus," Aquila and Priscilla emigrated to Corinth, although until Paul came they had not seen themselves as missionaries.

The three of them went to the synagogue the next Sabbath, and Paul exercised his right as a rabbi.

Paul disclaimed pretensions to oratory: "The word I spoke," he reminded Corinthians a few years later, "the Gospel I proclaimed did not sway you with subtle arguments; it carried conviction by spiritual power, so that your faith might be built not upon human wisdom but upon the power of God." There were Corinthians who rated him a contemptible speaker. Yet his preaching had a fine ring of assurance, every allusion crystal clear to his synagogue audience but the application startlingly fresh:

"Of legal righteousness Moses writes"—and Paul drew a text from Leviticus—"'The man who does this shall gain life by it.' But the righteousness that comes by faith says"—and he began his main exposition, a passage from Deuteronomy—"'Do not say to yourself, "Who can go up to heaven?" (that is to bring Christ down), or "Who can go down to the abyss?" (to bring Christ up from the dead). But what does it say? *The word is near you: it is upon your lips and in your heart.'*

"This means the word of faith which we proclaim! If on your lips is the confession, 'Jesus is Lord,' and in your heart the faith that God raised Him from the dead, then you will find salvation. For the faith that leads to righteousness is in the heart, and the confession that leads to salvation is upon the lips. Scripture says,"—and now Paul turned to Isaiah—"'Everyone who has faith in Him will be saved from shame.' *Everyone!* There is no distinction between Jew and Greek, because the same Lord is Lord of all, and is rich enough for the needs of all who invoke Him. For everyone, as it says again"—and now Paul was on the prophet Joel—"'*Everyone* who invokes the name of the Lord will be saved.' How could they invoke one in whom they had no faith? And how could they have faith in One they had never heard of? And how could they hear without someone to spread the Good News? And how could anyone spread the Good News without a commission to do so? And that is what Scripture affirms: 'How welcome are the feet of the messengers of Good News!'"[18]

Or were they? As Paul looked up southward from the agora, the skyline was dominated by a mountain 1,900 feet high and precipitous on all sides except the west: the volcano-shaped Acrocorinth, visible on a clear day from Athens; and above the rim of the mountain's saucer-like summit peeped the great Temple of Aphrodite. The cult was dedicated to the glorification of sex. One thousand girls were kept consecrated to the goddess, and their processions, rituals, and individual solicitude so aroused male devotees and set the tone of the city that the ancient world described habitual fornicators as "living like Corinthians," a phrase coined by the early Greek comedians and carried across to the new Corinth. In the city itself, the archaic Temple of Apollo had been restored by the Romans and now stood behind Paul as he gazed at Acrocorinth. This also glorified sex, as well as music, song, and poetry, for Apollo was the ideal of male beauty. The temple's inner recesses held nude statues and friezes of Apollo in various poses of virility, which fired his male worshippers to physical displays of devotion with the god's beautiful boys.

Corinth was the biggest city Paul had yet encountered, a brash new commercial metropolis founded in its current form less than a hundred years earlier after a century in ruins. It squeezed nearly a quarter of a million people into a comparatively small area, a large proportion being slaves engaged in the unending movement of goods. Slaves or free, Corinthians were rootless, cut off from their country background, drawn from races and districts all over the empire and, except for the Jewish community, without natural groupings; a curiously close parallel to the population of a twenty-first-century "inner city," the overcrowded materialistic heart of any great urban concentration, with the superficial difference that Corinthians masked their materialism, sexual appetites, and superstitions behind a cloak of religiousness. Paul had seen a Christian church grow and flourish in the essentially rural areas of southern Galatia and in the moderately sized cities he had found in Macedonia. Now, if the love of Christ Jesus could take root in Corinth—the most populated, wealthy, commercial-minded, and sex-obsessed city of western Europe—it surely must prove powerful anywhere.

He made converts—Stephanas, whom he baptized with all his household, and Gaius, a wealthy God-fearer with a large home; since "Gaius" is the first name, this was most likely one Titius Justus, whose house was next door to the synagogue. But progress was unsensational and the impact on pagan Corinth negligible, giving no indication of what would come. Paul was inhibited by the lack of his team and by the need to earn a living. He was impatient for the coming of Silas and Timothy.

When they arrived, his cup ran over. Closeted together for long hours above the shop, questioning Timothy closely, he learned to his relief that despite persecution the Thessalonian believers had not only endured with undiminished faith and love but also were growing in depth and number. To Paul, who had fussed at Berea and Athens, imagining calamities and failures, the news taught a lesson: that his Lord was perfectly able to keep those who put their faith in Him: "He who calls you is to be *trusted*."

He determined to express his love and gratitude immediately. "Timothy has just arrived from Thessalonica, bringing good news of your faith and love...." It was probably Timothy's pen that scratched away as Paul dictated, perhaps sitting in the winter sunshine in Gaius's garden or out on the slopes of Acrocorinth looking across the Gulf of Mount Parnassus. "He tells us that you always think kindly of us, and are as anxious to see us as we are to see you. And so in all our difficulties and hardships your faith reassures us about you. It is the breath of life to us that you stand firm in the Lord. What thanks can we return to God for you? What thanks for all the joy you have brought us, making us rejoice before our God while we pray most earnestly night and day to be allowed to see you again and to mend your faith where it falls short? May our God and Father Himself, and our Lord Jesus, bring us direct to you! And may the Lord make your love mount and overflow toward one another and toward all, as our love does toward you. May He make your heart firm, so that you stand before our God and Father holy and faultless when our Lord Jesus comes with all those who are His own."

The style of this First Letter to the Thessalonians reads quite differently from the exclamations Paul had thrown at the Galatians. Neither was it elaborately composed in the manner of contemporary men of letters who used the epistolary form to readers everywhere. Paul was writing for particular people and cared nothing if the style was "Pauline" or not. But Timothy did have problems to report from Thessalonica. Christians had died already (possibly under persecution) and survivors were worried whether they would all meet again; certain church members were being idle, sponging off others while saying that to earn a living was unnecessary because of the Lord's imminent return.

Paul therefore applied himself to untangling the misconceptions and elaborations that had grown up around his teaching. At the same time, unconsciously, he gave an insight into his own character when he urged the whole brotherhood, to whom the letter was to be read aloud, how they ought to live. Since he loathed deceit, he would not outline a manner of life if he did not aspire to it himself. Thus by slight paraphrase, a portrait of Paul in the closing months of AD 50 may be drawn from the extended summing up in the First Letter to the Thessalonians.

Paul endeavored to live at peace with his fellow believers—not that there were many yet in Corinth. He rebuked the idle and careless, encouraged the fainthearted, supported the weak, and was very patient with them all. He took care not to pay back wrong for wrong but sought to help his fellows whether they were Christians or unbelievers. He was always rejoicing, he prayed constantly, and he thanked God in every circumstance whether harsh or favorable, knowing that God as revealed in Christ particularly desired this. When some expounded texts or told him eagerly what they believed God had revealed to them individually, he did not crush them but tested their views, by Scripture and by the oral tradition of what Jesus had taught, and accepted gratefully every new insight that passed this test. He kept himself from every action or word he knew was wrong.

His constant prayer, with full confidence, was that the God of peace would purify him and, in all the defilements of a pagan city, keep him sound in spirit, soul, and body, "without fault when our Lord Jesus Christ comes."

Timothy had brought another money gift from the Philippians. Paul could now temporarily abandon the loom and leather to devote himself to preaching, aided by Silas and Timothy. He concentrated on the synagogue, longing to see a nobility of spirit like the Bereans', which would create a firm base for advance among pagans.

But Jews who refused to acknowledge Jesus as Messiah reacted like those in Pisidian Antioch: "They opposed and resorted to abuse"—and the word Luke used need not be limited to verbal abuse. Paul may have suffered once again a synagogue whipping, the "forty stripes save one," in the presence of Crispus, who was the ruler of the synagogue, and all the congregation. If so, there was a terrible irony in Paul's words when with bloodied back he picked up his torn clothes, drew himself painfully to full height, shook the clothes free of the synagogue's dust in a symbolic action that all recognized, and alluded to those words of Ezekiel by which a messenger is discharged of responsibility for the death of those who refuse his warnings. "*Your blood* be upon your heads!" cried Paul. "I am innocent. From now on I will go to the Gentiles."

His heart was as sore as his back. He longed that Jews and non-Jews should be one in Christ, a "new Israel"; Paul had nothing of the anti-Semite in him. He still hoped to win his "brothers according to the flesh," and it was for this reason, as well as the convenience and size of the house, and not because he wished to provoke and snub the Jews, that he accepted the offer of Titius Justus to make the house next door to the synagogue the place for preaching about Christ. And the first convert to be baptized, with his household, after Paul's withdrawal was none other than Crispus, the ruler of the synagogue. A man named Sosthenes took his place.

When the news spread in the city that Paul had been forced out of the synagogue, pagan Corinthians began at last to flock into the church, until early on any Sunday morning the lawn and mosaics round the fountain in the house of Gaius Titius Justus were covered by men and women, sitting separately, all eyes on Paul as he preached and on Silas or Timothy as they baptized afterward.

In Paul's mind, however, a seed of worry took root, that the pattern of previous cities was about to be repeated; rejection by Jews, progress among the pagans, fury from Jews, and then, just when the gospel gained a hold, expulsion by mob violence or judicial process. The fear grew in him that he would never find a city where he might lay a spiritual foundation and build unhurriedly. One night as he sat late by himself in the upper room at Aquila's, when the city's noise had ceased except for the occasional bark of a dog or the metallic tramp of guards on their rounds, depression, which was one of the strands of Paul's nature, seemed to gain the upper hand. He would never win another Corinthian to Christ and see the sparkle of new life in a Corinthian's eyes. And he dreaded the physical agony of another stoning or a beating with rods, the desolation of being flung out again with winter now on them, the seas turbulent, and nowhere to take his stiff, aging joints but the mountain trails of the Peloponnesus.

Suppose his faith was futile and Christ had never risen from the dead. Suppose the Presence was a figment of his imagination, and there was nothing, no one. He wanted to give up, stop preaching, take himself away to live quietly at peace, back to the Taurus, to Arabia, anywhere.

Suddenly he saw Him. As on the Damascus Road, as in the temple, he saw Him, the Lord Jesus, and the unmistakable voice, quiet, reassuring, "Do not be afraid, but speak and do not be silent. For I am with you. And no one is going to attack you in such a way as to hurt you. For I have many people in this city."

TWENTY ONE

THE HOUSE OF GAIUS

Before dawn on the first day of any week during AD 51, several scores of men and women entered the house of Gaius next door to the synagogue. Because Sunday was an ordinary weekday for Jews and all days alike to pagans, the Christians met at an hour that even slaves could keep.

As Paul looked around in the growing daylight while they sang hymns to Christ and the Father, he could reflect that "few of you whom God has called are men of wisdom, by any human standard ... few of you are powerful or nobly born." One of the few was Crispus, former ruler of the synagogue, and another the ex-pagan Erastus, the elected city treasurer and probably the most substantial of the converts. Instead of the wise and powerful, God had chosen the simple and the weak, the base-born, the despised, to shame the world in its pretensions, "so that no human being might boast in the presence of God." Many slaves were members of the church. Paul knew what some had been through: torn from home in forest, steppe, or mountain beyond the frontiers, hustled in gangs on a rigorous journey to one of the great slave centers; if young and healthy, put to hard labor in quarry or fields until their spirits broke, then shipped to Corinth, exposed naked for sale to good masters or bad. Their parents, wives, children were lost forever, unless chance threw them together again.

God had chosen unlikely raw materials. Paul could mentally list the previous characters of some of his friends: fornicators, debauchees, and whores; he mentioned homosexuals of both sorts, boys and the sodomites who used them; there were thieves, misers, swindlers, drunkards, extortioners, foul-mouthed slanderers, and of course idolaters. "But you have washed yourselves!" he would cry. "You have been consecrated, you have been justified through the name of the Lord Jesus Christ and by the Spirit of our God." The past was as if it had never been.

The stories converts must have told him privately would not only tear at his heartstrings but also sicken him. The Victorian natural scientist Henry Drummond said during D. L. Moody's evangelistic campaigns, "Such tales of woe I've heard in Moody's inquiry room, that I've felt I must go and change my very clothes after the contact." Paul must sometimes have stolen away to the remoter slopes of Acrocorinth where the scent of meadowsweet replaced the stench of garbage and offal, and the sight of the seas and distant mountains could refresh him while he prayed.

Corinth left him under no illusions about paganism. It was here, on another visit, that Paul wrote in the Letter to the Romans the diagnosis that precedes his unfolding of "God's way of righting wrong, a way that starts from faith and ends in faith." "All their thinking," he wrote in words unconsciously borne out by the evidence of contemporary pagan writers, "has ended in futility, and their misguided minds are plunged in darkness. They boast of their wisdom, but they have made fools of themselves, exchanging the splendor of immortal God for an image shaped like mortal man, even for images like birds, beasts, and creeping things.... In consequence God has given them up to shameful passions. Their women have exchanged natural intercourse for unnatural, and their men in turn, giving up natural relations with women, burn with lust for one another; males behaving indecently with males, and are paid in their own persons the fitting wages of such perversion....

"They are filled with every kind of injustice, mischief, rapacity, and malice; they are one mass of envy, murder, rivalry, treachery, and malevolence; whisperers and scandalmongers, hateful to God, insolent, arrogant, and boastful; they invent new kinds of mischief, they show no loyalty to parents, no conscience, no fidelity to their plighted word; they are without natural affection and without pity. They know well enough the just decree of God, that those who behave like this deserve to die, and yet they do it; not only so, they actually applaud such practices."

To such people Paul preached the gospel in Corinth. "First and foremost," he wrote, "I handed on to you the facts which had been imparted to me: that Christ died for our sins, in accordance with the Scriptures; that He was buried; that He was raised to life on the third day; and that He appeared to Cephas, and afterward to the Twelve. Then He appeared to over five hundred of our brothers at once, most of whom are still alive, though some have died. Then He appeared to James, and afterward to all the apostles. In the end He appeared even to me." Paul said his own spiritual birth was extraordinary—the strange word he used could be translated "an abortion" or "abnormal"—"for I had persecuted the church and am therefore inferior to all other apostles; indeed not fit to be called an apostle." He emphasized his own meeting with Jesus on the Damascus Road; his detractors, indeed, said he lacked a fitting humility. He ignored them: Christ knew his weaknesses too well for the criticisms of others to matter, though they got a little under his skin. He went on drumming home the message. "Thus we preached and thus you believed."

And when they believed, they leaped out of their old existence as completely as Paul had leaped out of his. He analyzed for them what happened: "When anyone is united to Christ, he is a new creature: his old life is over; a new life has already begun." As soon as a man had this "new life," Paul expected him to talk about it, so that the gospel spread with astonishing speed. At their assemblies, encouraged by Paul but with a strict eye to decorum, local Christians would expound and testify; again and again an unbeliever present would hear something that searched his conscience and brought conviction, and the secrets of his heart were laid bare, until in repentance and faith he cried, "God is certainly among you!" Day by day too in the marketplace and at the graceful Fountain of Peirene where Corinthians gossiped, in the gymnasia, perhaps even in the public baths, Paul led them in the work of an evangelist. Constantly he would see the miracle of new birth, because "my speech and my message were not in plausible words of wisdom, but in demonstration of the Spirit and power, that your faith might not rest in the wisdom of men but in the power of God."

But though Corinthians were quick to believe and to evangelize, they were slow to mature. Paul had much that he wanted to teach them and grieved that instead of strong meat that could form spiritual muscle and bone, he must feed them as it were on baby's milk, going over and over the simplicities of faith. Yet, if more slowly than he wished, they were undoubtedly displaying new characteristics and discernments, which Paul said were gifts of the Spirit of the Father and the Son, who was present among them, active if invisible, handing out different abilities to different people for the building up of His church.

In particular, many of the Corinthian Christians seemed to have been entering on a novel and satisfying yet perilous experience: "speaking in tongues." The meaning of "tongues" or *glossolalia* has been much debated, especially since its widespread revival in the early twentieth century: The Pentecostals, growing faster than any other denomination in many parts of the world, owe their origin and much of their warmth and fervor to their use of "tongues," and similar spiritual discoveries have been made here and there in the major historic churches. Yet "tongues" remain the most puzzling of the spiritual gifts described by Paul, whether they are "tongues of men or of angels," whether a suddenly acquired fluency in languages previously unknown or prayer and praise in ecstatic utterance unrelated to a human tongue.

Paul welcomed the gift. But when the Corinthians abused it after he left, he had to stress the risks that are inherent wherever tongues are practiced. He warned that the gift of tongues is easily counterfeited and easily leads to excess. Those who do not possess it must never condemn as fanatics those who do, who in their turn must not despise as less spiritual the far larger number of Christians without the gift. The grave danger of a church breaking up into factions must be resisted. Speaking in tongues should always be accompanied by the parallel gift of interpretation, for the primary function of every spiritual gift was not to comfort its recipient but to build up, encourage, and stimulate the whole church. "I thank God I speak in tongues more than you all," said Paul. "Nevertheless, in church I would rather speak five words with my mind, in order to instruct others, than ten thousand words in a tongue."

The church was already an influence in Corinth—neighbors could not fail to notice its new morality, even if they were blind to its source.

The morality taught by Paul and demonstrated by his converts was in stark contrast to the old, permissive morality of the ancient world. It was unconventional: It showed a love of man irrespective of his race, showed forgiveness instead of resentment for wrong, joy instead of grim endurance of adversity or oppression. A slave no longer followed the proverbial maxims that commended the love of other slaves but hatred for masters; the pursuit of robbery and sexual lust; the avoidance of telling the truth. Instead he sought by his behavior and prayers to win his master.

As at Thessalonica, there was a new conception of love. At Corinth it contrasted not only with the promiscuousness encouraged by the Aphrodite cult but also with the homosexuality of Apollo. By sheer moral force, the Christians were introducing a completely different concept of love.

There were failures too, for the pressures on the young church were enormous. The right attitude toward sex was inevitably a burning question to Corinthian Christians. Paul was so sure that misuse of sex damaged human personality, flouted divine law, and invited inevitable misery, that he could not let his converts adapt their ethics to the situation in which they were placed. Nor would he clamp them in the legal straitjacket, which was the Jewish answer; they must learn to live in Christ's freedom, by His strength.

Christians were surrounded by problems. They were few, and their lifestyle absurd beside the power represented by pagan processions up wide steps and under huge columns of temples that looked as if they would flourish for a thousand years. In the meat market it was difficult to find joints other than from animals sacrificed to idols; purchase of this meat implied public recognition of the idol's divinity. Family or craft dinner parties were often held in temples, with the idol as host. In the theater a play was in essence a heathen ceremony, the stories generally were of gods and goddesses, and the performances bawdy; live sex on stage was not unknown.

Small wonder that Paul would have to write in due course: "Let anyone who thinks that he stands take heed lest he fall. No temptation has overtaken you that is not common to all people. God is faithful, and He will not let you be tempted beyond your strength, but with the temptation will also provide the way of escape, that you may be able to endure it."

TWENTY-TWO

GALLIO'S DECISION

With churches springing up in other parts of Achaia, Paul was about to leave Corinth on a local tour of encouragement when further excellent news arrived from Thessalonica, so that during the tour he could boast happily (according to his habit of spurring one church by applauding another) that the Thessalonians' faith remained steadfast under all persecutions and troubles. It leaped ahead, and their love for one another found more and more practical outlets.

They had problems and discouragements too, and on his return to Corinth, Paul composed with Silas and Timothy the Second Letter to the Thessalonians. Their sufferings, he told them, were making them worthy subjects of the kingdom of God, and when the Lord Jesus came back in glory, the accounts would be squared; men and women who had utterly refused Him, spurned His Good News, and hurt His people would not escape justice but suffer the eternal ruin of being "cut off from the presence of the Lord and the splendor of His might." In this he followed the teaching of Jesus, who never hesitated to warn those who rejected His love; Paul could not speak softly about a second chance in another life. He was not afraid to preach judgment, even if he would need later to amplify and clarify his thought.

Some of the Thessalonians had swallowed rumors that this "Day of the Lord" had come already and were acting as though absolved from normal behavior. Paul begged them not to be "so easily confused" in their thinking, or for that matter "upset by the claim." He reminded them briefly but vigorously of his oral teaching about the signs which must precede the Day, though part of what he wrote remains the most obscure of all Pauline literature, possibly because he veiled certain topical or political allusions in a code to which his original readers had the key.

He was particularly concerned at the origin of the rumors, especially since one possible source was a "letter purporting to come from us." When Paul signed the letter he was now dictating, he took particular pains against forgery: "The greeting is in my own hand, signed with my name, *Paul*; this authenticates all my letters: this is how I write. The grace of our Lord Jesus Christ be with you all." Thus the Second Letter to the Thessalonians contains the earliest mention of forgery being used as a weapon to hurt Paul by confusing his friends. The forgers may have been the very Pharisees who had disrupted the church in southern Galatia, until routed by the arrival of Paul's letter to the Galatians, and who now took a leaf out of his book. The forged letter was an indication that Jewish opponents were infiltrating the church to destroy it from within; Paul was to cross their trails frequently until they came near to achieving their aim.

Meanwhile, he urged the Thessalonians to "stand firm and hold to the traditions which you were taught by us, either by word of mouth or by letter."

He gave strict instructions that no one should be idle or a scrounger, but work for a living after the example of the apostles. Next he laid down a principle for the rebuke and recovery of recalcitrants, in which he mixed firmness and love equally, giving guidance too frequently forgotten in the centuries to come: "If anyone refuses to obey what we say in this letter, note that man, and have nothing to do with him, that he may be ashamed. Do not look on him as an enemy but warn him as a brother."

And then, almost casually, Paul concluded with a brief tremendous prayer that expressed his belief that the Thessalonian Christians could triumph above the harshest circumstance: "May the Lord of peace Himself give you peace—at all times, in all ways. The Lord be with you all."

In the course of this second letter, Paul made a personal request: "Go on praying for us, that the Word of the Lord may speed on and be gloriously acknowledged, just as with you; and that we may be rescued from wrongheaded and evil men, for not all have faith."

Soon after the letter's arrival in Thessalonica, the prayer was answered at Corinth in a remarkable and decisive way.

During the early summer of AD 51, Sosthenes, who had succeeded Crispus as ruler of the synagogue, became a Christian. What is more, he retained his office, evidently agreeing with Paul that a synagogue was a natural sphere for Christian leadership. At that, the other principal Jews determined to break Christianity in Corinth. An opportunity came with the installation, on July 1, 51, of a new proconsul of Achaia, Lucius Junius Gallio, whose two years' proconsulship has been dated almost exactly by fragments found in 1905 at Delphi. Gallio was the brother of Seneca, the great philosopher who was a high favorite of the emperor Claudius. "No mortal," wrote Seneca, "is so pleasant to anyone as Gallio is to everyone." The Jewish leaders perhaps knew this reputation and hoped Gallio would be pleasant to them. They filed a prosecution against Paul.

When prosecutors, defendant, and their supporters ranged themselves before the raised open-air bema on the south side of the agora, Paul carried with him the promise that had come in the vision at night, that no attack on him should prosper. Yet Gallio's decision would be supremely important, both to Greece, because he was governor of the chief province, and throughout the empire because of his influence at court. As much as any one man, he could either stifle Christianity or, in Paul's phrase, cause it to "speed on and be gloriously acknowledged."

The Jews pursued their prosecution by arguing that Paul propagated a religion unrecognized by the State: "This man is persuading men to worship God contrary to the Law." Paul stepped forward. He was about to open his mouth in defense when Gallio stopped the case and addressed the Jews. Paul's legal mind would have grasped at once the enormous implication of Gallio's statement, for he took the Jewish charge about "the Law" in quite another sense than they had intended.

"If this were a matter of crime or grave misdemeanor," pronounced the proconsul, "there would have been good reason for me to listen to you Jews. But since it is a matter of words and names and your own Law, *I do not wish to be judge of these things*"—a precise legal expression, by which a Roman magistrate exercised his discretion not to interfere where he ruled that no statute had been broken.

Before the Jews could appeal, Gallio gave a brief order that drove them from the judgment seat by the butts of military spears. The moment they were out of the precinct they got their own weapons back. If Gallio ruled that this was a domestic matter, then they would act on his decision. They could not lay hands on Paul because he had withdrawn from their synagogue, but Sosthenes had not. They seized him, stripped him, and gave him the "forty stripes save one" in full sight of Gallio on the judgment seat. "And Gallio cared for none of these things." They were exercising their domestic right to punish those within their jurisdiction, just as he had ruled a few moments before.[19]

Even so, the proconsular decision left Paul and his converts free to preach where they wished, with no danger of sudden assaults and imprisonments. Rome had become their protector.

Farmers and goatherds must often have seen an aging Jew, his black beard flecked with grey, his head well wrapped against the strong light, striding purposefully with a team of young men along the trails that wound between the course scrub. Paul was on his way to some country town where he would receive a welcome from friends who had visited Corinth and heard the gospel. The faith spread possibly even to Sparta and Olympia and across the gulf and up the slopes of Parnassus to Delphi itself. Almost certainly, Paul and the Corinthian church evangelized among athletes and spectators at the biennial Isthmian Games of AD 51, for his First Letter to the Corinthians sounds a distinct note of mutual reminiscence when he employed the metaphor: "You know (*do you not?*) that at the sports all the runners run the race, though only one wins the prize. Like them, run to win! But every athlete goes into strict training. They do it to win a fading wreath; we, a wreath that never fades. For my part I run with a clear goal before me; I am like a boxer who does not beat the air; I bruise my own body and make it know its master, for fear that after preaching to others, I should find myself rejected."

The long stay at Corinth crowned by the proconsular decision was one of the watersheds of Paul's life. Southern Galatia had proved his conviction that Gentiles could be full Christians. Corinth proved that Christianity could take root in a great metropolis and from there spread throughout a province. With the freedom won by the legal decision, it was obvious to Paul that his next objective must be the other great metropolis of the Aegean—Ephesus. After that, to Rome and beyond. But while his mind—and his commission—drew him to Rome, his heart cried, "Jerusalem!" He still yearned to preach in the city of his race; the words of the exiled psalmist echoed in his spirit, "If I forget thee, O Jerusalem, let my right hand forget her cunning. If I do not remember thee, let my tongue cleave to the roof of my mouth; if I prefer not Jerusalem above my chief joy."

He decided, therefore, to take a furlough and attend Passover at Jerusalem before settling at Ephesus. And because he remained a Jew, he determined to celebrate his return to the Holy City by a Nazarite vow—the vow of those specially set apart to the Lord under the old order—and let his hair grow for thirty days. Before sailing it would be cut, placed in a bag, and at the temple he would solemnly cast it on the sacrificial fire.

In March 52, he was ready to leave at the opening of navigation. He had been based at Corinth eighteen months.

For the last time he gathered with the Christians at the house of Gaius. He knew that backsliding and errors would probably emerge after he left; he even may have had a shrewd suspicion of some of the forms these would take. But for the present, all was unity, peace, and love as they met at the atrium beside the fountain under flaming torches. Here they celebrated the Lord's

Supper, conducted according to the tradition that had come to him through the earlier apostles from the Lord Himself: "that the Lord Jesus on the night when He was betrayed took bread, and when He had given thanks, He broke it, and said: 'This is My body, which is given for you. Do this in remembrance of Me.' In the same way also the cup, after supper, saying, 'This cup is the new covenant in My blood. Do this, as often as you drink it, in remembrance of Me.'"

TWENTY-THREE

A SCHOOL AT EPHESUS

When Paul left Corinth, Aquila and Priscilla accompanied him to transfer their tentmaking to Ephesus. This seems to have been a deliberate decision of missionary strategy. While Paul took his furlough, they could prepare for his mission by making friends and beginning a business where he would earn his living.

Together they walked down to Cenchreae, the Corinthian port for the Aegean, near the narrowest part of the isthmus, where in a few years' time the Romans would attempt to build a canal by slave labor. Paul entered the synagogue, since he could not do so in Corinth, to discharge his vow by the ceremonial shaving of his head. After a night in the home of a believer named Phoebe, they took the ship through the islands of the Cyclades, beautiful in a wine-colored sea. Paul could enjoy it. Because Acts has no space for his personal feelings, he has been considered indifferent or loftily superior to scenery. Yet he wrote of the beauty of the stars, how one differs from another in glory; he was aware of the beauty of the human body and he noted how, in great houses he visited, some of the vases and bowls were works of art, others merely useful. He was full of the psalms too and on a voyage like this could echo their praise: "O Lord, how manifold are Thy works! In wisdom hast Thou made them all: the earth is full of Thy riches."

At length they entered the short Gulf of Ephesus, which is now silted up. The modern visitor who stands on the shore with his back to the sea and then walks inland across the fields has much the same view that Paul had when his ship sailed toward the harbor. On his left were the hills that separated Ephesus from the Gulf of Smyrna; on his right, Mount Coressos and part of the six-mile circuit of walls built by Lysimachus three hundred years before, and the watchtower at the seaward end, which would later be called Saint

Paul's Tower. The ship rounded the point. The breakwater, which worsened the silting it was built to cure, was now on his left. As the ship threaded its way up the dredged channel, overcrowded with vessels, the city lay all around. Passengers' eyes were dazzled in the sunlight by the massed houses of calcar stone and the marble public buildings, which filled the narrow plain and climbed steeply the hundred feet of Mount Pion ahead and up the higher Mount Coressos to the right. Paul could see, cut from the hillside of Pion, the theater that would be the scene of one of the great incidents in his story. And on the alluvial plain to the north of Pion, at the foot of a smaller sacred hill, glittered the huge Temple of Artemis, one of the Seven Wonders of the World. It had been burned down by the fanatic Herostratus on the night Alexander the Great was born far away in Macedonia but rebuilt to its former magnificence, a fitting crown for the "first and greatest metropolis of Asia."

Paul settled his friends, an easy task since Jews would always find a welcome from fellow Jews in a strange city. He then left Aquila and Priscilla and carefully did not associate them with his first approach to the synagogue, lest they be compromised should the elders reject him. On the contrary, the elders expressed interest in what Paul had to tell them about Jesus and asked him to stay longer in Ephesus. He declined, but when they came to the harbor to see him off on the pilgrim ship a day or two later, he said, "I will come back to you if it is God's will."

Paul seems to have traveled alone throughout this period of leave. The pilgrim ship took him to Caesarea. He went up to Jerusalem, one pilgrim among many. He kept the Passover and had an affectionate reunion with the Jerusalem church. It was now that he conceived a plan for raising money from all the new churches in Greece and Asia on behalf of the "poor saints in Jerusalem." Such a collection, put aside weekly with prayer, would unite these far-flung churches in a joint enterprise. It would also emphasize the honored position of the city where Jesus had been nailed to the cross, and be of distinct practical help because the Jerusalem church, lacking Gentile members, had less to draw on for charitable purposes yet could not expect money from charities administered by the temple authorities. Paul may have had a further hope. The money he brought them could be used not only for the aged and sick but also to release some of the able-bodied to undertake missionary work in the east, such as he did in the west; at present the Jerusalem church was not particularly missionary-minded.

Paul did not stay long in Jerusalem but went down to Antioch through Galilee, where he met again many who had seen Jesus alive after His resurrection and heard of the death of others. The city of Antioch refreshed him. It was his home. For a man who would not rest when on the mission field, the city where he had taught for a year remained the one place where he could fully relax.

At the end of a short summer, Paul set out early in August 52 for his next term of service. He walked north and took the opportunity of brief but invigorating visits to his old haunts in southern Galatia, through Derbe, Lystra, Iconium, Pisidian Antioch, "strengthening all the disciples" and launching his scheme for the Collection. The Western Text then adds a curious statement that, if not authentic, catches Paul's feelings: "But when Paul wished, according to his own plan, to go to Jerusalem, the Spirit bade him return to Asia." Once again, his heart cried, "Jerusalem!" while his Lord directed him west. Therefore he hurried back to Ephesus, taking the direct "horse road" over the uplands rather than the main trade route by which the slow camel trains wandered down the valleys through the big cities of the interior. Before winter he was settled in Ephesus.

The first news Paul learned from Priscilla and Aquila was of a brilliant Jew from Alexandria named Apollos, whom they had heard in the Ephesus synagogue.

To their delight, he had begun to speak persuasively, intensively, about Jesus of Nazareth, describing accurately the broad facts of His life, death, and resurrection. Apollos, however, talked as if Jesus were a figure of history rather than Someone still at work in the world. The only baptism Apollos knew was that of John the Baptist, who had baptized men in token of their repentance because the kingdom of God was imminent, urging them to behave like penitents. Priscilla and Aquila invited Apollos home and filled in the gaps, until he learned the secret of the personality re-created by the Spirit of the Father and of Jesus. His teaching now became yet more urgent and persuasive, but he did not wish to stay in Ephesus; his destination was Achaia. Priscilla and Aquila realized how valuable such a man would be in Corinth, and together with the little knot of believers who had already gathered round them gave him a warm letter of introduction. They could tell Paul how news had already trickled back from Corinth that Apollos "was a great help to those who through God's grace had become believers. For with his strong arguments he defeated the Jews in public debates, proving from the Scriptures that Jesus is the Messiah."

The aristocratic, motherly Priscilla and her husband certainly had not been idle during Paul's absence, but they had little conception of developing a church. They were primarily tentmakers, people who loved Jesus and shared the gospel with their neighbors, whereas Paul was a full-time worker for Jesus who made tents to pay expenses. The limitations of Priscilla's activities are indicated by a curious discovery that Paul made.

As he walked about the pillared agora at the foot of Mount Pion, or up and down the steep streets, with their sudden views of the sea, Paul was directed by someone who had heard his message to a little group who seemed to believe as he did. He met them, some dozen men, evidently Gentiles, who were believers but rather in the manner of Apollos before he reached Ephesus. Their origin is a mystery, and even in so extensive and populous a city as Ephesus it is odd that Priscilla and Aquila had never come across them. Paul detected at once that their faith, though sincere, was lacking, and the question he put forth revealed what he thought important.

"Did you receive the Holy Spirit when you became believers?" he asked.

"But we have not even heard there is a Holy Spirit."

"What baptism were you baptized with, then?"

"John's baptism," they replied.

"John baptized with a baptism in token of repentance," Paul said, "and told the people to put their trust in One who would be coming after him, that is, in Jesus."

They at once asked to be baptized into the Lord Jesus. Paul took them down to the river Cayster, and not far away from the magnificence of the Temple of Artemis, he held a simple ceremony. After they had come up from the water, they knelt and Paul laid his hands on their heads, praying that each might receive the Holy Spirit. Immediately came an extraordinary release of power. It was like the Day of Pentecost in Jerusalem over again. They spoke in tongues, praising and proclaiming the glories of the name of Jesus, then told everybody they met about the truths that suddenly had become clear to them in the Scriptures they already knew. The whole atmosphere was heady with joy. Many years later the survivors read some words in Paul's letter to Ephesus and other Asian churches that must have recalled that day: "Do not get drunk with wine ... but be filled with the Spirit, addressing one another in psalms and hymns and spiritual songs, singing and making melody to the Lord with all your heart, and for everything giving thanks in the name of our Lord Jesus Christ to God the Father."

The dozen men, with Aquila and Priscilla and their converts, were already the nucleus of a Christian church when Paul went again into the synagogue to take up the elders' invitation. Regularly, for three months of that winter of AD 52–53, Paul (in Luke's words) "spoke with utmost confidence, using both argument and persuasion as he talked of the kingdom of God." The Jews here were more open-minded than those of Thessalonica or Corinth; they disputed but did not refuse to listen. Many pagans entered the synagogue for the first time and believed, and once again Paul saw Christ break down the dividing wall of hostility between Jew and Gentile.

Obdurate Jews, however, began to gain the upper hand. In early spring of 53, they abused Christ's way until constructive teaching in the synagogue became impossible. Paul withdrew, and all disciples—Jew and

Gentile—withdrew with him, leaving many empty seats and a distinct drop in the offerings.

A spacious portico in the city gymnasium was offered to Paul by a schoolmaster with the apposite name of Tyrannus ("Tyrant"), acquired perhaps as a nickname, though presumably he was now a convert and less irascible; or he may have been the descendant of a "tyrant," the honored ruler of a Greek city-state. He needed the portico for his schoolboys at the normal times of teaching, the cool of the day, and, according to the Western Text, Paul had it from eleven o'clock until four, the hours of heat and siesta when all Ephesus shut up shop; even slaves could come to hear him. Then Tyrannus and the boys returned in the remaining hours of light, two or three according to season, while Paul went off to private houses, rich and poor. As Paul would remind the Ephesians, "You know that I kept nothing from you, that was for your good: I delivered the message to you; I taught you, in public and in your homes; with Jews and pagans alike I insisted on repentance before God and trust in our Lord Jesus." Nor was he ashamed of tears; he wept openly when men spurned Christ. Sometimes Paul would accept an invitation only to discover a trap laid by Jews who wanted to discredit him. He was equal to it. "They curse us and we bless. They slander us and we humbly make our appeal."

His chief work continued in the School of Tyrannus. Part of each session he would instruct converts. The letter to the Ephesians does not specifically remind them what he taught, as he reminded Galatians and Thessalonians, but it must contain echoes of the voice they heard as they sat in the shade of the portico during the heat of the summer days of AD 53: "Since you are God's children, you must try to be like Him. Your life must be controlled by love, just as Christ loved us and gave His life for us, as a sweet-smelling offering and sacrifice which pleases God.... Submit yourselves one to another, because of your reverence for Christ. Wives submit yourselves to your husbands, as to the Lord.... Husbands, love your wives in the same way that Christ loved the church and gave His life for it...."

"Slaves, obey your human masters, with fear and trembling, and do it with a sincere heart, as though you were serving Christ. Do this not only when they are watching you, to gain their approval, but with all your hearts do what God wants, as slaves of Christ.... Masters, behave in the same way toward your slaves, and stop using threats. Remember that you and your slaves belong to the same Master in heaven, who treats everyone alike." Again and again he would emphasize, "Pay close attention to *how* you live. You used to be in the darkness, but since you have become the Lord's people you are in the light. So you must live like people who belong to the light."

Often he would take them into deep waters of Christian doctrine to help them mature in the faith, "reaching to the very height of Christ's stature." Those who were literate would scribble down on scraps of papyrus what he told them, especially the facts about the life of the Lord Jesus. As the months passed, a convert would acquire a whole stack of these papyrus notes and sew them together. They could not conveniently be made into continuous rolls like the literary works in what was left of the famous Library of Ephesus (most of which had been removed to Pergamum before Roman times) but had to have separate pages instead. And thus the codex style, which would be universal for books in centuries to come, began in Ephesus and elsewhere simply as the form of Christian notebooks.

Paul held classes like any other teacher except without charge. He also held open meetings when converts brought pagan friends. He began to acquire fame in the city. With converts, especially those who were truly seeking maturity, a very special relationship grew. The Ephesians knew him as a lovable man who brought out the best in those who followed him. Nor did they resent his constant call, "Imitate the way I live"; for he added, "as I imitate Christ."

Paul at this time was cheerful, the old tensions eased. The work was happy, and Ephesus gave no hint of terrors to come.

TWENTY-FOUR

THE NAME

Philemon was a landowner and slaveholder of Colossae, a small city far up at the base of a sheer mountain on the south of the Lycus River, near where it flows into a broader valley to join the Meander. He came down to Ephesus to superintend the sale of his wool—for Colossae was noted for its glossy dark fleeces—and to worship Artemis at her temple. The temple at Ephesus was the largest building in the western world. The 117 Ionic columns, tall and slender, rose 60 feet and each weighed 15 tons; the column bases of the west portico had human figures sculptured life-size; and gold glittered inside and out. Behind the high altar stood the great Mother Goddess, identified by the Greeks with Artemis, by the Romans with Diana, a black meteorite roughly carved in the human form but with feet and legs fused together. Breasts by the score covered the torso as befitted the goddess of fertility, though the cult had not developed the sexual extravagances associated with Corinth's Aphrodite.

Cities throughout the province of Asia had contributed to the building of the temple and were represented in the carefully graded hierarchy of virgins and priests. Pagans farther afield regarded it as the center of their worship. Thus religion joined with trade to bring a steady stream of visitors down the valleys of the Cayster and Meander from the interior or along the coast from the north and south. They traded, they worshipped, and returned with small silver or terra-cotta replicas of the image of Artemis to watch over their homes. Philemon, however, went home with a very different loyalty. He came across Paul and was converted. "You owe your very life to me," Paul would remind him long afterward when begging a favor for another convert.

Landowner and missionary became warmly attached, and Paul sent with Philemon a mature, if recent Christian named Epaphras, a native of Colossae but a member of the Ephesian church.

Back at Colossae, Philemon let his light glow brightly. His wife, Apphia, and their son, Archippus, probably still a youth, were converted, together with some of their slaves. Neighbors soon joined the church, which met in their house. As Paul would write to them, "When the true message, the Good News, first came to you, you heard of the hope it offers. So your faith and love are based on what you hope for, which is kept safe for you in heaven. The Gospel is bringing blessings and spreading through the whole world, just as it has among you ever since the day you first heard of the grace of God and came to know it as it really is."

Epaphras did not confine his witness to Colossae. He evidently traveled a time with Paul, who, when writing from prison in Rome, called Epaphras "my fellow prisoner in Christ Jesus." Epaphras probably spread the gospel to cities near Colossae. A few miles northwest, on higher ground overlooking the broader valley, stood the twin cities of Laodicea and Hierapolis, the textile centers close to the petrified cliff of calcified stone that stands out like a white gash, visible for miles. Here churches sprang up, each with its own characteristics. The three were close, with much coming and going. In morning light, Colossians could look up at Laodicea and Hierapolis clear in the sunshine and perhaps pray for the Christians there. In the evenings, with the sun in the west, the twin cities in their turn could see across to Colossae below, and they too would pray.

The process at Colossae and the twin cities was being repeated throughout the province. By visitors returning from Ephesus, or by teams of converts going out at Paul's instigation, the gospel spread to Smyrna, to the royal city of Pergamum perched on its high rock, and to Thyatira, the birthplace of Philippian Lydia. From each new center it reached out into the surrounding countryside. Luke summed it up well when he said that in the course of two years "all the people who lived in the province of Asia, both Jews and Gentiles, heard the word of the Lord."

Paul longed to go on circuit to visit them everywhere, but too much was happening in Ephesus.

If Corinth was sex-obsessed, Ephesus, as Shakespeare said, was full of "dark-working sorcerers that change the mind." Magicians treasured scrolls of curses and spells and knew the grisly formulas to make them potent. ("It is a shame even to speak of the things that they do in secret," Paul told his converts.) They sold abracadabras written on strips of papyrus for wear next to the skin to cure aches and pains. ("Let no one deceive *you* with empty words," urged Paul.) It was famous for the study of the occult by those who boasted that they were in league with cosmic "principalities and powers," the superhuman forces of darkness.

Where evil went naked and arrogant, "God did extraordinary miracles by the hand of Paul." In Paul's estimation, workers of miracles and those with gifts of healing were normal in every Spirit-filled church, though less important than apostles, prophets, and teachers. Miracles are not recorded as usual in his own experience. Except for the healing of the lame man at Lystra and possibly (not certainly) the youth who at a later time fell out of the window at Troas, miracles are associated with Paul only at Paphos and Iconium where opposition was blatant, and at Ephesus. They can be no more explained than the miracles of Christ; they stand with His. The form of them at Ephesus, however, was precisely appropriate.

During early mornings, Paul was at his tentmaking and leatherwork in the close atmosphere of a small room at Aquila's house, a sweatband round his head and a cotton apron round his middle. Someone evidently begged him to come and lay hands on a sick or demon-possessed person. He could not go. But he knew that Christ was not limited to the hands of an apostle. If in Galilee He could heal without physical contact when faith rose strong enough, in Ephesus God could do "so much more than we can ever ask for, or even think of, by means of the power working in us"; for that power, as Paul would tell, "is the same as the mighty strength which He used when He raised Christ from death" and put Him above all principalities and powers. Christ was stronger than "any conceivable command, authority, power, or control," with a name "far beyond any name that could ever be used in this world or the world to come."

All this Paul told them. But these ex-pagans who had once worn abracadabras next to the skin needed a focus for weak faith. Paul tore off his sweatband and they took it and laid it on the patient, praying over him in the name of Jesus. He was healed. Many others begged similar aid, and Paul would send a convert, or Timothy, who had now joined him, with a sweatband or an apron he had used. Not that it was mechanical. Jesus in Galilee, when a desperate woman touched the hem of His garment in the middle of a crowd, knew instantly that strength had been drawn from Him to stop her hemorrhage; so Paul paid heavily in spiritual energy for these Ephesus healings as he gave his whole self in prayer. A comment in another letter and another context suggests he had an exceptional gift for entering into the very presence and need of those, however distant, for whom he prayed: "As you meet together, and I meet with you in my spirit, by the power of our Lord Jesus present with us...." It was the present Lord Jesus rather than the absent Paul of whom the patient and his friends would be aware. Each miracle was a meeting with the One who could heal the whole man.

The news that men and women were really healed and evil spirits were being driven out spread like wildfire. Gossip swept the harbor and shops that Paul's sweat rags had a potency far beyond any abracadabra papyrus, that the name of Jesus was the best name of all. A strolling Jewish exorcist named Sceva, who claimed to be a high priest and operated a partnership of nonsense with his seven sons, decided to add "the Lord Jesus" to his catalog of spells. The sons went around pronouncing it over clients. Nothing happened for a while. Then they entered the home of a demon-possessed man, stood around, and solemnly said in chorus: "I command you by Jesus whom Paul preaches—"

Before they could say, "Come out of this man," the patient interrupted. With beady eye and the strange voice of a body gripped by devilish forces, he said, "Jesus I know. Paul I am acquainted with. But *who are you?*" With that, he jumped on them and beat up the lot, tore their clothes off them and threw them out of his house "naked and wounded."

The incident shook Ephesus. "All the Jews and Gentiles were filled with fear and the name of the Lord Jesus was given greater honor." What is more, it had a decisive effect on the young Christian church. Many believers publicly confessed that they had dabbled in magic and not broken clean. They said they wanted to put an end to the habits of darkness. "And a number of those who practiced magical arts brought their books together and burned them in the sight of all." As rolls of spells and rare cabalistic writings went up in smoke, including some for which magicians would have given high prices; public opinion reckoned that professional secrets worth the very considerable sum of fifty thousand silver drachmae were destroyed.

The gospel's swift advance provoked inevitable counterattack. How it came is uncertain. Paul's story enters a brief though vital period when facts are obscure. Luke turns very discreet. If he wrote Acts during the reign of Nero (AD 54–68) and especially if partly to aid Paul's defense in Rome, he needed to avoid angering Nero unnecessarily by any reference, however indirect, to a certain political event in Ephesus that impinged on Paul's affairs though did not affect his case. Paul had no such inhibition, but his epistles and a speech he made about Ephesus are equally tantalizing because his readers and hearers already knew what he had been through, and he was not writing autobiographically.

What happened must be pieced together from clues scattered around the New Testament and in secular history. Much depends on whether Paul wrote Philippians from Ephesus, not Rome, a theory which has attracted important scholars but will remain controversial to the end of time.[20]

A biographer has to decide between slowing to a halt in a bog of conflicting possibilities or striding boldly across by a causeway of conjecture. I choose the second course and, without stepping aside to discuss all the alternatives, tell the story as I see it. Paul's next eighteen months unfolded somewhat as follows, though the tone of assurance in my narrative must not disguise that some of its conclusions are tentative and disputable.

The first counterattack came from unbelieving Jews. Knowing Gallio's decision in Corinth, they could not arraign Paul before the Romans for propagating an unlawful cult, nor apply domestic law since he had removed himself from Jewish jurisdiction. They thought up a charge, however, that could be fatal if proved.

By several decrees of Augustus and others, the Jews had secured imperial protection for money raised to support the temple in Jerusalem. Any tamperer, whether Roman official or private person, incurred the same severe penalties as for sacrilege against pagan temples. All Jews of the dispersion were expected to pay the voluntary temple tax, and Ephesus, as contemporary evidence shows, was the forwarding center for collections from synagogues throughout the rich province of Asia. In AD 53 the treasurers at Ephesus noticed a decided drop and were not slow to uncover the cause: Many Jews in Colossae, Smyrna, Pergamum, and other cities were transferring their contributions to swell Paul's fund for the "poor saints in Jerusalem." Paul had not told converts to stop supporting the temple, and most lacked his conviction that Jewish Christians should not repudiate their heritage; but those whom local synagogues had forced out because they followed Jesus Christ ceased paying the temple tax.

The decline in funds showed how rapidly the Christian Way had spread among Asian Jews. It also offered Paul's opponents a fresh line of attack. They lodged a formal accusation of temple robbery before the proconsul of Asia, Marcus Junius Silanus, alleging that Paul had misappropriated money that lawfully should go to the temple of Jerusalem. Silanus, a member of the imperial family and thus a cousin of the reigning emperor Claudius and of Nero, was an indolent man but upright; he could not ignore so serious a charge yet would neither hurry to hear the case nor decide it except on evidence. He ordered Paul's arrest in the autumn of 53.

The slow process of taking evidence throughout Asia gave the prospect of a long imprisonment on remand. Being a Roman citizen, Paul was confined in reasonable comfort in a room of the Praetorian Guard at the proconsular palace. When eventually the case should come to trial, Paul could expect a horrible death if found guilty of such a felony. Unless he appealed to Caesar, he would be thrown into the underground dungeons until the next gladiatorial games at Ephesus, and then, as the last item on the program, he and other criminals, naked and with no weapons but their hands, would be driven with whips into the arena. At the opposite end, wild beasts, starved for two days to ensure that they should be both ravenous and furious, would be released from their cages, and the sadistic entertainment would begin.

Meanwhile, Paul's conditions were not oppressive. Timothy and other friends, including Priscilla and Aquila, were able to visit him frequently. He was allowed to go about the city attached by a light chain to a soldier and to continue teaching in the School of Tyrannus for short periods. The pace of life slowed, and he entered a phase when he was more than ever at peace. He had no sense of frustration and could say at last that he had learned in whatsoever state he was to be content. He had more leisure to pray. Long hours passed as his spirit joined friends far away—in Galatia, Thessalonica, in Corinth from which already ugly rumors trickled in; and to the Philippians, who by their prayers had shared his brief but violent imprisonment at Philippi.

Paul prayed audibly. When he turned to his scrolls of Scripture, he read audibly as well, for the ancients had not discovered the modern knack of reading with the eyes alone. But his prayers were not incantations; he talked quietly, reverently, to Someone present if invisible. Thus each soldier on duty, roster by roster, had an unexpected demonstration of the roots of Paul's personality. They were captivated, too, by his courtesy toward them, his patience and laughter and lack of resentment, his interest in their homes and backgrounds. They heard his conversation with friends, and they noted curiously that when friends left he seemed conscious of Someone still in the room. Not surprisingly, the soldiers talked with Paul and thus the whole guard and the proconsular court quickly appreciated that his imprisonment had nothing to do with temple robbery but was for Christ. Before long there were Christians in the palace, and Paul's sentries became his companions in prayer.

On a more exalted level, the Asiarchs, presidents, and ex-presidents of the provincial council,[21] who would not have stooped to attend Paul's teaching at the School of Tyrannus, were intrigued enough by palace gossip to send for him. Several became friendly, a fact which would have an important consequence. In other ways too, Paul could recognize that "whatever has happened to me has really advanced the Gospel." Most of the local Christians, far from being intimidated, stepped forward to fill the gap. Paul found that his imprisonment gave "most of the brothers more confidence in the Lord, so that they grew bolder all the time in preaching the message without fear." And though the false Christians, whose activities had dogged Paul elsewhere, hurried into Ephesus when they heard he was confined and began to set up a rival church "meaning to stir up fresh trouble for me as I lie in prison," Paul did not mind. They could do little harm when he was still around. "What does it matter? One way or another, in pretense or in sincerity, Christ is set forth, and for that I rejoice."

Paul was happy. Whichever way he looked, the future shone bright.

TWENTY-FIVE

THE HAPPIEST LETTER

A messenger arrived from the Philippian church. His name was Epaphroditus, and he brought the sympathy of the Philippians in practical form, not only their assurance of prayers for Paul's release but another gift of money, timely because a prisoner had to pay for his lodging yet could not earn wages. Epaphroditus gave all the news, of Luke and the jailer and the rest, until Paul longed to be with them again. He made himself Paul's servant, accepting the rough quarters allotted to prisoners' slaves. But then he fell ill, and Paul sent verbal warning by a Christian traveler that the Philippians might never see their friend again. Happily he recovered, and Paul determined to send him back.

Paul seized the opportunity of writing to the Philippians to thank them, and to promise them Timothy as soon as Paul's trial was over, to be followed—he was sure—by himself. The next day therefore Timothy's pen was poised to take the happiest letter Paul ever dictated.

"Paul and Timothy, slaves of Christ Jesus, to all the saints of Christ Jesus at Philippi, with the elders and deacons: Grace to you and peace from God our Father and the Lord Jesus Christ.

"I thank my God every time I think of you, and every time I pray for you I pray with joy because of your partnership in the Gospel from the first day until now, being sure of this, that He who has begun a good work in you will go on completing it until the Day of Christ Jesus—it is right for me to think this of you all, because I have you in my heart!"

Words of love and encouragement flowed as fast as Timothy could write them down. Next, Paul told how imprisonment had worked for the best and the future held no shadow. He admitted being in a dilemma—whether to long for acquittal and years of fruitful service or for death and a yet more joyful release. His one fear was lest he might betray Christ publicly in the agony and humiliation of the arena. But their prayers and the inexhaustible strength of the Spirit of Christ Jesus would be decisive: "It is my strong expectancy and my hope that I shall never be ashamed but now, and always, I shall be full of courage so that Christ will be uplifted—whether by my life or by my death. For to me, *to live is Christ and to die is gain*—"

Timothy looked up. Paul had put into that brief, immortal sentence the intense conviction of them both and of so many others, whether in Ephesus, Philippi, or elsewhere: "To live is Christ and to die is gain." Timothy's pen put it on the papyrus. Paul was dictating again, thinking aloud: "I am not sure which I should choose. I am caught from both sides: I want very much to leave this life and be with Christ, which is a far better thing; but it is much more important, for your sake, that I remain alive—I am sure of this. *And so I know that I will stay.* I will stay on with you all, to add to your progress and joy in the faith."

He turned to practical affairs, urging the Philippians to live in a way that commended the gospel to neighbors and urged them not to be terrified by opposition. To make him really happy, they must be one in love and heart and mind, concerned about one another's needs, unselfish, unconceited. He warmed to his theme and, as was his way, moved effortlessly from mundane matters into a massive statement of Christian truth.

Whether or not he was quoting a hymn that he and Silas had extemporized in the Philippi jail, his deep feelings expressed themselves, as on other occasions, in words that had the rhythm and clarity of true verse that no translation from the Greek can convey:

> Let this mind be in you
> That was in Christ Jesus,
> Who being in the form of God,
> Did not cling to His equality with God,
> But emptied Himself—

Took the form of a servant
And was born in the likeness of men!
And letting Himself seem a mere man
He humbled Himself,
Took the path of obedience,
To death—
Death on a cross!
Wherefore God has highly exalted Him,
Granted Him a name above every name,
That at the name of Jesus
Every knee should bow,
In heaven, on earth, under the earth;
And every tongue confess
That Jesus Christ is Lord
To the glory of God the Father!

The cell seemed full of music. The whole letter sparkled with golden phrases about Christ, forged to emphasize or explain everyday concerns: "That I may *know* Him, and the power of His resurrection and the companionship of His sufferings." "I can do all things through Him who strengthens me." And, in thanking them for the sacrifice they had made to send money: "My God shall supply all your needs according to His riches in glory by Christ Jesus." The letter breathed affection for the Philippians that no distance could weaken and a joy no prison bars could quench. During the dictation, friends and soldiers wandered in and out and thus, in the chill of a late autumn evening, as Paul and Timothy neared the end of their work, some of them were the first to hear words that have since warmed and heartened men and women in more than a thousand tongues: "Rejoice in the Lord always. Again I will say, Rejoice! Let your gentleness be known to all. The Lord is near: do not worry about anything, but in everything by prayer and supplication with thanksgiving, make your requests known to God. And the peace of God which passes all understanding shall guard your hearts and minds in Christ Jesus.

"Finally, brothers"—and Paul's call to the Philippians lights up the furnishing of his own mind, for otherwise his words were hollow, and Timothy and the Ephesians would have known it—"Finally, whatever is true, whatever is honorable, what is just, what is pure, what is lovely, what is gracious, if there is any excellence, anything praiseworthy, fill your thoughts with these things. What you have learned and received from me, and heard and seen in me, do: and the God of peace shall be with you."

Paul's "finally," the second of the letter, did not bring it to a close. Just as in the letter of Galatia, though for a different reason, he was reluctant to break off his message to "my brethren dearly loved and longed for, my joy and crown." But at last he reached the farewells. "Greet every saint in Christ Jesus. The brethren who are with me greet you." Paul's Christian guards begged to be included, the soldiers of Ephesus to the soldiers of Philippi. So Paul added, "All the saints greet you, especially those of the Caesar household.

"The grace of our Lord Jesus Christ be with your spirit."

In the course of his letter, Paul had said, "I am not already perfect ... but one thing I do: forgetting what lies behind and straining forward to what lies ahead, I press on toward the goal, the call to heaven from God in Christ Jesus."

The next months were to prove the honesty of the admission "I am not already perfect." They would force him to turn his mind to things that were not honorable, pure, or lovely and eventually would place a strain on him as he ran his race that made past troubles seem trivial. The joy, forbearance, lack of anxiety, sense of peace about which he had written would be tested to the limit.

The actual court case, before Proconsul Silanus early in the spring of 54, produced an anticlimax. Evidence collected in the province offered no proof that Paul had misappropriated money dedicated to the temple of Jerusalem. If Jews preferred Paul's fund to the voluntary temple tax, that was not temple robbery and Silanus refused to convict. This showed strict Roman justice, not favoritism; yet Paul's acquittal had the effect of marking him as a man protected by Silanus—which would have unforeseen and most damaging consequences.

Meanwhile, Paul had an immediate problem. All was not well across the Aegean in Corinth. Whether the bad news came with Apollos, who was certainly at Paul's side a little later, or by one of the stream of travelers between the two ports in the normal run of trade, Paul's concern ran so deep that he rushed over for a brief visit that left a painful impression both on him and on them. He would not stay until happier times; his place lay in Asia where he had planned an extensive tour, while his policy toward Corinth and other churches was that, however much he cared, each must learn to stand alone; he even seemed to have taken away Sosthenes, the former ruler of the synagogue, to assist on the upcountry Asian tour.

When they were back in Asia, further adverse news followed—of Corinthian Christians entangled in the snares of that city of unbridled love. Paul wrote a letter of advice that has not survived; and when Timothy set off on his promised visit to Philippi, Paul instructed him, young as he was, to go on afterward and sort out the Corinthians' muddle before Paul should return once more on his way to Macedonia.

Paul had not yet gone upcountry when Ephesus was stunned by the assassination of Proconsul Silanus.

Some weeks previously, Claudius Caesar had died, poisoned by his cousin and fourth wife, Agrippina; they were both great-grandchildren of Augustus, and Claudius had adopted Nero, her son by a previous marriage, as his heir. As she intended, Nero was immediately proclaimed *princeps*—emperor. Agrippina feared that her cousin Silanus, who had as good a title in blood as Nero, would plot to avenge Claudius and seize the throne by murdering both mother and son. To forestall this, she made Silanus the first victim of the new reign. At her orders the knight Publius Celer and the freedman Helius, controllers of the emperor's personal property in Asia, "administered poison to the Proconsul at a banquet," as Tacitus records, "in a manner too open to escape detection."

Celer and Helius took over the province, pending the arrival of a new proconsul and proceeded to liquidate their enemies. No man, however unpolitical, who was reckoned to have been protected by Silanus could count life secure. And that included Paul.

Paul's upcountry tour was thus shadowed by menace. When he and Sosthenes, the Macedonians Aristarchus and Gaius, and possibly Apollos traveled from city to city, they suffered more than the hardships, heat, and fatigue of the road. They were not only in peril from implacable Jews, from worshippers of Artemis who resented conversions to Christ, although Paul never insulted the goddess; they also had to contend with the contempt and ill will of petty officials anxious to shed their former loyalty to Silanus. "To this very hour," Paul wrote shortly afterward, "we go hungry and thirsty; we are clothed in rags; we are beaten; we wander from place to place, we work hard to support ourselves. When we are cursed, we bless; when we are persecuted, we endure; when we are insulted we answer back with kind words." They were looked on as the scum of the earth; people felt well rid of them. But others listened. Doors were open, opportunities unlimited.

The tour ended prematurely because of more grave news from Corinth. Paul received a report that a Corinthian Christian had committed incest in a manner disgusting even to pagans in sex-mad Corinth; and this man had not been expelled from the brotherhood. Paul saw the church rapidly becoming a byword to the heathen. Then a letter reached him from the elders of Corinth seeking clarification of several matters he had discussed in the letter that has not survived. But they showed no compunction about the disgraceful state of affairs.

Corinth had never been long out of his mind. The hardships of pioneering did not blunt his responsibility for districts already worked: On top of everything else, as he once wrote, "there is the daily pressure of my concern for all the churches." He now decided to return to Ephesus and devote the next days or weeks to the composition of a letter to deal thoroughly with the situation and to bring the Corinthians to a better mind before he visited them again.

TWENTY-SIX

"THE GREATEST OF THESE ..."

When Paul arrived in Ephesus, several Corinthians awaited him—"Chloe's people," who were either members of a family or traders of a firm—to give him a yet more disquieting report.

Christians were suing one another in pagan courts, and the church was being torn apart by quarreling. Some boasted they were "Paul's party," others that their loyalty was to Apollos, and some were "Peter's men," whether converts of an unrecorded visit or merely using his name. And one or two boasted that they owed nothing to any apostle: "I belong to Christ." With quarreling went arrogance, as if they were superior in the eyes of God and man; and there were other faults, until Paul wept. There could be no greater contrast between the happy letter to Philippi and the pain he faced in writing to the Corinthians, "with a greatly troubled and distressed heart, and with many tears, not to make you sad but to make you realize how much I love you all."

Corinth was displaying the paradox at the heart of Paul's activity. For him, the aim and the possibility was every Christian morally and spiritually perfect in Christ; yet in each church human weakness marred, and false teaching confused. Christ had warned it would be so, for He wanted the love of free people not puppets on a string, but Paul took it personally and rather hard when his converts preferred dissension to unity, self-advancement to service, half-love to full devotion, despite Christ's willingness to give them every fine quality and all the strength they needed.

Paul settled down to dictate to Sosthenes an expression of gratitude and faith astounding in the circumstances, then went straight to an appeal for unity: "Is Christ divided? Was *Paul* crucified for you? Or were you baptized in the name of Paul?" He was glad he had baptized nobody himself except

Crispus and Gaius; he added as an afterthought the household of Gaius but could remember no other. "Christ did not send me to baptize but to preach the Gospel, and not with eloquent wisdom, lest the cross of Christ be emptied of its power." Paul pressed the point and emphasized, as if to lift the whole discussion at once to a higher plane, the stark contrast between the world's philosophies, which seek goodness by the application of human thought and effort, and the gospel, which philosophy and common sense regarded as ludicrous: "God in His wisdom made it impossible for men to know Him by means of their own wisdom. Instead, God decided to save those who believe, by means of the 'foolish' message we preach. Jews want miracles for proof, and Greeks look for wisdom. As for us, we proclaim 'Christ on the cross,' a message that is offensive to the Jews and nonsense to the Gentiles, but for those whom God has called, both Jews and Gentiles, this message is Christ who is the power of God and the wisdom of God."

The foolishness of God was wiser than men, the weakness of God was stronger. By the time Paul had unfolded a long argument, he had made plain that no man could discover God by force of intellect. Had Paul known what marvels of knowledge would emerge in the next two thousand years, that the human mind and anatomy were infinitely complex, the universe so vast that the earth spun as a mere grain in space, he would have said the same. He would have considered it ironic that, the more men discovered the insignificance of their planet, the more highly they would rate themselves, all the more sure that they could explain everything without reference to God.

They knew nothing. "The wisdom we speak is the wisdom of God, secret, hidden, which God prepared for our glory before time began; which none of the rulers of this age has known, for if they had known they would not have crucified the Lord of glory.... The man who is merely natural does not receive the things of the Spirit of God; they are ridiculous to him and he is not able to know them because they can only be understood by a spiritual man. 'For who,' [Paul quoted from Isaiah] 'has known the mind of the Lord? Who can instruct him?' But we have the mind of Christ."

Having forced the Corinthians, when his letter should be read aloud, to face the rest of it on the plane of the spiritual, not the merely human, Paul disposed of the question of party spirit rapidly by showing that each apostle or messenger was a servant in the Lord's field—"I planted, Apollos watered, but God gave the increase"—or a workman building His temple. As for the arrogance that went with party spirit, "None of you should be proud of one man and despise the other. Who made you superior to the others? Didn't God give you everything you have? Well then, how can you brag, as if what you have were not a gift?" Paul slipped into irony that ran close to sarcasm, "You are rich already! Without us you reign as kings!" In contrast, the apostles were like despised criminals who were sent last into the arena to die. "We are fools for Christ's sake, but you are 'wise in Christ.' We are weak, but you are strong. You are held in honor, but we in disrepute." And he described the rough treatment on his missionary tour. "I am saying all this," he added, "not just to make you ashamed but to bring you, as my dearest children, to your senses." He would soon be with them and deflate the arrogant. "What do you wish? Shall I come to you with a rod, or with love in a spirit of gentleness?"

By now, when he seemed to have stopped dictating until at least the next day, it was clear that this letter would be longer by far than any he had written to date. It might also be his last, were he to be engulfed in the political storm that threatened Ephesus. It bore therefore the aspect of a testament.

He knew that his writing held equal authority with his speaking, the authority of an apostle and of a prophet, as truly commissioned to convey God's word as was Isaiah or Jeremiah. His opponents rated this conviction boastful, but, he would tell the Corinthians, he had nothing of which to boast: "I am the least of the apostles, unfit to be called an apostle, because I persecuted the church of God." As an apostle and prophet, he must give them the word of God. Like Isaiah or Jeremiah, however, he must speak to the immediate condition of his hearers, and when he contemplated what to say in correcting Corinthian abuse of sex, he suffered uncertainty.

In this letter to Corinth, and in no other, he was ready to admit that one or two of his judgments lack the authority of a clear ruling given by Jesus, and though Paul believed he interpreted the Spirit's wisdom, he would not go beyond the phrases, "But in my judgment ... and I *think* I have the Spirit of God." The very uncertainty underlines Paul's profound belief that his writings had the same authority that impelled his predecessors, using a different form, to cry, "Thus saith the Lord."

Like them, he had a hard message. With utmost distaste, he had to look at apostasy and uncleanness and root it out. The Corinthian church must expel the incestuous man and send him back to the world where Satan reigns. Paul's actual words, "consigned to Satan for the destruction of the body, so that his spirit may be saved on the Day of the Lord," caused confusion in the centuries that followed and were misinterpreted to justify the burning of heretics; but Paul's concerns were equally the purity of the church and the good of the offender. When, later on, he heard that the punishment had been effective, he was almost afraid lest he had been too ruthless. "Something very different is called for now," he wrote in a later letter. "You must forgive the offender and put new heart into him; the man's sorrow must not be made so severe as to overwhelm him. I urge you therefore to assure him of your love for him by a formal act."

And they must all flee fornication. To the church in a Corinth dominated by the sexual license of Aphrodite's temple, Paul determined to stress the importance of sexual purity. "Every other sin that a man can commit is out-side the body; but the fornicator sins against his own body. Do you know that your body is a shrine of the indwelling Holy Spirit, and the Spirit is God's gift to you? You do not belong to yourselves; you were bought at a price. So then, honor God in your body."

He agreed with those who in their letter had asked if it were not better for a man never to touch a woman. Anxious to conciliate the ascetic group within the church (possibly those who called themselves "Christ's party"), and to preserve unity, he admitted his preference in the present distresses for an unattached state like his own, and not least because the Lord would return soon; but he refused to let them think marriage or sexual relations were sinful in themselves. Nor must married couples suppose they would serve God better if they separated. Paul's words on chastity, fornication, and marriage, the subject of endless discussion and commentary ever since, have left him with somewhat of a reputation as a woman-hater, and he certainly betrayed traces of impatience with women as a sex. Yet close study shows his acute awareness that in all consideration of sex, in its dignity and beauty as much as in its abuse, man and woman matter equally. Indeed, he took a view exactly opposite to those in later ages who condemned a "fallen woman" while condoning the man provided he were discreet. Paul's condemnation is reserved for the man.

In his discussion of relations between man and woman, the keynote was his desire to help rather than to harass: "I am saying this because I want to help you. I am not trying to put restrictions on you. Instead, I want you to do what is right and proper, and give yourselves completely to the Lord's service without reservation."

The good of all and the glory of God were the decisive factors, just as when he turned to problems such as whether to eat meat that had been consecrated to idols before it had been sold or served. In another long, careful discussion he showed that Christians were free to do as they liked, but such freedom must never hurt others. An idol was a mere piece of wood or stone, yet pagans—and many a new Christian convert—thought otherwise. If therefore the butcher, or the host, should make plain that the meat had been offered to an idol, the mature Christian should refuse it, not for his own conscience's sake but for others, lest the weak brother or the pagan suppose the Lord Jesus is on supping terms with gods and goddesses.

"Whether you eat or drink, or whatever you are doing, do all for the honor of God: give no offense to Jews, or Greeks, or to the church of God." Paul told them that he tried to be helpful to everyone at all times, to meet them halfway, to please them, "not anxious for my own advantage but for the advantage of everyone else, so that they may be saved. Imitate me, then, just as I imitate Christ."

When he dealt with their questions regarding the form and order of a Christian church, sorting out their aberrations, correcting and criticizing but praising where he could, his aim was to urge them toward building up the church and not selfishly to please themselves. They should recognize that they were Christ's body "and each of you a limb or organ of it." In a physical body there were different functions, each indispensable to the other. "If the body were all eye, how could it hear? If the body were all ear, how could it smell? … God has combined the various parts of the body, that all its organs might feel the same concern for one another. If one organ suffers, they all suffer together. If one flourishes, they all rejoice together."

In the same way, God had distributed gifts in the body of Christ, the church: first and highest, apostles; then, prophets; next, teachers, workers of miracles, healers, helpers, and administrators, speakers in tongues, and interpreters of tongues. And some were appointed to very humble functions and should thereby be honored, not despised.

Paul said that all should aim at the higher gifts. Then he added, "And now I will show you the best way of all."

Days had passed in dictating, each passage in the letter needing deep thought and prayer. Paul had covered many emotions. Much of his teaching had related to the theme of love, the problems caused by Corinth's obsession with *eros*, sexual love. He now wanted to leave them with a true understanding of that higher, peculiarly Christian love, which the disciples termed *agapē*. If he could convey the meaning of this kind of love, they would indeed have an example to aim at, a way in which to live.

His mind turned to all he knew of the Lord Jesus, both from the traditions of the life lived in Palestine and from the daily companionship of the Spirit of Jesus, so very real as He guided and trained through the years. "Imitate me as I imitate Christ," he had told the Corinthians.

Somewhere in Ephesus, or in the hills overlooking the sea, alone with his Master, Paul looked once more at Perfect Love. He could perceive Him only dimly, as if through a colored glass or reflected in a metal mirror, and longed for the day when he would know the Lord Jesus as fully as the Lord knew him: The Lord Jesus—patient and kind; never jealous, not possessive, envying no one. Not boastful nor anxious to impress; not arrogant, proud, or haughty, nor giving Himself airs. Not rude or discourteous. The Lord Jesus did not insist on His own way, pursue selfish advantage, or claim His rights. He was not touchy or irritable or quick to take offense. He did not brood on injuries, bear a grudge, or show resentment; He did not gloat over other men's sins, feel pleased when others went wrong, nor did He condone injustice. Instead, He was gladdened by goodness, delighted in it, and always took the part of truth. Yet He was slow to expose and could overlook faults. There was no limit to His endurance, no end to His willingness to trust, no fading of His hope.

With the face of Perfect Love filling his mind, Paul resumed dictating, to deliver the best known of all his works, a prose poem that, besides its profound spiritual value, entitles Paul to rank among the greatest masters of literature. Numerous translations have unfolded shades of meaning; every generation finds apposite words to express the Greek, yet the English language has few finer passages than the rendering of the thirteenth chapter of First Corinthians in the *King James Version*:[22]

"Though I speak with the tongues of men and of angels, and have not charity, I am become as sounding brass, or a tinkling cymbal. And though I have the gift of prophecy, and understand all mysteries, and all knowledge; and though I have all faith, so that I could remove mountains, and have not charity, I am nothing. And though I bestow all my goods to feed the poor, and though I give my body to be burned, and have not charity, it profiteth me nothing.

"Charity suffereth long, and is kind; charity envieth not; charity vaunteth not itself, is not puffed up. Doth not behave itself unseemly, seeketh not her own, is not easily provoked, thinketh no evil; rejoiceth not in iniquity but rejoiceth in the truth. Beareth all things, believeth all things, hopeth all things, endureth all things.

"Charity never faileth; but whether there be prophecies, they shall fail; whether there be tongues, they shall cease; whether there be knowledge, it shall vanish away. For we know in part, and we prophesy in part. But when that which is perfect is come, then that which is in part shall be done away. When I was a child, I spake as a child, I understood as a child, I thought as a child: but when I became a man, I put away childish things. For now we see through a glass, darkly; but then face to face: now I know in part; then shall I know even as also I am known.

"And now abideth faith, hope, charity, these three; but the greatest of these is charity."

TWENTY-SEVEN

AFFLICTION IN ASIA

One major Corinthian problem remained. Some of them said that Christ's blessings were for this life only: no life after death, no resurrection into eternity.

This doubt looked peculiarly pertinent to Paul's own situation. The storm clouds were gathering fast as those whom Silanus had favored or protected were murdered or thrown into jail. Paul knew his turn might come; he faced death daily, stood in jeopardy every hour. It was like the thunderclouds he must have watched from the city walls high up on Mount Coressos at the turn of the season, black and threatening, deepening each minute but giving no indication whether the torrential rain would pass by or drench him. "A wide door for effective work has opened to me," he told Corinth, "but there are many adversaries."

If he became a mangled corpse, a mess of blood and sinew to be pushed off the arena floor and piled in a cart while slaves sprinkled sand ready for the next item, was that the end?

Paul saw that the question was bound up with the resurrection of Christ. The two were mutual. He therefore reminded the Corinthians what he had taught them, as a first and foremost component of his Good News, how Christ had not only "died for our sins" but also had been "raised to life again on the third day," at Passover time in Jerusalem twenty-five years ago. He listed the witnesses who had seen Him, "most of whom are still living." He reminded them that he too was a witness of the risen Christ, how meeting Christ had revolutionized him, so that "I worked harder than any of them, though it was not I but the grace of God which is with me." If he and the other witnesses were proclaiming Christ as risen from the dead, "how can some of you say that there is no resurrection of the dead? But if there is no resurrection of the dead, then Christ has not been raised."

If Christ had never, in precise historic fact, risen from the dead, then Paul's preaching and the Corinthians' faith were futile: "You are still in your sins." Conversely, if no dead are ever raised, Paul had willfully misrepresented God, had committed perjury by swearing that Christ had risen. And those who had died believing in Him had perished utterly. If it were all a mere shadowy hope, "if our love in Christ is good for this life only, and no more," wrote Paul, "then we deserve more pity than anyone else in all the world.

"But Christ *has* been raised from the dead!" Sheer dogmatic certainty rang through Paul's words, backed by the Corinthians' knowledge of his moral integrity and of his careful examination of the evidence. They knew that no man who so hated deception, who consciously lived as responsible to the all-seeing God of truth, who had taught them new conceptions of goodness and honesty, could propagate a lie as a pious way of explaining that Jesus survived as a Spirit. Paul believed the murdered Jesus had stepped out of the grave.

When Paul turned to forestall the inevitable further questions, "How can the dead be raised to life? What kind of body will they have?" he rejected the coarse materialism that supposed flesh, blood, and bones could inherit the kingdom of God. "You fool!" was his reaction to anyone with such an idea.

Instead, the continuity and transformation were like the relationship between seed and crop. "When you plant a seed in the ground, it does not sprout to life unless it dies. And what you plant in the ground is a bare seed, perhaps a grain of wheat, or of some other kind, not the full-bodied plant that will grow up.... This is how it will be when the dead are raised to life. When the body is buried it is mortal; when raised it will be immortal. When buried it is ugly and weak; when raised it will be beautiful and strong. When buried it is a physical body, when raised it will be a spiritual body.... We will wear the likeness of the Man from heaven."

Paul's contemplation of so glorious a future carried him into another sublime passage, as full of literary beauty as of prophecy. And once again its concluding words, the last of the entire epistle except for a few practical points about immediate arrangements, have never been more finely rendered into English than by the *King James Version*: "Behold, I show you a mystery; we shall not all sleep, but we shall all be changed, in a moment, in the twinkling of an eye, at the last trump: for the trumpet shall sound, and the dead shall be raised incorruptible, and we shall be changed.... So when this corruptible shall have put on incorruption, and this mortal shall have put on immortality, then shall be brought to pass the saying that is written, 'Death is swallowed up in victory. O death, where is thy sting? O grave, where is thy victory?' The sting of death is sin; and the strength of sin is the law. But thanks be to God, which giveth us the victory through our Lord Jesus Christ.

"Therefore, my beloved brethren, be ye steadfast, unmovable, always abounding in the work of the Lord, forasmuch as ye know that your labour is not in vain in the Lord."

In the months following his dispatch of the letter to Corinth, Paul himself needed every ounce of that final exhortation and encouragement.

The storm broke. Sometime at the end of 54 or early 55 Paul was swept into calamity. He had planned to stay in Ephesus until spring, seizing the evangelistic opportunities presented by a great pagan festival and by the public's unhappiness and disquiet after the murder of Silanus, and then to return to Macedonia; he had abandoned his intention of revisiting Corinth immediately, having written instead, and would go there after Macedonia.

All this was thrown into the melting pot. A time of terror, such as even the hard campaigning Paul had never known, brought him to the sharpest crisis of his life, "the affliction we experienced in Asia."

"We were so utterly, unbearably crushed that we despaired of life itself." "Pressed above measure, above strength." "Completely overwhelmed, more than we could bear." "The things we had to undergo were more of a burden than we could carry, so that we despaired of coming through alive." "Crushed, overwhelmed, and desperate. I feared I would never live through it." Thus translators attempt to convey what Paul wrote shortly afterward. It can never be known exactly what happened. He was probably arrested and beaten with rods severely, possibly tortured, for the murderers of Silanus were administrating Asia arbitrarily. Thrown into a dungeon, he probably fell grievously ill with a recurrence of the "thorn in the flesh," for the memory of this terrible time lay fresh in mind on the occasion when he described how the "thorn" had buffeted him until he implored the Lord to remove it.

More than this, he passed into mental and spiritual affliction. Research cannot uncover the details, but certain clues are available. Ephesus was the center of witchcraft. We dare not dismiss the possibility that a curse was laid on Paul, causing severe mental agony. Those who have known something of the mysterious powers of voodoo in tribal communities, or experienced the mystifying exploitation of evil in certain types of Western spiritualism, would certainly not eliminate this theory. And it would help to explain a choice of words in the famous passage, "Who shall separate us from the love for Christ?" which Paul composed about eighteen months later: "I am convinced that there is nothing in death of life, in the *realm of spirits or superhuman powers* ... in the forces of the universe, in heights or depths—nothing in all creation that can separate us from the love of God in Christ Jesus our Lord."

Whether or not Paul suffered from sorcery as well as brutality, it seems unquestionable that he descended into a spiritual valley in which his soul endured stresses that nearly shattered him. He had the taut nerves of the genius, on which physical or mental suffering—his own or others—grated with a roughness unknown to less sensitive men. He recoiled from pain, though never fleeing; felt hurt when abused, though bearing no resentment; grew agitated when a church was threatened by those he had won to faith: "Who is weak and I do not feel weak with him? Who is made to stumble and I do not burn with indignation?" In the slime and stench of an Ephesus dungeon, his mind turned restlessly: the problems of Corinth, the problem of evil, the apparently limitless resources of those who hated Christ. "Perplexed; afflicted; persecuted; struck down" are some of the words he used. As distress increased, he seemed to have entered a dark night of the soul and suffered a loss of will.

In a notable section of the letter to the Romans, when the events at Ephesus were still recent, he used terms about himself that (unless purely rhetorical) suggest he had been through deep waters of spiritual agony. Though his words are often assumed to describe the period before the Damascus Road, a closer study indicates that they refer to Paul the Christian, and unless he was saying his mental conflict continued endlessly, which the context denies, he would seem to be drawing general conclusions from a particular struggle. "I cannot understand my own behavior," he wrote. "I fail to carry out the things I want to do, and I find myself doing the very things I hate.... I know that nothing good dwells within me, that is, in my flesh. I can *will* what is right, but I cannot do it.... Every single time I want to do good it is something evil that comes to hand." Paul delights in the Law of God, yet sin battles against this and makes him "a prisoner of that law of sin which lives inside my body. What a wretched man that I am! Who will rescue me?"

"O wretched man that I am! Who shall deliver me?" The cry echoed through nights of pain and despair until profound realization of weakness led to a surge forward in the Spirit: "Who shall deliver me? I thank God through Jesus Christ our Lord!"

As Paul slipped into suffering, to a depth he had never previously known, he began to learn more of the power of Jesus: "He said to me, 'My grace is sufficient for you, for My strength is made perfect in weakness.'" "Blessed be the God and Father of our Lord Jesus Christ," he wrote specifically of this crisis, "the Father of mercies and God of all comfort, who comforts us in all our affliction," so that Paul could comfort others in any sorrow, with the comfort he had received himself. He realized, as never before, that he was sharing in Christ's sufferings so that he might share Christ's comfort. He saw the purpose of it all, that he might describe to his converts the reality of Christ's extraordinary power and love.

"It has taught us not to rely on ourselves but only on God, who raises the dead to life." God had delivered and would deliver; Paul could never doubt this again, as the future would show. Against the record of calamity, he could write the assurance of rescue. Against the word *afflicted*, he wrote "but not crushed"; against *perplexed*, "not driven to despair"; "persecuted but not forsaken, struck down but not destroyed: always carrying in the body the death of Jesus, so that the life of Jesus may be manifested in our bodies." He repeats it: "Always being given up to death for Jesus' sake, so that the life of Jesus may be manifested." Paul's difficulties and pain actually helped Jesus to show Himself, to spread abroad the aroma of His love, just as the scent of rose petals grows stronger when they are crushed.

"So we do not lose heart." Paul had been tempted. Despair had nearly cut him off before some of his finest work. But now he could face whatever might come. "Though our outer nature is wasting away, our inner nature is being renewed every day. For this slight momentary affliction is preparing for us an eternal weight of glory beyond all comparison, because we look not to the things that are seen but to the things that are unseen; for the things that are seen are transient, but the things that are unseen are eternal."

Physical deliverance, the rescue from certain death to unconditional liberty, came somehow through the intervention—at fearful risk—of Aquila and Priscilla. They were ready to die in Paul's place. "Give my greetings to Priscilla and Aquila," Paul wrote after they had returned to Rome the next year. "They risked their necks to save my life, and not I alone but all the Gentile congregations are grateful to them." He emerged from the spring of 55 weak in health put purified in spirit.

Almost immediately after release, his life was in peril again. This time Luke could describe the incident in detail, for the riot in Ephesus had nothing to do with Silanus and showed Roman government at its best.

Every spring, devotees of the Mother Goddess converged on Ephesus for Artemisia, the great festival that worship, trade, and gaiety made the highlight of the city's year. Processions marched from the Temple of Artemis to the north gate, on below the theater and along the marble way, then up the hill by the city hall and out by the Magnesia Gate. Between excitements the crowds thronged the streets. This was the coming opportunity that had caused Paul to decide not to leave Ephesus earlier.

It was also the prime sales season for the important guild of silversmiths, whose replicas of the Artemis idol were normally in heavy demand. This year 55, however, the silversmiths suffered a slump, a remarkable testimony to the success of Paul's mission. Hundreds of visitors were refusing to buy; some because, as Christians, they were treating Artemisia merely as an annual outing, a chance to hear Paul again and meet fellow believers but no longer to purchase silver goddesses to take to the temple for blessing, and others because they were converted to Christ during the festival.

The silversmiths had lost sales enough already. One of the biggest employers, Demetrius, in a rage called a protest meeting of his own craftsmen and others, including presumably some Christians who gave Luke an eyewitness account. What Demetrius quite intended to achieve is not clear, for his speech so inflamed his hearers that matters were soon out of his hands.

He made no bones about the chief reason for his fury, whatever lip worship he gave the goddess. "Men," he cried, "you know that from this trade comes our prosperity. And you see and hear that not only in Ephesus but almost everywhere in Asia this fellow Paul has persuaded and turned away masses of people, telling them that handmade gods are not gods at all. And there's danger that not only will this trade of ours fall into disrepute, but the temple of the great goddess Artemis will count for nothing, and her greatness be destroyed, she whom all Asia and the inhabited world worship!"

At that the audience roared the city's worship cry: "Great is Artemis of the Ephesians!" They poured into the street and began to run where citizens instinctively converged in time of emergency—the theater cut from the hillside of Pion, meeting place of the monthly Popular Assembly, which every adult male might attend. As they ran up the steep street toward the entrance at the top, shouting, "Great is Artemis of the Ephesians," people dropped what they were doing and joined the rush, certain that a great danger or a great decision must be at hand. Some of the silversmiths seized two of Paul's companions, the Macedonians Aristarchus and Gaius, and swept them along. More and more citizens spilled through the gate at the upper end of the theater and ran down the gangways, until tier after tier filled up, while below on the stage Demetrius and his men swayed around Aristarchus and Gaius. On the scaffolding above the proscenium (the theater was being enlarged and improved throughout Paul's period in Ephesus), workmen laid down their tools and looked on astonished.

When Paul in another part of the city heard what had happened, he determined to go to the theater and address the crowd. Apart from intervening to rescue his travel companions, he saw a supreme opportunity to reach the biggest audience of his life. The theater was filling rapidly and it held nineteen thousand. The acoustics were marvelous. Once he had stilled the people, as he knew he could, he could preach about Jesus.

The disciples implored him not to go. While they were still arguing, messengers came from the Asiarchs, the eminent friends Paul had made during his first imprisonment. They too begged him not to risk his life in the theater. Respect for their understanding of the crowd's mood caused him reluctantly to abandon the plan.

Meanwhile in the theater, as Luke dryly described, "Some cried one thing and some another, for the assembly was in confusion, and most of them did not know why they had come together." Leading Jews feared a pogrom and hastily put up a spokesman, Alexander. Thrusting his way onto the stage, he lifted his hand for silence. His intention was to tell them the Jews were not the culprits and in fact hated Paul as much as they did.

The crowd recognized Alexander as a Jew. Someone shouted at him, "Great is Artemis of the Ephesians!" Then, "Great is Artemis of the Ephesians," yelled the rest. Mass hysteria swept the tiers. The worship cry came again and again until the entire theater reverberated the rhythmic chanting of four Greek words, *"Megalē hē Artemis Ephesiōn!"*

"Megalē hē Artemis Ephesiōn!" The cry echoed across the city and over the water to the ships in the harbor and across to the hills beyond the gulf. They could hear it in the Temple of Artemis. The chant floated to soldiers on the walls along the height of Coressos as they looked down amazed. In the theater itself, all but the lowest tiers had a splendid view of the lower city, with the wide porticoed street to the harbor gate, and of the gulf, but they had no eyes for these. Work lost, dinners uncooked, the fierce heat of the sun meant nothing. The monotonous and now almost meaningless cry went on and on, "Great is Artemis of the Ephesians!"

The chief executive of Ephesus, holder of the highest elected office and responsible for civic order, was thoroughly alarmed. The Romans objected to any irregular assembly. They could treat one that behaved like this as a riot and punish the city by canceling yet more of what little self-government remained. He was, however, a man of sense. He waited for the vast concourse to exhaust itself. And so for two hours, while the sun moved steadily along the ridge of Coressos, the chant drummed through his head.

At last he thrust himself forward and put up his hand. The crowd knew him as the one official who rightly should conduct the business of a Popular Assembly. The noise died away.

"Men of Ephesus," he said, his voice sounding back from the specially toned bronze and clay vessels placed round the theater. "What man is there anywhere who does not know that the Ephesians' city is temple warden of the great goddess Artemis and her image which fell from heaven? This being beyond dispute, your proper course is to calm down and do nothing rash. These men who you dragged here are not temple robbers, nor blasphemers of the goddess. If therefore Demetrius and his fellow craftsmen have a case against anyone, there are assizes and there are proconsuls"—a tactful admission that since Silanus's death his murderers were joint rulers, de facto proconsuls—"so let them accuse each other there. But if you have something general to discuss, it must be settled in the lawful Assembly. We are in danger of being charged with riot because of what has happened today. There is no excuse for this illegal and uproarious concourse, and we shall not be able to give a reason for it."

Then, having made them thoroughly ashamed of themselves and produced a total anticlimax, he declared the assembly closed.

TWENTY-EIGHT

A TREATISE FOR ROME

After the uproar, Paul knew it was time to move on, as he had always intended after Artemisia. His plan included a return visit to Macedonia and southern Greece, then Jerusalem with some Asian and European converts to hand over the Collection. "After I have been there, I must also see Rome."

Before the riot, being nervous lest his letter to Corinth had been too strong and had discouraged his "children," he had dispatched young Titus of Antioch to investigate the situation, Timothy being detained in Macedonia. Titus was to return, not to Ephesus but to Troas where Paul intended to preach before crossing to Europe. When Paul reached Troas, almost certainly by sea, he found an excellent opportunity for preaching, "but my mind could not rest because I did not find my brother Titus there. So I took leave of them and went on to Macedonia" to find Titus, who would be coming up through Greece.

In Philippi, Paul's first visit since the flogging, the church was enduring persecution and deep poverty with remarkable joy, their customary generosity unquenched. But they suffered from false apostles and counterfeit Christians, so that for Paul "there was still no relief for this body of ours: instead, there was trouble at every turn, quarrels all around us, forebodings in our heart. But God, who brings comfort to the downcast, has comforted us by the arrival of Titus." Titus brought good news. The Corinthians had taken the punishing part of Paul's letter in the right spirit. It hurt, but they accepted the pain as deserved and were eager to vindicate themselves. They longed to see Paul again. And they had treated Titus with such respect and affection that Paul could write to them, "We have been delighted beyond everything by seeing how happy Titus is: you have helped to set his mind completely at rest. Anything I may have said to him to show my pride in you has been justified."

The situation in Corinth was far from perfect. They still needed rebuke and appeal. Worse, they were disgruntled about Paul himself. They complained that by abandoning his plan to cross direct from Ephesus, he had played fast and loose: They hinted he was untrustworthy. Paul had little difficulty in answering that. "It was to spare you I refrained from coming to Corinth." He had written instead, in order that his third visit should not be as painful as the second.

More seriously, they had been unsettled by the arrival of preachers with impressive panache, carrying apparently impeccable credentials, who seemed all the more superior to Paul in that they charged a stiff fee. Their propaganda was such that the Corinthian church, Paul's very own foundation, actually demanded proof of his commission. The new arrivals had denied him the qualities of a true apostle, pointing out that he carried no letters of commendation from Jerusalem, refused payment, did not live like a genuine Jew, and behaved much too meekly, was contemptible in body and despicable in speech; an apostle should boss his flock, they said. They conceded Paul could write weighty letters.

He was not unprepared for these people turning up in Corinth. He did not demur from naming them: "Counterfeit apostles, they are dishonest workmen disguised as apostles of Christ. There is nothing surprising about that; if Satan himself goes disguised as an angel of light, there is no need to be surprised when his servants too disguise themselves as servants of righteousness. They will come to the end that they deserve." Paul was astonished at some of their assertions about him, but whereas he had reacted indignantly to similar circumstances in Galatia, his attitude now, ten years later and after the Ephesus crisis, was more one of amusement ("I am a nobody.... I will talk like a fool"). Nevertheless, he felt he must answer the Corinthians' inquiries about his status. They forced him to boast, rather wryly, that he indeed bore all the marks of a genuine apostle. He seemed aware that they had noticed an overreadiness to vindicate his genuineness, "but you drove me to it"; and anything he said was to build them up and strengthen them, his very dear friends.

Thus the long Second Letter to the Corinthians, written from Macedonia when Timothy rejoined him, was not so much a defense as a means of demonstrating what an apostle should be like. It contains intimate personal revelations of Paul's life and character past and present, his weakness and sufferings, and is the source of much of the material for his biography. It also contains a rationale for his motives, revealing his conceptions of both the task and the message of the true ambassador for Christ.

Paul and the other apostles were not proclaiming their own excellencies "but Christ Jesus as Lord, and ourselves as your servants, for Jesus' sake." "The love of Christ controls us," he wrote, "because we are convinced that One has died for all: therefore all have died. And He died for all, that those who live might no longer live for themselves but for Him who, for their sake, died and was raised.... If anyone is in Christ, he is a new creation, the old has passed away, the new has come. All this is from God, who through Christ reconciled us to Himself and gave us the ministry of reconciliation; that is, God was in Christ reconciling the world to Himself, not counting their trespasses against them, and entrusting to us the message of reconciliation.

"So we are ambassadors for Christ, God making His appeal through us: 'We beseech you on behalf of Christ, be reconciled to God! For He has made Him to be sin who knew no sin, so that in Him we might become the righteousness of God.'"

Paul decided not to go to Corinth too quickly. Titus, eager to return, took the letter, and Paul sent two other Christians, one of whom he called "the brother who is famous among all the churches for his preaching of the Gospel." Tradition believed this to be Luke and that his earliest writings were circulating already.

Paul wanted Corinth to settle down completely before his own arrival. He did not wish to find "quarreling, jealousy, anger, selfishness, slander, gossip, conceit, and disorder." He did not wish to be forced into the role of strict judge. Nor did he want to stir them up to complete the contribution they had promised to the Jerusalem Collection. They should have it ready willingly, each according to his means, their generosity measured by the only true gauge: "You know how generous our Lord Jesus Christ has been: He was rich, yet for your sake He became poor, so that through His poverty you might become rich."

At the end of his letter, after urging them to "mend your ways, heed my appeal, agree with one another, live in peace, and the God of love and peace will be with you," Paul used a farewell that is without doubt the most quoted sentence of all he ever wrote: "The grace of our Lord Jesus Christ and the love of God and the fellowship of the Holy Spirit be with you all."

The letter dispatched, Paul continued in the north for an entire year. After encouraging the churches of Macedonia, he began evangelizing fresh territory, the neighboring province of Illyricum, a mountainous land bordering the Adriatic. No word of his exact movements survives, but his activity must have been much as he had described in his recent *apologia*: "Giving no offense in anything, that the ministry be not blamed, but in all things approving ourselves as the ministers of God, in much patience, in affliction, in necessities, in distresses, in stripes, in imprisonments, in tumults, in labors, in watchings, in fastings; by pureness, by knowledge, by long-suffering, by kindness, by the Holy Ghost, by love unfeigned. By the word of truth, by the power of God, by the armor of righteousness on the right hand and on the left, by honor and dishonor, by evil report and good report: as 'deceivers' and yet true; as unknown and yet well-known; as dying, and, behold, we live; as chastened and not killed; as sorrowful, yet always rejoicing; as poor, yet making many rich; as having nothing, yet possessing all things."

While in the north, Paul nearly crossed the Adriatic to visit the Christians of Rome, but the opportunities of Illyricum left no time before he moved south at last, to spend the three winter months of 56–57 in Corinth. When he arrived in mid-December, their troubles had subsided. No breath of controversy is heard. Instead, in a happy atmosphere, he could give much time to a new project: a letter to the Christians of Rome that should be the distillation of his thought, his nearest approach to the writing of a book, a carefully constructed literary composition, which, if he had never written or spoken another word, entitles Paul to rank with Socrates, Plato, and Aristotle among the greatest intellects of the ancient world and, indeed, of all time.

Paul already had several friends and distant relations in Rome before Aquila and Priscilla returned there from Ephesus. Ease of communication in the empire induced constant coming and going to the world's center, and he could send greetings to his foster mother from Antioch and her son Rufus, "that outstanding worker in the Lord's service"; to two Jews of his own tribe or family whom he described as his fellow prisoners, probably when they were in Ephesus, "who were Christian before I was"; to the first convert in Asia; and to others.

He looked forward to renewing acquaintance and to the fresh experience of enjoying the company of a church he had not founded. Far from being jealous, he had been thrilled to hear about their faith and prayed for them regularly, yet his previous plans to visit Rome had yielded in the face of unending calls to pioneer where Christ was unknown, to push onward, to watch more and more men and women receive the grace of God so that thanksgiving and praise flowed ever wider.

Paul was determined to go "where Christ was not named"; not therefore to Alexandria and Egypt, or Carthage and other cities of north Africa. He had his sights on Spain, the highly civilized, most westerly province of the empire, and he could call in at Rome on the way. He would not stay long. His policy remained never to build on another's foundation. But because his commission was to all pagans, whether civilized or savage, educated or ignorant, "I am eager to preach the Good News to you also who live in Rome" and to win converts there. Moreover, the visit would be of mutual benefit: "For I long to see you that I may impart to you some spiritual gift to strengthen you, that is, that we may be mutually encouraged by each other's faith, yours and mine."

Meanwhile, since he must first take the Collection to Jerusalem, and already may have had a premonition that he would not reach Rome as quickly as he hoped, he decided to give them the fruit of his years of experience and learning at the side of Christ. He had now been a Christian for a quarter of a century and was in his late fifties: mature, assured of the supreme excellence of his Master in all the changes and chances of life. In contrast with previous letters, he was not obliged to combat aberrations, or to rebut criticisms—except once, when he snubbed slanderers who twisted his words to "sin away, to give God's forgiveness more opportunity!" Only once too did his tendency to justify himself break through, when he said, "In Christ Jesus, I have reason to be proud of my work for God.... What Christ has wrought through me to win obedience from the Gentiles by word and deed, by the power of signs and wonders, by the power of the Holy Spirit"; but even then he disclaimed personal credit.

Instead, there is a calmness, a magisterial confidence in this letter to Rome, the longest he wrote, which distinguishes it from those to Galatia and Corinth.

It contains some of his profoundest, most difficult writing and much of his most beautiful. The subject of great commentaries from Origen to Barth, of thousands of pages of exposition and meditation, its every word examined under theological, philosophical, and textual microscopes, it has been also one of the world's decisive books. It formed the seedbed of Augustine's faith and Luther's Reformation. It was reading Luther's *Preface to the Epistle to the Romans* that caused John Wesley's heart to feel strangely warmed. He wrote that he "did trust in Christ, Christ alone, for salvation; and an assurance was given me that He had taken away *my* sins, even *mine*, and saved *me* from the law of sin of death."

Paul's words were first heard by one Tertius, his scribe for this letter. With greetings and preliminaries over, the theme rang out in the room at

Corinth where they worked: "I am not ashamed of the Gospel: it is the power of God for salvation to everyone who has faith, to the Jew first and also to the Greek. For in it the righteousness of God is revealed through faith for faith ..." and Paul announced his text, a quotation from the minor prophet Habakkuk; six words in Greek that have become familiar in six words of English: "The just shall live by faith," or "He who is right with God by faith shall live."

Paul then showed that man has an instinctive awareness of God and has rejected and excluded him. In consequence, pagans have slipped into the moral cesspool that lay all around Paul in Corinth. Nor could Jews, with all the privileges stemming from God's revelation of Himself, and their pride in their destiny as His people adopt a smug superiority toward the pagan, for Jews too had stubborn and rebellious hearts, which God would punish. Paul cannot offer a condoning God. His burden as a missionary stems not only from delight in displaying the excellencies of Christ but also from crystal-clear, terrifying awareness that judgment will come on all men and women because all have sinned. The whole world is accountable to God, whether consciences excuse or accuse, "on that day when, according to my Gospel, God judges the secrets of men by Christ Jesus."

"But now"—and this was the part Paul loved—"God's way of putting men right with Himself has been revealed.... God puts men right through their faith in Jesus Christ." All have sinned and come short of God's glory, but Jew and pagan alike are justified by receiving His grace as a gift, "by being redeemed in Christ Jesus, who was appointed by God to sacrifice His life so as to win reconciliation through faith." God's justice is thus made plain, in the past by His overlooking sins, in the present "by showing positively that He is just, and that He justifies everyone who believes in Jesus. So what becomes of our boasts? There is no room for them!"

Paul devoted a long section, with special reference to the Jews, to elaborate his thesis that forgiveness cannot be earned; a man or woman can only be "accepted as righteous" by believing "in Him who raised Jesus our Lord from the dead—Jesus who was put to death for our sins and raised to life to justify us."

And thus Paul reached the first great autobiographical passage of the treatise: "Therefore, since we are justified by faith we have peace with God through our Lord Jesus Christ. Through Him we have obtained access by faith into this grace in which we stand, and we rejoice in our hope of sharing the glory of God. More than that, we rejoice in our sufferings, knowing that suffering produces endurance, and endurance produces character, and character produces hope, and hope does not disappoint us, because God's love has been poured into our hearts through the Holy Spirit which has been given to us. While we were yet helpless, at the right time God died for the ungodly. Why, one will hardly die for a *righteous* man! Though perhaps for a *good* man one will dare to die. But God shows His love for us in that *while we were yet sinners* Christ died for us...."

After a discourse on the origin of sin, Paul turned to a topic that had exercised him grievously ever since he wrote to Galatia and that Corinthian problems had made the more urgent: the answer to backsliding, how the Christian may overcome the sin that continues to trouble him. He proceeded to expound to the Romans at considerable length his conviction that they should treat the pre-Christian self as dead and realize that a "resurrection life" was created in them when they believed. He switched metaphors and told them to look at themselves as no longer slaves under orders to sin but slaves of Jesus. Then Paul bared his soul, admitting, "I fail to carry out the things I want to do, and I find myself doing the very thing I hate"—until he cried, "Who shall deliver me? I thank God through Jesus Christ our Lord!"

After that he could expand with zest on the glorious fact that "if the Spirit of Him who raised Jesus from the dead is living in you, then He who raised Jesus from the dead will give life to your own mortal bodies through His Spirit in you. So there is no necessity for us to obey our unspiritual selves or live unspiritual lives." Anyone who does not have the Spirit of Christ "does not belong to Him. But if Christ is in you ..." and here Paul warmed to the theme that was his favorite after the cross, the marvel of "Christ in you": how Christ's Spirit leads, takes away fear, gives and directs the urge to pray, and creates a consciousness "that we are children of God."

Paul's rapture at the glory of the life with Christ, now and in the hereafter, mounted in tempo and glowing language until from the depth of his own experience he cried, "What then shall we say to this? If God is for us, who is against us? He who did not spare His own Son but gave Him up for us all, will He not also give us all things with Him? Who shall bring any charge against God's elect? It is God who justifies; who is to condemn? Is it Christ Jesus who died, yes, who was raised from the dead, who is at the right hand of God, who indeed intercedes for us? Who shall separate us from the love of Christ? Shall tribulation, or distress, or persecution, or famine, or nakedness, or peril, or sword? ... No, in all these things we are more than conquerors through Him who loved us. For I am sure that neither death, nor life, nor angels, nor principalities, nor powers, nor height, nor depth, nor anything else in all creation, will be able to separate us from the love of God in Christ Jesus our Lord."

In a later section of the letter Paul urged the Romans to worship God by a manner of life worthy of people whose minds had been renewed, not modeling themselves on the behavior of the world around them. And once again he revealed, if unconsciously, many features of his own character. As when he wrote to the Thessalonians during his first stay in Corinth, his exhortations needed only to be adjusted to a slightly different focus to provide a pen portrait of himself.

The Paul of Corinth AD 57 was determined to use every spiritual gift up to the very limit of his faith, which, too, he recognized as a gift of God. He worked for the Lord "with untiring effort and with great earnestness of spirit," keeping the inward fires well stoked. He was steady in times of distress and gloriously happy in prospect of the future. Prayer was as natural to him as breathing. He was a hospitable, generous man; Paul loved to help people, was cheerful, not doing his acts of kindness sanctimoniously, grudgingly, or smugly. His love was genuine, unsimulated, and he had a marked touch of sympathy, rejoicing with those who rejoiced, weeping with those who wept. Nor did he choose his company with an eye to class, wealth, or position; the humblest Christian found him ready to walk out of his way to do a good deed or share an experience, and Paul had a gift for counting every person as better than himself. He loved his fellow Christians and was indeed a lovable man, despite any rough edges. He counted it most important to live harmoniously with fellow believers.

As to non-Christian Jews and pagans, Paul did his utmost to live at peace with them however much they disliked him. He hated evil and would not let mockery, discouragement, the malice of antagonists, or impostors loosen his grip on what he knew to be good. Instead he blessed his persecutors and prayed for them, as the Lord Jesus had instructed in the Sermon on the Mount, which he virtually quoted. Paul repaid evil with good: feeding his enemy, giving him drink if thirsty, not seeking revenge but leaving the Lord to look after the question of just recompense.

"Do not be overcome by evil, but overcome evil with good." Paul's aim was to be so full of Christ that no room was left for the un-Christlike, in himself or in anyone around.

More than anything else, this letter was Paul's manifesto for the Christian life.

PART FOUR

TO CAESAR YOU
WILL GO

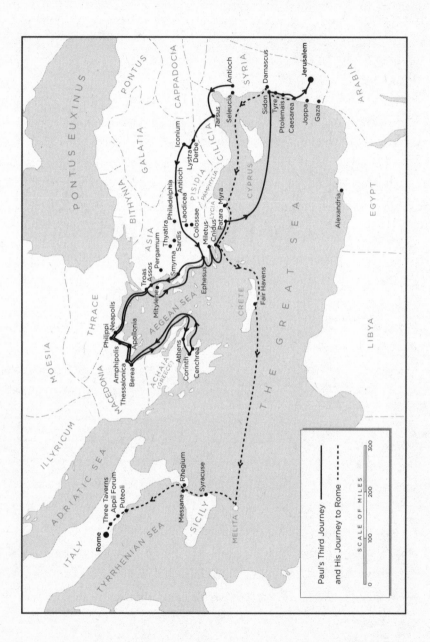

Paul's Third Journey ——— and His Journey to Rome - - - - - -

SCALE OF MILES
0   100   200   300

TWENTY-NINE

FACING THE FUTURE

While writing to Rome, Paul ranged in his mind over an acute distress of the past twenty-five years: Why should Jews as a nation reject Jesus, refusing to acknowledge Him as their Messiah, the Christ?

Paul had debated in himself and among friends whether God had rejected the Jews. He concluded forcefully that this was not so, in that he and many other Jews were Christians. On the other hand, if the Jews had flocked as a race and nation to the standard of the risen Jesus, the Gentiles might always have taken second place in the Christian church. In the letter to the Romans, Paul described good coming out of the evil of the Jews' refusal and acknowledged the unsearchable depth of wisdom in God's plan: When the Gentiles have been brought into the kingdom, the Jews will follow in a yet more glorious day.

But he could not quite swallow this delay. Not only did he continue to love his own race; but this love reached a pitch of extraordinary intensity that could only be compared with the weeping of Jesus as He looked across at the temple from the Mount of Olives or His sigh on another occasion, "O Jerusalem, Jerusalem, how often would I have gathered your children together as a hen gathers her brood under her wings, and you would not!" Paul uttered his own longing in terms that, in the context of what Christ meant to him, are almost unbelievable: "I am speaking the truth in Christ. I am not lying; my conscience bears me witness in the Holy Spirit, that I have great sorrow and increasing anguish in my heart. For I could wish that I myself were accursed and *cut off from Christ* for the sake of my brethren, my kinsmen by race.... My heart's desire and prayer to God for them is that they may be saved."

He regarded his coming return to Jerusalem with the Collection as a last opportunity to demonstrate his love and to declare Christ to his own people, perhaps before a vast concourse, before going west. He was aware of danger there. He appealed to the Romans, "by our Lord Jesus Christ and by the love of the Spirit, to strive together with me in your prayers to God on my behalf, that I may be delivered from the unbelievers in Judea, and that my service for Jerusalem be acceptable to the saints."

Paul had intended to take passage as before on a pilgrim ship from Cenchreae to reach Jerusalem for Passover. Corinthian Jews learned his plans and plotted accordingly: All the sailors in a pilgrim ship would be Jews; sailing at night at the time of new moon, the decks unlit except for navigation lights, Paul was to be tricked into coming to the gunwale. A stunning blow, man overboard, no cry raised....

Paul got wind of the plot. He had no intention of dying in a corner. He decided to miss Passover and go overland through Macedonia and sail across to Troas. Troas would be a rendezvous. For at Paul's request, each important church had selected their representatives who should accompany him and deliver the money to the Jerusalem sick and poor, and thus display the essential unity of the worldwide church. Timothy of Lystra and Gaius of Derbe represented Galatia, Aristarchus and Secundus were the Thessalonians, and Sopater the Berean. Trophimus and Tychicus, both Greeks, would come from the province of Asia.

Paul and his friends walked north through the unforgettable Greek springtime on roads bordered by wild irises and roses, potentillas and poppies, and what later ages would call the Judas tree. But in each city, their foreboding of Jerusalem was intensified by the reaction of Christian leaders. Those who had the gift of interpreting the Spirit's foreknowledge were emphatic in warning Paul not to go up to Jerusalem.

At Philippi, having dispatched his traveling companions ahead, Paul spent Passover week with his Philippian friends. Then he and Luke sailed from the nearby port of Neapolis. If the winds had wafted him swiftly to

Europe after the vision in the night seven years before, they now seemed
to echo the Macedonian warnings. The voyage took five days instead of
two to reach Troas.

Here, in the upper part of a tenement house, the Christians gathered together
on the Saturday night, the last of Paul's visit. He had found a ship and his
party would be leaving next morning.

The little church of Troas, fruit of his two brief previous calls and of
the evangelization that had spread from Ephesus, evidently lacked a wealthy
member who could invite them to worship on his lawn. They were using the
attic, and were crushed in, every man and woman, and their children who
could not be left at home. Sweaty bodies made the air close, smoke curled
from the spouts of little vegetable-oil lamps; the room grew hot and stuffy,
for though the night temperature in April was moderate, Troas stood in a
sheltered, narrow coastal plain.

A young man called Eutychus had wedged himself on the windowsill and
listened fascinated as Paul unfolded mysteries of the faith. They had eaten a
light meal, their *agapē*, and later would break bread and sip the wine of the
Lord's Supper, the beginning of the Lord's Day.[23] Meanwhile, Paul and his
hearers equally were determined to use this last opportunity. But Eutychus
had put in a hard day's manual labor, for his pagan master knew nothing of
Sabbath rest, and as he listened, his head nodded despite himself. Midnight
came and went. All eyes were on Paul, and when Eutychus's head dropped
lower on his chest, none of the other youths noticed to prod him awake.
Paul's voice floated in and out until it was lost altogether.

Suddenly there was a crash and a commotion. Eutychus had fallen right
out of the window onto the narrow street below. It was not a deep drop, some
fifteen feet, but he fell hard. By the time Paul had followed the agonized
rush of the boy's friends and relations down the stairs, Luke had pronounced
Eutychus dead. They stepped aside for Paul. He knelt and pressed the body

close to his own, and those who knew their Scripture would recall that this is what both Elijah and Elisha did with young men who had died. Paul said, "Do not worry. He is alive!"

Whether Paul had consciously used a form of artificial respiration that revived the heartbeat before clinical death had supervened or was doing as the Spirit moved him without understanding cause and effect, Luke left open the question of miracle. Eutychus almost certainly remained unconscious for a time when they took him upstairs again, yet such was Paul's calm and confidence that they were able to resume while the boy lay recovering. Paul talked on and the people listened. They shared the bread and wine. They could not stop asking questions or hearing more of "the Word," until at break of day, without resting, he left.

"They took the boy away alive and were greatly encouraged." And it may be that the hymn Paul would quote in his circular letter to Asia (Ephesians) had its origin that night: "Awake, thou that sleepest, and arise from the dead, and Christ shall give thee light."

Paul had chosen a ship not scheduled to call at Ephesus. Hurrying to reach Jerusalem by Pentecost, he did not wish to be sucked into the affairs of the vigorous Ephesus church or risk provoking Jews or pagans into another uproar that might cause arrest and detention. He arranged that his party should go aboard while he went by road. The first leg of the journey was to Assos, about thirty miles by land and longer by sea as the ship must round Cape Lectrum. Very unusually, Paul insisted on walking alone; he had set off at dawn and could make it in a day at that time of year.

He wanted to face the future. He had been warned in every city that persecution and prison awaited him in Jerusalem. Should he accept these warnings as divine orders to turn on his tracks and go straight to Rome? Could he take what was coming to him in Judea? He climbed from the coastal plain into the low hills and walked southwest until the road turned east with the land. By midday, from this clifftop road, he had one of the superb panoramas of Asia Minor: On his right hand across the narrow strip of sapphire water lay a dark blue of hills, the island of Lesbos. Ahead, the white clouds of springtime made sun and shade dance. Far in the distance at the end of the gulf he could see more distant blue hills in which lay Pergamum. His heart could go out to the Christians there, and to Smyrna, Ephesus, and away to Colossae and Laodicea.

As he walked, he reached the final crisis of his life: whether to turn or to press forward. Undisturbed except by sheep with their bells, guard dogs to bark at him, and donkeys and a camel or two, he was able to learn his Master's will and reach the conclusion that would steady him through the tumults to follow.

For the last few hours of the walk, as the sun dropped, the light behind him was full on the fantastic rock of Assos, a great block of granite dominating city and countryside and crowned by a temple.[24] Out of sight at the bottom of the cliff lay the harbor with its breakwater. Here Luke and the others were already waiting, a little anxious that Paul should be out there alone.

When he reached them and went on board, they could see by his face that he was utterly at peace.

Luke's log of the voyage marks where they hove-to each evening when the wind dropped: off Mitylene, capital of Lesbos and once home of the poetess Sappho, whose poems gave rise to the word *lesbian*; off the island of Chios, a good run; then another good run to the western side of Samos, the large island southwest of Ephesus and birthplace of Pythagoras, the philosopher and mathematician, five hundred years before; and then, early on Thursday, April 28,[25] they slipped in past the great marble lions that marked the Miletus harbor, a losing rival to Ephesus yet still a fine port.

Finding that the captain wanted two or three days' wait, Paul leaped at the opportunity of seeing the Ephesian elders once more. A Christian of Miletus sped posthaste the fifty miles. To cross by water that afternoon to Priene, borrow a horse from a Christian, ride over the hills, wake up the Ephesus presbyters in the middle of the night, and get them somehow back to Miletus in about forty hours was an amazing effort, but the Ephesians were as eager as the messenger to drop all business at the moment's notice for Paul's sake.

They gathered in a Miletus house, and Luke was there to take down the speech and watch its effect.

"You yourselves know," Paul began, "from the first day I set foot in Asia, how I lived among you, serving the Lord the whole time with humility, with sorrows and trials which came on me because of the plots of the Jews. You know I kept back nothing that was good for you." He reminded them how in public and private, to Jews and Gentiles, he had urged repentance, and "trust in our Lord Jesus. And now, look, I am going to Jerusalem, driven by the Spirit. And what will happen to me there I know nothing, except that in every city the Holy Spirit makes plain that chains and rough treatment await me. But none of these things moves me! I do not count my life at any value to myself—provided I may finish my race nobly and fulfill the commission I received from the Lord Jesus, to 'give full witness to the Good News of the grace of God.'

"And now look: I know that none of you, among whom I have gone in and out proclaiming the kingdom, will ever see my face again! So I declare to you this day that I am absolved from responsibility for any man's blood, for I kept back nothing in proclaiming to you all the whole purpose of God. Be on guard, therefore, for yourselves and for all the flock of God, of which He has made you shepherds." Paul warned them, in words that surely derive from Jesus' warnings about the wolf that scatters the flock when the hireling flees because he does not care, that "after I am gone savage wolves will come in and not spare the flock." Even among these men in front of him some would "distort the truth, to induce disciples to break away and follow them. So be on guard, remembering how night and day over three years I did not cease counseling each one of you, with tears.

"And now I commend you to God and to His gracious word, which has power to build you up and give you your heritage among all who are dedicated to Him. I have not wanted anyone's money or clothes for myself;

you all know that these hands of mine earned enough for the needs of me and my companions. I showed you that it is our duty to help the weak in this way, by hard work, and that we should keep in mind the words of the Lord Jesus, who Himself said, 'Happiness lies more in giving than in receiving.'"[26]

Already tears were on some of their faces. Paul knelt, and they knelt with him. He prayed in words too intimate for Luke to record (he had probably used a medical shorthand to take down the speech), and when Paul stopped, the men of Ephesus sobbed unashamedly. They hugged him and kissed him, "sorrowing most of all," Luke realized, "because of the word he had spoken, that they should see his face no more."

They went together to the ship. The parting was hard. Luke said, "We tore ourselves away from them."

THIRTY

RIOT IN JERUSALEM

About a week later a somewhat similar scene occurred on a beach the other side of the Mediterranean, at Tyre on the Syrian coast.

They had sailed by way of Rhodes and changed from their coaster at a big port in southwestern Asia Minor to a large merchantman, which used the summer westerlies to cross the open sea south of Cyprus direct to Tyre. Here the captain needed a week to unload cargo. Paul and his party sought out the Christian disciples. Once more he was warned against going to Jerusalem, and he recognized that the local church leaders spoke "by the Spirit." He made no comment. Warm affection sprang up between the small group of Tyrian Christians and the nine or ten travelers, and when it came time to sail, all the men with their wives and children came to see them off. Tyre at that time was an offshore island connected to the mainland by a mole, on either side of which sandy beaches had formed. Before the travelers rowed out to their ship, everybody knelt on the sand under the cloudless Mediterranean sky for prayer.

The merchantman sailed twenty miles and put in for a day at Ptolemais (Acre). They again called on the local Christians. The next morning another short run round the headland of Carmel completed the voyage to Caesarea, capital and principal port of the province of Judea, where the procurator's palace, with which Paul was to become so well acquainted, may have caught his eye among the sun-drenched marble buildings as he landed. At first, there were no more warnings. Paul and his companions were welcomed as guests of Philip, the notable evangelist and once fellow deacon with the murdered Stephen, whose influence had spread into Africa far up the Nile. Philip had four unmarried daughters; the family later migrated to Hierapolis near Colossae where the daughters were mines of information about the earliest days of Christianity. Each also had the gift of prophecy. But they remained silent about Paul's future.

Some days afterward, the famous prophet Agabus arrived from the hill country. Agabus, whose prophecy of famine when he visited Antioch had been the immediate cause of Paul's return to Jerusalem after the Hidden Years, suddenly pulled Paul's tasseled cord off his waist. The travelers and Philip's family looked on with a premonition that prophetic warning, by symbol and word, was imminent. Agabus squatted on the ground. He tied the cord round his feet and hands. "Thus says the Holy Spirit: So shall the Jews at Jerusalem bind the man who owns this girdle and deliver him into the hands of the Gentiles!"

Agabus had drawn no conclusion or moral; he had stated Paul's future. Luke and others could bear it no longer. "We and those who were there begged him not to go up to Jerusalem." They wept and pleaded. Why shouldn't Paul stay quietly at Caesarea while the rest of them carried the money to Jerusalem and returned, and they could then set out for Rome? They thought he was wrong to ignore the warnings. Many commentators in subsequent centuries have agreed, contrasting Paul's obstinacy now with his quick acceptance when forbidden by the Spirit to preach in Asia or enter Bithynia.

Their loud lamentation had an effect. Paul felt (to judge by the word he used) squeezed and pummeled like the washing under the wrists of a washerwoman. He knew that their urgings sprang from deep affection, from desire to protect him. Yet he had been sure, at the very least since the road to Assos, that the higher love of the Lord Jesus called him to Jerusalem. Maybe death there would exert the same decisive influence for Christ as had Stephen's death, perhaps be the linchpin in the reconciliation of Jew and Gentile, the reconciliation of Jews the world over to Christ. If, in passionate love for his people, Paul was ready to be "cut off from Christ" for their sake, he was certainly ready to die.

"What are you doing," cried Paul, "weeping and pummeling my heart? I am ready not only to be bound but to *die* in Jerusalem for the name of the Lord Jesus."

Luke recorded, "And so, as he would not be persuaded, we gave up the attempt, saying, 'The Lord's will be done.'"

The Caesarean Christians had arranged mules to carry the money bags of the Collection, and riding mules for Paul's party, and had sent ahead to ensure lodging in a Jerusalem overcrowded with pilgrims for Pentecost: They had arranged a stay with one of the earliest disciples, a Cypriot named Mnason, whose background made him sympathetic toward the ex-pagan Christians whom many Jerusalem Christians would despise. All the way up the sixty miles into the hills the bends of the road disclosed parties of pilgrims drawn from every province of the empire, from Persia, from Arabia and the southern incense countries, from north Africa and the upper Nile, everyone zealous to display devotion to the temple and the Law of his fathers, and rejoice at the Festival of First Fruits.

After a happy welcome at Mnason's, the Christians from Europe and Asia Minor were eager to enjoy the sights. As Paul observed the beauties of Jerusalem and the outer wall of the temple, he was seen in the crowded streets by some of his bitterest enemies, Jews of Asia, who recognized Trophimus of Ephesus too. If Paul took any of his friends except the circumcised Timothy into the temple's court of the Gentiles, he would not have let them step through the low barrier, the "wall of partition," past warning notices that if a Gentile went farther and defiled the holy courts, he would have only himself to blame for his death.

The next day Paul and the accredited representatives of the Gentile churches were formally received by James the Lord's brother and the Jerusalem elders to hand over the gift of the alms. Peter and the other apostles were abroad spreading the gospel; Thomas, according to tradition, had already reached northern India. The ascetic James continued to maintain a cautious policy so that the priests and rulers of the nation should tolerate those Jews, now a large number, who acknowledged Jesus as Messiah while observing the traditions of their ancestors. Most of the elders were convinced that Paul did his best to destroy this policy wherever he went. Paul knew their estimate of him and for months had been nervous lest they should not accept the gift in the spirit in which Europe and Asia offered it.

Luke noted the grave kiss of peace between Paul and each elder; next, the delegates brought forward their moneybags. Then Paul narrated, detail by detail, "the things that God had done among the Gentiles through his ministry." It was a missionary speech with a plain implication, that the elders of the overweighted Jerusalem congregation should spur their people to go out and follow up the initiative won by Paul among the Gentiles, until there should be one flock under the one Shepherd.

The reaction was disappointing. The elders made appropriate noises of praise to God and turned promptly to a much more pressing affair.

"Brother," they addressed Paul, "you see how many thousands of converts we have among the Jews, all of them staunch upholders of the Law. Now, they have been given certain information about you: it is said you teach all the *Jews* in the Gentile world to turn their backs on Moses, telling them to give up circumcising their children and following our way of life." The elders did not venture to suggest they believed the calumny, nor were they concerned with Gentiles, for the letter sent by the Council of Jerusalem had settled that question. But they felt some action by Paul, rather than a pronouncement of their own, must remove the misconception.

"What is to be done therefore? You must do as we tell you." Paul must follow the practice whereby rich men showed their love of the Law by paying the expenses and sharing the vigil of poor men. (They had four under a Nazarite vow who had incurred ritual defilement but were too poor to buy sacrificial birds and animals to purge the defilement and complete the vow.) "Then everyone will know that there is nothing in the stories they were told about you, but that you are a practicing Jew and keep the Law yourself."

Paul could scarcely be more dashed. Since they knew he had no money of his own, they must have insinuated he should use part of the Collection; yet

Europe and Asia had hardly supposed their ill-afforded present would be used to discharge ceremonial vows. Besides, he was being invited to dissemble. The elders openly intended to exploit his action to assert that Paul kept the Law. Yet he did not. He honored it; he was ready to be like a Jew to the Jews and "put myself under that Law to win them, although I am not myself subject to it," and he had taken a Nazarite vow himself. But this would be acting a lie.

And yet such was his love for the Jews that he agreed to the elders' plan, hoping it might somehow help more Jews to believe in Christ. "Let love be without dissimulation," he had recently urged the Romans. Never do evil that good might come, he had taught; yet now he would reject his own advice. In no way was his love for the Jews more evident than in this error of judgment at Jerusalem.

Paul immediately left the home of Mnason to live in one of the inner courts of the temple, with four men he had never seen before, for the last two or three days of their vigil. He paid the money, joined the rituals, kept the fasts. And all along he knew he was living in the very mouth of the lion. The crowds of pilgrims who milled through the temple in these days following the feast were at their most excitable; not many years earlier they had risen in fury when a bored Roman soldier looking down from the citadel of Antonia had gestured obscenely. Jews from Asia and Europe who loathed Paul's very face might see him and resent his presence in the sacred interior of the temple.

The purification drew to a close. The next morning the four men would have their heads shaved and the hair burned at the sacrificial fire. Paul would return to Mnason's home and soon embark for Rome.

The continual traffic of pilgrims around him in a temple and city pulsating with national and religious pride, together with his memory of prophetic warnings, kept him alert for danger. It came suddenly. The Jews from Asia who had recognized the ex-pagan Ephesian in the streets of Jerusalem saw

Paul from a distance in the inner temple courts with four men and jumped to the conclusion that they were Greeks like Trophimus.

"Men of Israel, help!" they yelled. "This is the man who preaches to everyone everywhere against our people, against the Law and against this place! And now he has defiled the Holy Place by bringing Greeks into the temple!"

Those within earshot rushed to lynch a renegade and defiler, until a milling mass swirled about Paul. Then they were dragging him out of the sacred precinct where no blood might be shed. Pummeled, torn, with screams of frenzy in his ears, Paul was borne down the steps, every yard bringing a bruise. He heard the great doors of the temple clang, heard the roar of the mob swelling. Now if ever was the time to prove his own words, "Rejoice in the Lord always. The peace of God, which passes understanding, shall keep your heart and mind."

He remained on his feet, but it was a losing struggle. Soon he would be on the ground and torn limb from limb. Someone was twisting an arm; one ear was split already. His eyes were bruised and swelling. Was he to die without being able to say one word?

He heard above the uproar the metallic clank of soldiers at the double on the flat roof of the portico. The riot had been immediately reported by Roman guards to Claudius Lysias, the garrison commander or *chiliarch* (colonel of a thousand), who at once saw from his tower that all Jerusalem was converging on the temple in that blind instinct that reacts to outrage without knowing the cause. A serious civil disturbance was building up. He took command of the operation himself. With the precision of long training, two hundred men quickly marched out of the citadel of Antonia, which dominated the north-west corner of the temple, down the steps onto the portico roofs designed for ease of maneuver, and straight to the center of trouble.

The crowd ceased lynching Paul and made way for the soldiers. In the last riot they had resisted, and in the ensuing fight and panic, thousands had been trampled to death. Claudius Lysias came up, arrested Paul, and ordered his wrists clapped in double-chained irons. Then he inquired who Paul was and what he had done.

The howling made inquiry impossible. Lysias ordered his men to take Paul into the citadel. This infuriated the crowd. As the soldiers began to escort him, with Lysias at his side, across the court toward the main stairs of Antonia, the mob yelled, "Kill him! Kill him!" and pressed on the circle of spears and shields, until by the bottom of the steps Paul had to be literally carried up the stone stairway. Lysias had decided the man must be the illiterate Egyptian who had recently led a tragic uprising, inducing thousands to carry hidden daggers and stab political opponents by stealth, then to camp on the Mount of Olives in expectation of the miraculous collapse of the city walls and the defeat of the Romans; the military had routed the armed rabble, hundreds of survivors had been crucified or sent to the galleys, but the Egyptian escaped. Surely he had now returned, and the Jews were venting their rage on the foreigner who had duped their sons.

At the top of the steps, with the howling mob below and with peace and quiet, through imprisonment, a few feet ahead, Paul said to Lysias in Greek; "May I have a word with you?"

Lysias was surprised to hear this panting, bleeding little specimen of matted humanity speak Greek and asked if he were not the Egyptian. Paul, who could detect by Lysias's accent that he was Greek by race, replied, "I am a Jew, from Tarsus in Cilicia, a citizen of 'no mean city.'"

Lysias was even more surprised. The battered criminal must be a scholar and a gentlemen; he had just escaped death by inches yet had the wit to quote a tag of Euripides. When Paul added, "Please let me speak to the people," Lysias gave permission.

Paul turned and raised one bruised, chained hand. Lysias was yet more astonished: Paul's gesture quieted the crowd. The yells died to murmurs.

Paul began to speak in Aramaic. Lysias would have known a little of it but not enough to follow the speech. He had only Paul's word that he was no rebel aiming to rouse the Jews, but Lysias did not interfere. He could marvel to hear a man whose head must throb and every joint ache deliver a powerful extemporaneous speech that held this blood-lusting crowd enthralled, but Lysias could not know of Paul's tactful choice of words, his sensitivity to this audience, which he was determined to conciliate and then to win. With blood trickling from broken lips, Paul was making one of his most winsome speeches, even if it failed.

"Brethren and fathers," cried Paul. "Hear the defense which I now make before you." The time-honored, respectful formula, together with the realization that he spoke in Aramaic, brought total silence.

"I am a Jew! Born at Tarsus in Cilicia but brought up in this city at the feet of Gamaliel, educated according to the strict manner of the Law of our fathers, being zealous for God. As you all are this day! I persecuted this Way unto death, binding and delivering to prison both men and women, as the high priest and the whole council of elders can bear me witness. From them I received letters to the brethren, and I journeyed to Damascus."

Paul told the story of his conversion. And they listened. At last he was preaching to a vast crowd of Jews. The opportunity had come and he had seized it. All pain was forgotten as he described his sudden experience on the Damascus Road and echoed the words that had transformed him: "He said to me, 'I am Jesus of Nazareth whom you are persecuting.'" Paul told of the blindness, of Ananias, "a devout man according to the Law, well spoken of by all the Jews living there," of his baptism, until he reached what must have been the hardest part for them to accept. He had more to say, but first he explained why he went to the Gentiles; he spoke of his trance in Jerusalem, recounting his argument with the Lord when forbidden to preach in Jerusalem. "And I said, 'Lord, they themselves know that in every synagogue I imprisoned and beat those who believed in You. And when the blood of Stephen Your martyr was shed, I also was standing by and approving, and keeping the garments of those who killed him.'

"And He said to me, 'Depart; for I will send you far away to the Gentiles—'"

The word struck like a match in dry straw. Paul's speech was drowned in yells of "Kill him!" "Away with him!" "He's not fit to live!"

The crowd surged onto the stairway. Others farther back waved their cloaks or threw dust. With the whole place in a frenzy, Lysias pulled Paul inside the citadel.

Puzzled, not knowing what he could report to his superiors, his respect for Paul destroyed by the mob's violence against him, Lysias gave an order to a centurion and walked swiftly away to his quarters.

THIRTY-ONE

THE TORTURE CHAMBER

The citadel seemed dark in contrast to the strong sunlight. The noise died as they marched Paul to the lower floor, on down narrower stairs into vaulted cellars lit by flickering torches, through a low archway and into the torture chamber.

They removed his chains, stripped him, then bound his ankles to a bar and tied his wrists to long thongs, which they threw over a beam above and slightly ahead of him. They pulled on the thongs until his arms were stretched high above his head and his whole body, leaning forward, hung taut. The position was painful in itself and every blow would fall on tightened nerves and muscles. Paul was not bent over a whipping post for punishment, because the aim was the extraction of information; someone would stand near his mouth, expecting between screams to hear him confess his crimes.

By now Paul knew what was intended. He was to be given the dreaded *flagellum*, a murderous scourge of heavy rawhide loaded with jagged bits of zinc, iron, and bone. Whether to force evidence out of slaves and those without rank or as the prelude to crucifixion, which Jesus had endured, the weight and lacerating of the scourge could kill a man. A survivor would have torn nerves and damaged kidneys, and might even be out of his mind.

If Paul lived through it, he would never preach again.

When the centurion in charge stepped forward to check that all was ready, Paul said, "Is it legal for you to flog a Roman citizen, and one who has not been convicted?"

The centurion acted instantly. He hurried off to find Lysias. Paul remained stretched from the beam, but the husky slave who held the *flagellum* laid it down, and the clerk who must note agonized gasps of confession stepped back. The garrison commander's alarm may be gauged from the speed with which the centurion came.

Looking at the naked little Jew in front of him, Lysias had a moment's doubt when he saw the scars from whip, rod, and stones.

"Tell me, *are* you a Roman citizen?"

"Yes."

Lysias remembered heavy bribes to intermediaries. "It cost me a great sum to acquire this citizenship."

"But it was mine by birth," said Paul.

Lysias was very distinctly worried. There might be powerful relatives who would cause a fuss and ruin him for tying up Paul to be examined under the lash. He was immediately taken down. The husky slave and the clerk disappeared quickly, for all who were involved could suffer if Paul took proceedings. Paul was helped into his clothes and taken for the night to a cell away from the vermin that infested the general dungeons and left unbound except for the usual light chain.

Lysias still had nothing to report to explain the riot. Therefore, the next day he exercised his right as a military governor of Jerusalem to order an emergency session of the Sanhedrin to investigate what charge lay against Paul. He had already released him from chains and now conducted him personally to the court, as if to emphasize that Roman citizenship was more honorable than Jewish. Then he withdrew from the Hall of Polished Stones and waited outside.

Paul stood in the precise spot where Stephen had stood. The seventy-one judges included a few from the time of Stephen's trial. The president was Ananias ben Nedebaeus, one of the most rapacious men ever to disgrace the office of high priest. Paul did not know him by sight, and the damage done by the mob's violence made sharp vision difficult. It had not, however, reduced the strength of personality he could exert through his eyes. He gripped the council with the intense gaze that had quelled Elymas the Cypriot long ago, and thereby he seized the initiative and opened the proceedings himself.

"My brothers," he began, "I have lived all my life, and still live today, with a perfectly clear conscience before God. I—"

The president barked an order. One of the court ushers struck Paul a stinging blow on the mouth.

The old Paul flared at such totally illegal behavior. Forgetting his own teaching, "When we are cursed, we bless, when insulted we answer with kind words," he shouted at the indistinct figure of the president: "God will strike you, you whitewashed wall! You sit there to judge me according to the Law; yet you break the Law by ordering them to strike me!"

The ushers were horrified. "You are insulting God's high priest!"

Paul was abashed. "My brothers," he said mildly, "I did not realize he was the high priest. Scripture says, 'You must not speak evil of the ruler of your people.'"

Balked of orderly argument, Paul made a move that was brilliant if reckless. He knew the Sanhedrin was divided between Pharisees, who believed in a resurrection at the Last Day and in the existence of angels and spiritual beings, and the party of the Sadducees, who held rationalist, materialist views. Paul was sure that many of the Pharisees would believe in Jesus if only they saw Him as he, a Pharisee, had seen Him on the Damascus Road; belief in the risen Jesus was the only honest conclusion for a true Pharisee.

He called out to the Sanhedrin: "Brothers! I am a Pharisee and the son of Pharisees. It is for our hope in the resurrection of the dead that I am on trial!"

At that the Sanhedrin erupted, just as it had erupted at Stephen's cry, but instead of rushing at the prisoner, the judges began to argue furiously among themselves. "We find nothing wrong in this man," shouted Pharisees. "Suppose a spirit or an angel has spoken to him!" Sadducees, who included the high priest, shouted back angry denials until the judges came to blows, some even leaping into the well of the court, intending to seize or to protect Paul's person. Lysias heard the commotion, feared that Paul would be torn to pieces between them, and immediately ordered a squad into the hall. They rescued him forcibly and hurried him back to the citadel.

Lysias was no closer to a resolution. He still had nothing to report. Paul too felt frustrated. His attempts to testify about the Lord to his countrymen had failed and now he might never see Rome. As the day wore on and the patch of June sky through the prison bars turned from azure to red, and soon to stars, he slipped into one of his moods of melancholy. His friends had not been allowed into the castle. He felt alone—except that he could pray.

Suddenly, as in Corinth at another time of uncertainty, as during other crises, he saw the Lord Jesus. The Spirit, whose constant presence Paul had often mentioned in his letters, revealed Himself for a moment of time to Paul's eyes and ears, standing right beside him: "Courage! You have given your witness to Me here in Jerusalem, and you must bear witness in Rome too."

Paul did not doubt that he had seen Jesus, nor that the words would come true. The peace of God flooded into his heart and mind. He knew for a certainty what he had taught as a certainty: that all things work together for good for those who love God and are called according to His purpose.

The next morning the way was opened unexpectedly when the guards brought a visitor, his sister's son, whom Paul probably had not seen since a child. This young man, who would have been brought up to regard his turncoat uncle as dead to the family, had evidently reached a position of influence sufficient to gain admittance to the citadel. Almost certainly he had been present, unknown to Paul, in the Hall of Polished Stones, and possibly in the crowd who had heard Paul's unfinished oration from the stairs. Admiration had combined with thickness of blood to override the prejudice of years. What is more, the arrival of the nephew seemed to have been the first step in a reconciliation that included the release of the patrimony, which the family had kept from Paul. From this point in the story he had money at his disposal again; in fact, he was sufficiently well-off to be rated a likely source of bribes.

More immediately the nephew's intervention forced the situation. He reported a murder plot. Whether he had been present at its hatching by over forty young zealots or in attendance when the Sanhedrin approved it in secret session, the nephew risked his future, possibly his life, by betraying the plot. A formal request, he told Paul, would be made the next day that Lysias should send him down to the Sanhedrin for further questioning. He would be ambushed on the way. Some of the zealots inevitably might die in the scuffle with the escort, but all had taken a solemn religious oath neither to eat nor to drink until Paul was dead: By killing him they would do God service.

Paul did not hesitate. He called a centurion and told him to take the nephew to Lysias. The centurions were already attached to Paul beyond the claims of his Roman citizenship and hurried to do his bidding. Lysias too showed an immediate kindness, taking the young man by the hand where he could talk without being overheard by the staff. Lysias thanked the young man, warning him to preserve complete secrecy, and then took immediate action.

That night a strong force of two hundred infantry, two hundred spearmen, and seventy cavalry marched out through the new walls. In the center of the cavalry, muffled more for disguise than against the cool mountain air of June, Paul rode on horseback. By the next morning, they were at Antipatris at the foot of the hills. The conspirators had been outwitted. The road led on through the cultivated plain peopled mostly with Gentiles, and the infantry could therefore return to Jerusalem, leaving the seventy cavalry to escort Paul to the praetorium at Caesarea, where he was immediately brought before the procurator of Judea, Antonius Felix, successor to Pontius Pilate.

The officer commanding the escort handed Felix a letter from Lysias. Its gist was later given to Luke by one of the clerks, or published in the government gazette, and Luke incorporated it in Acts without comment. His sense of irony must have derived considerable amusement from what was claimed and what was tactfully omitted.

"Claudius Lysias to His Excellency the Governor Felix, greeting. This man was seized by the Jews, and was about to be killed by them, when I came upon them with the soldiers and rescued him, having learned that he was a Roman citizen. And desiring to know the charge on which they accused him, I brought him down to their Council. I found that he was accused about questions of their law, but charged with nothing deserving death or imprisonment. And when it was disclosed to me that there would be a plot against the man, I sent him to you at once, ordering his accusers also to state before you what they have against him."

Felix formally asked his province, since if he were from a native state he must be referred to the appropriate jurisdiction. On learning that Paul was Cilician, Felix remanded him in custody, in the praetorium built by Herod the Great.

The high priest hurried down to Caesarea despite his great age and in his entourage brought an advocate named Tertullus. Paul's friends had probably followed too so that Luke was present in court for the hearing. He must have derived further ironic amusement from noting the florid flattery of the opening speech of the prosecution, for Tertullus knew perfectly well that since the appointment of Felix in AD 52, Judea had suffered widespread bloodshed from the insurrections he provoked and from the increase in political murders after he had arranged for the ex–high priest Jonathan to be assassinated in the temple itself. Felix's greed was notorious. He had been born a slave, had risen to power on the shoulders of his brother the freedman Pallas, a favorite of Claudius, and his character is well summed up by Tacitus: "He exercised the power of a king with the mind of a slave."

Tertullus puffed out his cheeks and hitched his robes in the immemorial manner of advocates with weak cases.

"Your Excellency," he began, "we owe it to you that we enjoy unbroken peace. It is due to your provident care that, in all kinds of ways and in all sorts of places, improvements are being made for the good of this province. And now, not to take up too much of your time, I crave your indulgence for a brief statement of our case." First, Paul had been found "a perfect pest," fomenting unrest among Jews throughout the civilized world. Second, he was a ringleader of the sect of Nazarenes, the implication being that the Romans did not legally recognize this cult. Third, by attempting to profane the temple, he had broken the Jewish domestic law that Rome promised to enforce. "But we arrested him—" Tertullus ended rather lamely by saying that if Felix examined the prisoner, he would soon see the force of the charges.

The high priest's party supported counsel vigorously, but the Asian Jews who had sparked the whole affair were conspicuous by their absence. Felix called the defendant, appearing in person.

Paul showed himself entirely at ease, able to offer appropriate courtesies without flattery and to argue with a legal skill that had not withered in the long years since he had practiced.

"I know that you have administered justice over this nation for many years," Paul said, "and I can therefore speak with confidence in my own defense. As you can verify for yourself, it is no more than twelve days since I went up to Jerusalem on pilgrimage, and it is not true that they ever found me arguing with anyone or stirring up the mob, either in the temple, in the synagogue, or about the town." Paul had deftly shifted the locality of the charge from the "civilized world" to Jerusalem only. Even there they could not prove their accusations.

"What I do admit to you is this: It is according to the Way, which they describe as a sect, that I worship the God of my ancestors, retaining my belief in all points of the Law and what is written in the prophets; and I hold the same hope in God as they do, that there will be a resurrection of good men and bad men alike. In these things I, as much as they, do my best to keep a clear conscience at all times before God and man."

Paul described the events leading up to the outbreak in the temple. He had brought alms for his nation, and he had been ritually purified. "There

was no crowd involved, and no disturbance. But some Jews from Asia—"
Paul broke off in the middle of the sentence, and must have looked around
the courtroom meaningfully. "*They* ought to be here before you and make
an accusation if they have anything against me. Or else let these men themselves"—indicating the high priest and his followers—"say what wrongdoing
they found when I stood before the council, except this one thing that I cried
out while standing among them: 'It is for our hope in the resurrection of the
dead I am on trial before you this day!'"

Paul closed his case.

Felix had already made some investigation of the Christian Way and was
probably aware also of Gallio's decision. He could recognize that the Jews
had no case under Roman law and that he should acquit. However, he was
not averse to keeping the high priest guessing and less disposed to be trouble-
some; Felix was a prevaricator by nature. He adjourned the court on the thin
excuse that he would reserve judgment until Lysias came down.

He ordered Paul to be kept in open arrest and gave particular instructions
that friends should be allowed to visit as much as they liked and bring him
all he needed.

THIRTY-TWO

KING, QUEEN, AND GOVERNOR

The wet Mediterranean winter gave way to a hot summer, made bearable for Paul by sea breezes and by permission to walk on the shore or where he wished, while chained lightly to a soldier. Aristarchus of Thessalonica accepted the status of prisoner in order to serve Paul. Timothy had left for missionary travel in Europe or Asia Minor; now about thirty years old, he still retained some of his youthful timidity but had Paul's single-mindedness. The other delegates had returned to Asia and Europe too, except Luke, who took the opportunity for a thorough investigation of the oral and written evidence for the life, death, and resurrection of Jesus and for subsequent events.

It must have been encouraging to Paul each time Luke arrived back in Caesarea after long talks with Mary, the Lord's mother, or Mary Magdalene if she still lived, or Zacchaeus and the once-blind beggar at Jericho; or as they sat together, accompanied by Paul's soldier, while Philip the Evangelist told of the early days after the coming of the Holy Spirit and described Stephen as he knew him, which Paul could confirm from a different angle. Some hold that the Epistle to the Hebrews was composed at this time. The epistle carries no signature and its authorship can never be determined. About 150 years after Paul's day, Clement of Alexandria stated that Paul wrote it in Hebrew and Luke translated it into the Greek, which survived; modern scholarship doubts that this version can be a translation. Clement's successor, Origen, believed Paul merely supervised the writing. Tertullian decided that Barnabas did it. Others held it to be the work of Apollos, a view held by Luther.

Whatever Paul did in these quiet years, he had at last an opportunity, though limited, for reaching his own race. He also had two potential converts of eminence right beside him. Procurator Felix had seduced a member of the Jewish royal family, the very young Herodian princess Drusilla, who divorced the king of Commagene to marry Felix as his third wife. Whether from a guilty conscience, as an adulteress and a Jewess who had broken the Law by marrying a Gentile or because she had a full ingredient of Herodian curiosity, Drusilla persuaded Felix to send for Paul in private audience.

Paul did not resent Felix's authority. He was not an anarchist. He had urged the Roman Christians, living uncomfortably close to Nero, to regard Caesar as God's servant whose authority had been given by God. Paul's recipe for changing governments was not to foment political revolution but to transform the hearts of rulers, and when Felix offered the opportunity, he went to it with a will. He talked freely about faith in Jesus Christ without fear of this slave-hearted governor who, like Pilate before him, supposed he had power to release or to condemn—even though in Paul's view, as in his Master's, he had no power except it were given him from above. Felix, with his political crimes and his lust, found that Paul's preaching cut too near the bone. Luke wrote, "As Paul went on discussing goodness, self-control, and the coming Day of Judgment, Felix trembled and said, 'That will do for the present; when I find it convenient, I will send for you again.'"

Drusilla lost interest, but Felix summoned him often, and if he groped toward repentance, he hoped too that Paul would bribe him, after which the case would be settled in Paul's favor. Paul, Luke, Aristarchus, and old Philip and his daughters must all have prayed for the procurator's conversion. But Felix was not to turn.

In the spring of 59, after a riot in Caesarea, Felix was recalled to Rome in disgrace. His brother's influence saved him from execution or enforced suicide, but Felix was never again employed in the public service. Before he left, he could easily have released Paul, but he wished to curry a few last crumbs of favor with Jewish leaders. At least he did not want to give them grounds on which to charge him with maladministration of the case. Mean to the last, he left Paul in custody.

The new procurator of Judea was Porcius Festus, a man of better background and higher principles, whose endeavors to rule the turbulent province broke his health: He would die in office after two years.

As soon as he had been installed at the beginning of July 59, Porcius Festus left Caesarea to visit Jerusalem. Inevitably, among many other matters, the high priest and the Sanhedrin raised the question of Paul. They assumed Festus would wish to ingratiate himself, and asked that the trial be held speedily, and in Jerusalem: the young zealots who had rashly vowed neither to eat nor to drink until they had killed Paul, and presumably had walked around for two years under a dispensation, would be waiting to ambush him in a *wadi* or a wood. Festus ruined the plan, probably quite unintentionally. He merely suited his own convenience when he refused to order Paul to Jerusalem and informed the Jewish authorities that they must appear in Caesarea. He promised to expedite the hearing.

After eight or ten days, Festus returned with his retinue to Caesarea and the next morning took the bench as chief justice of Judea. The first case was Paul's. The moment Paul entered, the Jews from Jerusalem converged on him in the pent-up fury of two years' frustration, restrained only by the presence of the procurator. At first they hardly conducted the case in a way likely to impress Festus, for they let it go right over his head. As Festus described the scene: "When confronted with him, his accusers did not charge him with any of the crimes I had expected; but they had some argument or other with him about their own religion and about a dead man called Jesus, whom Paul alleged to be alive." Later they steered the prosecution more on the lines of Tertullus's pomposities before Felix but called no witnesses; if Festus asked for legal proof, none was offered.

Paul simply denied there was a case to answer. "I have committed no offense whatever: against Jewish law; or the temple; or against Caesar."

Festus saw the force of the defense. But puzzled by the religious quarrel, and not averse to humoring his new subjects, he was ready to hand Paul over to the Sanhedrin. He addressed Paul: "Are you willing to go up to Jerusalem and stand trial on these charges before me there?"

Paul knew that even if he should reach Jerusalem alive, he could more easily be done away with once there. The Jews, however, had opened an escape route: had they restricted their charges to the local matter of his alleged profaning of the temple, he could hardly have refused to be tried in Jerusalem without implying that Festus could not protect him or would treat the accused less fairly there. But now the Jews had raised the far wider charge of fomenting disaffection throughout the civilized world. Both charges, the religious and the political, carried the death penalty; but even though the second was the graver, Paul elected to be tried on this, the political issue, which directly concerned the Romans.

Very deliberately, Paul answered Festus, "I am standing at Caesar's tribunal and this is where I should be tried. I have done the Jews no wrong, as you very well know. If I am guilty of committing any capital crime, I do not ask to be spared execution. But if there is no substance in the accusations these persons bring against me, no one has a right to surrender me to them. *I appeal to Caesar.*"

At that appeal, duly delivered in legal form, precedent demanded a short adjournment while the procurator consulted his advisers whether to give leave. A Roman citizen had an inalienable right of appeal to the emperor, a privilege not accorded other provincials, but a governor must decide whether the case had sufficient weight to be referred to that august court.

Paul's appeal, though unexpected by Festus, was no sudden decision. In the past two years, as the case dragged on, Paul had thought out his next step. He must go to Rome. This offered a way. Moreover, the ruling of Gallio—that Christianity was a recognized cult—might not hold much longer: Another governor could rule differently. The only certain freedom for the future was a favorable decision handed down by the supreme court in Rome, the emperor himself. The emperor was Nero. But the young Nero of AD 59, despite the dubious way in which he had gained the throne, still remained under the wise influence of Gallio's brother, Seneca, the greatest philosopher of the day. Neither Paul nor any provincial could forecast in 59 the awful degeneration of Nero into the despot whose name has been a byword for lust, cruelty, and bad government. As for the heavy cost involved in an appeal to Caesar, despite its being technically a free process, Paul did not trouble. God had supplied all his needs when wants were simple, and would continue, whether or not it was by the restoration of the patrimony.

All depended on Festus's willingness to grant Paul his right. After that, the wheels of justice would grind slowly but could not be reversed.

The court reconvened. Festus took his seat, then uttered the time-honored legal response.

"Have you appealed to Caesar? Unto Caesar you shall go."

Festus was now in a quandary. He had ruled that a *prima facie* case lay for appeal, yet this first prisoner of the governorship to be referred to Rome had no charges against him that would be clear to Caesar, since Festus could not understand them himself. Fortunately, the Jewish king of the native state, which the Romans had set up to the northeast of Palestine, Herod Agrippa II, was due on a state visit. The Herods were proselytes, not full Jews by blood, but Agrippa could act as assessor to advise on the form of indictment.

He was thirty-two years old, the son of Herod Agrippa I, the king of Judea who had sought to execute Simon Peter and died miserably at Tyre shortly after Peter's escape. The son had been considered too young for Judea, which reverted to direct Roman rule, but four years later had been allowed to succeed an uncle as king of the handkerchief-size state of Chalcis, the narrow plain between the Lebanon mountains and Mount Hermon. This tiny kingdom had been extended gradually to a respectable size, totally dependent on the pleasure of the Romans. Agrippa was unmarried but according to gossip lived in incest with his sister Bernice, who was a queen dowager, widow of their uncle whom Agrippa had succeeded. Drusilla, wife of the disgraced Felix, was their sister.

Festus put his problem to Agrippa toward the end of the state visit. Agrippa expressed a wish to hear Paul. A time was arranged for the next day. Paul prepared his speech with great care, for he looked on it less as a defense than an opportunity of preaching before an exalted influential audience.

To this state function all the great men of Caesarea were invited, Jews and Gentiles, including the general officers of the military command. Many of the procurator's household were present in the audience hall, its pillared sides open to catch the air stirring lazily toward the Mediterranean, and Luke would have had no difficulty in securing a seat: his account of the proceedings bears all the marks of an eyewitness. He noted the "great pomp" with which King Agrippa and Queen Bernice were escorted to their thrones, with blare of trumpets, waving of peacock feather fans, and rigid salutes of the generals. No doubt it amused Luke to watch Festus obsequiously giving precedence to a king he could topple at a flick of his finger.

Paul was brought in. Small, almost stooping, but alert and vigorous in manner, gray-bearded now, a little less thin and wiry after years in moderate comfort, safe from stonings or beatings or long treks from city to city, yet with a frailty and a scarred face in sharp contrast to the hearty young soldier who led him, politely enough, by a chain.

Festus opened the proceedings. "King Agrippa! And all who are present with us: You see this man here about whom the whole Jewish people petitioned me, both at Jerusalem and here, shouting that he ought not to live any longer. But I found that he had done nothing deserving death; as he himself has appealed to the emperor, I decided to send him. But I have nothing definite to write to my lord about him. Therefore I have brought him before you—and especially before you, King Agrippa!—that after we have examined him I may have something to write. For it seems to me unreasonable, in sending a prisoner, not to indicate the charge against him."

Festus resumed his seat. Agrippa said to Paul, "You have permission to speak for yourself."

Paul raised his hand, not to command silence but in courtesy, almost as if blessing this young king whose soul he glimpsed behind the immoral and perfumed façade, and began on a quiet note.

"I consider myself fortunate, King Agrippa, that it is before you I am to make my defense today upon all the charges brought against me by the Jews, particularly as you are expert in all Jewish matters, both our customs and disputes. And therefore I beg you to give me a patient hearing.

"My life from my youth up, the life I led from the beginning among my people and in Jerusalem, is familiar to all Jews." They could testify if they wished that he had lived as a Pharisee, "the strictest part in our religion." And—reverting to the point that had split the Sanhedrin at his Jerusalem hearing—he stressed that he was on trial for his hope in the age-old promise God had made to their ancestors. "Why," asked Paul, addressing Agrippa but with every one of his audience in mind, "should it be thought a thing incredible with you that *God should raise the dead?*

"I myself was convinced that I ought to do many things in opposing the name of Jesus of Nazareth." Paul described the violence of his persecution of the early Christians. By personal testimony, as the surest way of introducing the gospel to his audience, he led steadily onward to the heart of the matter. He told of the Damascus Road. He did not mention Ananias, who as an obscure Jew would have meant nothing to Agrippa and Bernice, and he conflated several incidents and divine messages to make plain that Jesus Christ personally had sent him to open the eyes of Jews and Gentiles, to turn them from darkness to light, from the power of Satan to God, "so that [Paul quoted Jesus] 'by trust in Me, they may obtain forgiveness of sins, and a place with those whom God has made His own.' And so, King Agrippa, I did not disobey the heavenly vision, but I preached this message first to those in Damascus, then to those in Jerusalem and in all Judea, and to the Gentiles also, urging them to repent and turn to God and prove their repentance by their deeds."

Paul's words were not lost on Agrippa and Bernice. They too should repent and turn to God and prove their repentance by deeds.

Many of the distinguished audience may have grown increasingly embarrassed at this bold discourse, which, if taken seriously, must overturn the entire domestic existence of the king and queen.

Paul was in full course: "That is why the Jews seized me in the temple and tried to do away with me. But I had God's help, and so to this very day I stand and testify to small and great, saying nothing beyond what the prophets and Moses foretold: that the Christ must suffer, and that He, as the *first to rise from the dead*, would proclaim the dawn to the people and to the Gentiles—"

"Paul, you are mad! You are mad!" Festus shouted, his manners before royalty entirely forgotten. Up to that minute, he had supposed they were arguing about whether Jesus was dead, as the Jews said, or still living. It suddenly broke in on Festus that Paul was actually claiming Jesus had come alive again after being killed, that this was what Paul staked his life upon. The absurdity of it hit Festus between the eyes. "Paul, your great learning is turning you mad!"

"I am not mad, Your Excellency," Paul replied mildly. "What I am saying is sober truth. The king is well versed in these matters, and to him I can speak freely. I do not believe he can be unaware of any of these facts, for this has been no hole-and-corner business." And Paul ignored Festus. "King Agrippa, do you believe the prophets? I know you do!"

Then Agrippa spoke: "In a short time you think to make a Christian of me?"

"Short or long," Paul echoed, "I would to God that not only you but also all who hear me this day might become such as I am—except for these chains!"

Agrippa had heard enough. The *Authorized Version*'s "Almost thou persuadest me to be a Christian" does not translate accurately a statement that conveyed reproof and refusal rather than fervor.

At Paul's dramatic rejoinder, with its tremendous conviction that happiness for king and commoner lay only in the love of Jesus Christ, Agrippa rose from his throne to end the audience. The queen and all the company rose too. Royalty and governor withdrew, and only on reaching the private quarters did they admit how impressed they had been, telling each other that Paul had done nothing worthy of death or prison and could have been released had he not appealed.

Agrippa and Bernice continued ruling together until the Great Rebellion seven years later, which the queen strove to prevent. They left for Rome, where Bernice eventually became the mistress of the Emperor Titus, the general who captured Jerusalem, slaughtered its inhabitants, and leveled the temple and city to dust.

THIRTY-THREE

SHIPWRECK

Festus handed Paul to a centurion named Julius serving with the imperial or Augustan cohort, whose officers and men traveled throughout the empire on escort and courier duties. Julius commanded a detail of about a dozen soldiers: Paul was the only prisoner of rank, permitted to take two attendants who were listed as his personal slaves: Aristarchus and Luke the physician. The other prisoners would be convicts on their grim way to "make a Roman holiday," either as lion fodder at the games or, if burly enough, for training as gladiators. These would all be chained to timbers below decks; Paul and his attendants could move about freely, though he must always wear a loose chain as a symbol of his status.

In Caesarea harbor, Julius found a coastal vessel out from Adramyttium, east of Assos in the province of Asia, about to sail home with a Levantine cargo.[27] He took passage, confident of finding a vessel for Rome at one of the ports where the coaster would call; if she sailed so slowly that the season grew late, he could cross from Adramyttium to Neapolis near Philippi and conduct the party by land, then over the Adriatic to Brindisi. Either way, he expected to have them in Rome by the end of October.

They sailed from Caesarea in the last week of August 59, before a light westerly breeze, and put in for a day at Sidon, sixty-seven miles northeast. Julius let Paul ashore, thus immediately showing a kindness that was more than the respect to be accorded an unconvicted Roman citizen. Like other military men, Julius had fallen quickly under Paul's charm and air of authority. The Christians of Sidon gave Paul—and presumably Luke and Aristarchus—warm hospitality and fitted them out with any remaining needs for the long voyage.

The westerly, the prevailing wind of late summer in the eastern Mediterranean, prevented a crossing of the open sea south of Cyprus, the direct route that Luke remembered from the reverse voyage two years previously. They had to keep between Cyprus and the Cilician shore. Once more Paul saw the Taurus range, blue in the distance beyond the plain where he had lived as a boy. When the mountains came closer to the sea, the vessel hugged the coast, using the offshore breezes and the west-flowing current, and heaving-to each evening. Luke noted it all. He was not a seaman but described his observations in landlubber's language so accurate that when, in the mid-nineteenth century, a Scot with a yacht and great knowledge of seamanship (James Smith of Jordanhill) retraced Paul's route, he found that Luke's entire account of this most famous voyage with its disastrous end fitted exactly the facts of wind, sea, and coast.[28]

Tacking along the southern Anatolian shore was slow, hot work. For fifteen days, Paul and his friends never put into a harbor. Calm and pleasant Mediterranean weather meant heat and misery for the chained-up convicts below and impatience for the soldiers cooped up in this small ship among the sacks of dried fruit, which probably made most of the cargo. Julius had plenty of opportunity for getting to know his chief prisoner; if conversion followed, Luke was too discreet to mention it, but Julius's subsequent actions point toward the probability.

They crossed the Gulf of Attalia into which Paul had sailed with Barnabas on that first pioneering journey long ago. The rough hills of Lycia lay ahead. The weather could be changeable by now, in mid-September, with the mountaintops disappearing into cloud, and the lowland—where it narrowed to a point—etched against clearer evening skies to the west. Paul had never penetrated these mountains, but the faith may have been spreading already into the valleys from his missionary churches to the north and east. When at last the ship put into the great landlocked harbor of Myra, two miles from the city at the mouth of a great gorge, a church could have already been there. Myra, which now is deserted, grew into an important bishopric, where by a peculiar contortion of history and folklore Saint Nicholas of Myra became Santa Claus.

In the bay among the naval galleys propelled by slave power and the coastal shipping, Julius found a fine large merchantman of the Egyptian corn run, the lifeline of Rome, importing wheat under a system of privately owned vessels commissioned into imperial service. Myra, due north of Alexandria, was a principal port of call in summer, when the wind did not allow sailing direct to Rome.

Julius transferred his soldiers and prisoners. No other military officer was aboard, and thus by Roman practice in the corn fleet, he took precedence over the captain and the owner or supercargo; in any emergency, Julius would have the last word. His party increased the complement of the ship to 276 souls—Italian and Egyptian merchants, even an Indian or a Chinese, possibly a string of African slaves from the upper Nile, army veterans returning on retirement, priests of Isis, entertainers, scholars from the great University of Alexandria, together with women and children. With all of these, and a big cargo of wheat, the Alexandrian ship must have been over five hundred tons, by no means the biggest known to have been afloat at that period, and no smaller than many merchantmen that plied the Mediterranean at the time of Nelson and the last age of sail.

Paul's, however, differed from a nineteenth-century vessel in several vital respects. She had only one large mast carrying a huge mainsail, thus putting heavy strains on her timbers. Her stem and stern both looked like a modern bow. She was steered by detachable rudders rather like large paddles, and her captain had no compass or chronometer and only the roughest of charts, so he never knew his position unless he could see sun or stars to take a bearing, which he did by a primitive form of quadrant.

The ship's intended course on leaving Myra was to sail past Rhodes through the archipelagoes, then by the southern tip of Greece (now Cape Matapan) to reach Italy by the Strait of Messina; and so to Ostia, the port of Rome. But when the vessel tacked out of Myra Bay, the wind was still unfavorably northwest and strong. The captain had to work up above Rhodes near the mainland and its promontories to get smooth water and the shore breezes. "We sailed slowly for a number of days," recorded Luke, "and arrived with difficulty off Cnidus," the spacious port at the very end of a narrow, mountainous peninsula, the westernmost of the southern Anatolian coastline. Cnidus was the last point where they had protection from the full strength of the contrary wind, and "the wind did not allow us to go on." The captain would not enter harbor, though Cnidus had plenty of anchorage, but ran southwest through the Dodecanese toward the mountains of Crete. He rounded Cape Salmone and began to sail under the south of Crete, hoping that the wind would veer before he must turn north. And so "we struggled along the coast until we came to a place called Fair Havens, near the town of Lasea."

They had reached a roadstead well sheltered by the mountains and by islands, which was as far as they could sail into a northwest wind. Immediately beyond Fair Havens lies Cape Matala where the rocky coast turns sharply north for some twenty miles before turning west again, and if they tried to cross that open gulf, they would be wrecked on a lee shore. The captain anchored, windbound. Days passed. Fair Havens was pleasant enough but had no port; small parties might go ashore to visit Lasea, but the entire ship's company would need to live aboard if they wintered. October 5 came and went, the Jewish Day of Atonement that year of AD 59. The "Dangerous Days," when navigation was risky but still feasible, were slipping away. With November 11, all navigation would cease on the open sea, because then the sun and stars might be overcast for days, with no opportunity for bearings; this, rather than the inevitable hazard of storms, was the factor that stopped sea traffic in winter.

They had lost all prospect of reaching Italy that season. Julius convened a conference to decide the best plan and invited Paul to attend; by now Julius appreciated Paul's judgment as well as his seafaring experience.

The captain urged that they seize the first opportunity to round Cape Matala and reach the port of Phoenix, not far down the coast; probably he feared disaffection in passengers and crew if they wintered in isolated Fair

Havens, which had the additional disadvantage, as an anchorage, of being open to nearly half the compass, so that in a heavy gale the vessel might drag her anchors and go aground. If the wind changed to the south, they could just make Phoenix. He was a skilled seaman, as his future actions show, and would know that during autumn in these seas a south wind will often be followed by a violent northeaster, a levanter. His professional advice was to risk it. The owner backed him, for while the ship lay in Fair Havens, he was responsible for keeping the company from starvation, whereas at Phoenix the passengers would disembark.

Julius turned to Paul.

"Paul gave them his advice: 'I can see, gentlemen, that this voyage will be disastrous: it will mean grave loss, not only of ship and cargo but also of life.'"

Julius decided in favor of the captain and the owner.

About October 10, the captain noted that the wind had changed. Luke disassociated himself from the crew's reaction as if he thoroughly disapproved: "When the south wind blew gently, supposing they had obtained their purpose, they weighed anchor and sailed along Crete, close inshore."

They turned the cape and began merrily across the gulf, the dinghy bobbing behind as was customary on short runs inshore. If the sun shone on them, the clouds were ominously thick on Mount Ida, the highest point of Crete and now full on their starboard bow. Suddenly the wind changed. A tremendous blast roared down from Ida, striking them full force; Luke called its strength "typhonic." The air whirled and twisted; a drenching rain blacked out the coast. Their mast, under full sail, shuddered at the sudden gale, proving the foolhardiness of the ancients' practice of sailing single masted: The vibration was so excessive that water began to seep into the hull.

Within a few minutes, the captain knew he could never keep the ship headed into this northeaster: The levanter was upon them, and they must act accordingly. "We had to give way and run for it," to the lee of the small island of Cauda, or Gavdos, which lay some forty miles off the exact path of the wind. They had no hope of making its little port, which was on the wrong side, nor could they dare to anchor, but they used the comparatively smooth water and temporary, risky shelter of its cliffs to prepare as best they could for whatever lay ahead. First, they secured and hoisted the dinghy, now waterlogged. Passengers helped, and Luke recorded feelingly, "We managed with some difficulty." Then they used tackle to put cables under the hull in order to brace the timbers, a common precaution in ancient times (and occasionally in Nelson's day) against the strain of wind and turbulent water. The chief fear of all on board was that the ship would either break up or the timbers leak until she became waterlogged: More ancient ships were lost by foundering than by any other cause.

They lowered the yard with its mainsail, for if she ran with this wind under full sail, the end—if she did not founder first—would be the shallows and quicksands of the north African shore, the notorious Gulf of Syrtis Major off Libya. Their one hope was to set stormsails, lay her on a starboard tack (with her right side to the wind), and let her drift slowly to ride out the storm.

Leaving the shelter of Cauda, they were soon enduring the full agony of rough seas. Without much weight of sail, "we were violently stormtossed"— bobbing about like a cork, with the spray and rain preventing fires and drenching supplies, clothes, and everything above and below decks. What little was eaten would be thrown up by retching stomachs. The heaving, slippery boards made any movement painful. Paul, Luke, the convicts now released from their irons, and every able-bodied man would take turns at the pumps, but with the seeping of water through strained timbers, the level in the bilge rose remorselessly and the ship settled lower. On the second day, to lighten her, the captain ordered loose cargo jettisoned: all livestock and much else. On the third day, he ordered overboard the spare tackle—cables, spars, anything not essential.

Day after miserable day, night after terrifying night, they rose and fell in mountainous seas. Thick, unbroken clouds prevented any reckoning: The captain had no idea of the ship's position. To Luke, it seemed they were toss-ing on a crazy course, but in fact they drifted very steadily at a mean rate of one and half miles an hour in a direction about eight degrees north of west; had they possessed charts and the means to make dead reckoning, they would have spared themselves much worry, for they could not have set a more advantageous course—provided they did not founder. The main cargo of wheat had become thoroughly waterlogged—the sacks too heavy and sodden to move in a pitching ship and all the time increasing in weight.

The water level rose, the ship settled lower, until by the eleventh or twelfth day of the storm "all hope of our being saved was abandoned." Foundering was inevitable now—a matter of a few days at most even if the storm abated—and would mean the loss of all hands if they abandoned ship.

Little is known of the interior design of ancient ships, but all passengers would have been very much on top of one another, sharing their miseries without the slightest privacy. Yet Luke had not seen what Paul saw, until the morning when Paul struggled forward to where the captain and many of the crew huddled dejected. Paul threw his voice above the wind, and they gathered round him.

His first words were a chip of the old Paul with the tendency to justify himself, but his hearers respected him too much to notice. "Men," he said, "you should have listened to me and not have sailed from Crete; then we should have avoided all this damage and loss. But now I beg you, take courage! Not one of you will lose his life; only the ship will be lost. For last night, an angel of the God to whom I belong and whom I worship stood by me. And he said, 'Do not be afraid, Paul. You must stand before Caesar. And look, God has given you the lives of all who sail with you.' And so, men, take courage! For I believe God that it will be just as I was told. But we must be cast on some island."

On the fourteenth night since they had left Crete, with no decline of the gale, the sailors suddenly detected the sound of breakers from leeward. They could see nothing, but if they could hear above the storm they must be drifting close to a rocky shore. They took soundings and found twenty fathoms. A little later they found fifteen. At this rate they would soon be wrecked on the rocks. They could see the breakers now but not the shore, for they were in fact off the low point of Koura at the opening of what is now Saint Paul's Bay; Smith of Jordanhill discovered that this was the exact spot a drifting ship would have reached on the fourteenth night and that the soundings were accurate too.

The captain ordered no less than four anchors to be moved aft from their usual place forward, and dropped through the alternative stern hawseholes with which ancient ships, unlike modern, were fitted. By his seaman-like action, the ship would be prevented from falling on the rocks at night and better positioned to run on shore when daylight allowed a choice. Then "they wished for day." There was nothing else to do.

The sailors thought otherwise. Paul, alert, spotted what they were up to: The men on whose skill the safety of officers and passengers depended were quietly lowering the dinghy, under pretense of dropping anchors from the bow, determined to sneak away before the ship broke up. Paul said to the centurion and soldiers: "Unless these men stay in the ship, you cannot be saved." The soldiers cut the ropes and the boat fell into the sea and drifted away.

Just before dawn, Paul made another suggestion. The captain had been far too concerned with the crisis to think of it.

Paul addressed the officers and everyone in hearing. "For the last fourteen days, you have lived in suspense and gone hungry: you have eaten nothing whatever. So I beg you to have something to eat; your lives depend on it. Remember, not a hair of you will be lost."

Taking a sodden moldy loaf, he gave thanks to God, praying in the presence of all; he broke it and deliberately began to eat. They plucked up their courage and a general meal was organized. The ship's motion being less than for the past fourteen days, the feeding of 276 persons until all had eaten offered no difficulty. With new strength they dumped the rest of the wheat into the sea.

By now it was daylight. The ship lay at the entrance to a bay. No one recognized it; not knowing the rate or direction of drift, they might be anywhere off Sicily or Tunisia. Ahead stood a rocky shore, but they could see a sandy beach.

The captain carried out a complicated maneuver. The crew, in Luke's description, "slipped the anchors and let them go; at the same time they loosed the lashings of the steering paddles, set the foresail to the wind, and let her drive to the beach." The captain had her completely under command and half a mile to go. Soon she would be beached and they would wade ashore.

But he could not realize when he gave the order, that the rocky spit of land close on their starboard beam was in fact a little island (Salmonetta) linked to the mainland by a shoal, "a place where two seas meet," as Luke described it. Because of this the vessel was caught in a crosscurrent and swept onto the shoal until the forepart stuck fast in a bottom of mud and clay while the breakers began to pound the stern to pieces. The company began jumping out. The soldiers reacted instantly, in fear the convicted felons or Paul might try to swim off and escape. According to standing orders, they sought leave to slaughter the lot.

"But the centurion, willing to save Paul, kept them from their purpose; and commanded that they which could swim should cast themselves first into the sea, and get to land: and the rest, some on boards and some on broken pieces of the ship. And so it came to pass, that they escaped all safe to land."

THIRTY-FOUR

CAPITAL OF THE WORLD

Seeing a wreck, the natives rushed to the shore. Unlike the Cornish wreckers of fable and fact, they did all they could to help. It had started raining again, and everybody was drenched from seawater, so the natives lit a great bonfire on the beach, and the ship's company began to dry out.

The seamen had learned by now that this was Malta. The soaking had turned Luke rather Greek and superior; he dismissed the Maltese, even though they "showed us no little kindness," as barbarians because of their dialect and thick accent, though Malta had been Latinized for centuries. He was amused by their reaction to the next incident. Paul had sensibly warmed himself and helped affairs by scavenging around, despite his chain, for brushwood to feed the fire. He threw on a bundle; one of his sticks leaped out at him and fastened on his hand—he had picked up a torpid poisonous snake.

"When the natives saw the creature hanging from his hand, they said to one another, 'No doubt this man is a murderer. Though he has escaped the sea, Justice has not allowed him to live.' Paul, however, shook off the creature into the fire and suffered no harm. They waited, expecting him to swell up or suddenly fall down dead; but when they had waited a long time and saw no misfortune came to him, they changed their minds and said that he was a god."

Paul had not panicked at the snake, and he was equal to the next call. In the neighborhood of the wreck was the estate of Publius, the chief magistrate of Malta, who at once offered temporary hospitality. The crew and most of the passengers were probably disposed around the huts and cottages of his people, while Julius, Paul, and their attendants were invited to the villa, where they discovered that Publius's father lay sick. It was not Luke the physician but Paul who effected the cure. "Paul visited him," Luke recorded generously, "and, after prayer, laid his hands upon him and healed him; whereupon the other sick people on the island came and were cured."

Paul and Luke were only a few days at the chief magistrate's villa. Julius may have rented a house, where the healing and evangelism continued all that winter. Paul, Luke, and Aristarchus became greatly loved so that the people gave them many gifts and on their departure stocked them up with provisions. Tradition in Malta marks Paul's stay as the beginning of an unbroken Christianity; the Maltese kept in memory the site of the wreck for the eighteen centuries before Smith of Jordanhill confirmed their legend with evidence.

Another large grain ship from Alexandria, sailing under the figurehead of the twin gods Castor and Pollux, had wintered in the nearby harbor. When, early in February 60, her captain decided to take advantage of fair weather to make the short run onward, though the sailing season had not started, Julius booked passages. The voyage was uneventful, and at length Paul sailed into the Bay of Naples, saw Mount Vesuvius with its lazy curl of smoke and the city of Pompeii, unaware that nineteen years later she would be in ruins. The grain ship docked at Puteoli, then chief port of the bay, where they found Christians. Julius permitted a week's visit as their guests, whether because he was not yet expected in Rome and wished Paul to enjoy a last taste of comparative freedom; or because he had to send ahead to Rome for orders; or because he was simply in no hurry to bring the companionship of Paul to an end.

When at last they set out to join the Appian Way, Paul was a little nervous and depressed at what might lie ahead, both before Nero and among the Christians of Rome to whom he had once written so joyfully and vigorously, even though they did not owe their faith to him. Forty-three miles out of Rome, at the town of Appii Forum, he met Roman Christians hurrying to welcome him. At Tres Tabernae, Three Taverns, a halting place thirty-three miles out, was yet another group. "When Paul saw them, he thanked God and took courage."

Rome was the greatest city Paul had ever seen. More than a million free citizens and about a million slaves lived on or between the seven hills, some of which boasted wide gardens and luxurious villas: Below Nero's palace on the Palatine a large ornamental lake was being excavated for his pleasure, where the Colosseum stands now. Paul had little opportunity to view the forum and the great public buildings; after Julius handed over the prisoners to his superior officer and the convicted felons were taken off to be prepared for butchery by one means or another, Paul was placed in custody in a house rented at his own cost. It was not in the labyrinth of narrow streets and flimsy dwellings from which the mob emerged for periodical riots. He would have had a home of reasonable size—or small but with a roomy garden—just within the walls near the camp of the Praetorian Guard on the Caelian Hill in the north of the city.

The rumble of traffic down the narrow cobbled street at night, when the country carts were allowed to bring produce to the markets; the babble of jostling pedestrians by day; the distant roars of excited crowds in the Circus Maximus during chariot races or gladiatorial combats; the stench of a great city even in winter when Paul arrived, and the risk of malaria in summer did not make for ease or luxury. And the regulations demanded the never-ending presence of a soldier to whom he must be chained. But he was not in prison; he could have friends at his side and invite all whom he wished.

After three days he sent for the local Jewish leaders. And they came.

"Brothers," Paul said, "although I have done nothing against our people or the customs of our ancestors, I was arrested in Jerusalem and handed over to the Romans. They examined me and would have set me free, since they found me guilty of nothing deserving the death penalty; but the Jews lodged an objection and I was forced to appeal to Caesar, not that I had any accusation to make against my own nation. That is why I asked to see you and talk with you, for it is on account of the Hope of Israel that I wear this chain."

The Jewish leaders could not tell whether Paul might receive the emperor's favor and protection, and at that period in Nero's reign they lacked influence in the palace. They replied, "We have received no letters from Judea about you, nor has any countryman of yours arrived here with any report or story of anything to your discredit. We think it would be as well to hear your own account of your position; all we know about this sect is that opinion everywhere condemns it."

Since many Roman Christians were Jews by birth, the leaders knew more than they admitted, but Paul welcomed the opportunity for his normal sequence of preaching on arrival in any city: "to the Jew first." On the appointed day a considerable number came to his lodgings. Paul expounded and debated from early morning until evening, "testifying about the kingdom of God and trying to persuade them about Jesus, arguing from the Law of Moses and the prophets." Some were convinced, others skeptical. When they left him, Paul quoted Isaiah to them, the text used by Jesus in which God rebuked Israel's self-imposed blindness: "The heart of his nation has grown coarse, their ears are dull of hearing, and they have shut their eyes, for fear they should see with their eyes, hear with their ears, understand with their heart, and be converted and be healed by Me." Paul added, "Take notice: this salvation of God has been sent to the Gentiles. *They* will listen!" And the Jews left, arguing vigorously.

That was the beginning of a period that, despite his sixty years, was as strenuous as any in Paul's life. "He stayed there," wrote Luke in the final words of Acts, "two full years at his own expense, with a welcome for all who came to him, proclaiming the kingdom of God and the facts about the Lord Jesus Christ quite openly and without hindrance."

Luke's words are borne out by Paul's writings. "I have been made a servant of the church by God," he wrote from Rome, "who gave me the task of fully proclaiming His message, which is the secret He hid through all past ages from mankind, but has now revealed to His people. For this is God's plan: to make known His secret to His people, this rich and glorious secret which He has for all peoples. And the secret is this: *Christ in you*, which means you will share the glory of God. So we preach Christ to all. We warn and teach everyone, with all possible wisdom, in order to bring each one into God's presence as a mature individual in union with Christ. To get this done I toil and struggle, using the mighty strength that Christ supplies, which is at work in me."

His days sped by in the same task as at Corinth or Ephesus: winning converts, building up teachers and evangelists who should go out to win and teach others. The church in Rome had already become numerous and vigorous, whether or not Peter was there already, which the research of centuries has been unable to fix with certainty; yet there were many ancient hilltop cities in southern Italy awaiting evangelists and great cities of the northern plains and villages of the Apennines. Furthermore, Rome was the port of call for so many of every race and color in the Mediterranean world, and beyond that Paul never knew who might be brought to see him or to what distant land they might take the message. And Romans small and great sought him out. Tradition has it that even Seneca, still powerful as a statesman and philosopher, corresponded with him; but their "Letters" are a third-century forgery and prove nothing.

No one could leave that hired house untouched, if only to "argue vigorously." It had an atmosphere of happiness, with the music and singing that Paul mentioned in both the chief letters he wrote from it. His character had not been soured or hardened by troubles. To judge by what he thought important, he was kind, tenderhearted, forgiving, just as Christ had forgiven him. He walked in love, the element that bound his qualities together. He was still the great encourager, welcoming any who were weak in faith and refusing to argue about secondary matters. The Romans learned that he lived as he had taught them when he wrote three years before: "We that are strong ought to bear with the failings of the weak, and not to please ourselves.... Owe no one anything except to love one another." Like his Master he did not emphasize shortcomings but potential, and he would not pass judgment on others unless they betrayed their Master by open sin, when he could be severe, although always with the aim of restoring and strengthening.

In that Roman house, bitter people softened; anger, wrath, clamor died away. Paul had more than ever a sense of his littleness, his unworthiness—"less than the least of all saints"—and of the marvel of being entrusted with a commission "to preach the unsearchable riches of Christ." He seemed to delight in the contrast between the majesty of the message and the insignificance of the messenger: such a gentle little man now, yet with what steel and strength.

The soldiers, turn and turn about, knew where that strength had its chief contact with infinity. In the early mornings, the guard chained to Paul had no option but to join the time on his knees and hear the words of thanksgiving and intercession.

Paul's heart was far away in Greece or Asia Minor. "Father of glory," the soldier must have heard him pray, for the Ephesians, for the Colossians, and for "all who have not seen my face": "God of our Lord Jesus Christ, give them a spirit of wisdom and of revelation. May they know what is the hope to which You have called them, what are the riches of Your glorious inheritance, what the immeasurable greatness of Your power.... May they live a life worthy of You, fully pleasing to You, bearing fruit in every good work and increasing in their knowledge of You ... Father, of whom the whole family in heaven and earth is named, according to Your riches in glory grant them to be strengthened by might in the inner man. May Christ dwell in their hearts by faith. May they be rooted and grounded in love, and comprehend with all saints what is the breadth and length and height and depth—and know the love of Christ which passes knowledge, that they be filled with all Your fullness."

Mentioning many by name, entering into their needs and problems as best he knew them, Paul prayed, sometimes alone except for the soldier, sometimes with Aristarchus and Luke and whoever was with him. His prayers were shot through with praise, and it may have been a soldier, whether Christian yet or not, who first heard in Rome the thanksgiving that would ring out to the world: "Now unto Him who is able to do exceedingly abundantly, above all that we ask or think, according to the power that worketh in us, unto Him be glory in the church by Christ Jesus throughout all ages, world without end. Amen."

Old associates found their way to Paul, joining Aristarchus and Luke "the beloved physician." One was John Mark, whose desertion in Pamphylia long ago had split Paul from Barnabas. Whether Mark had been in Rome with Simon Peter or had traveled from Cyprus or Alexandria, Paul was completely reconciled and soon described him as "a great comfort to me." Timothy was back at Paul's side, and Tychicus too, who had been an Asian delegate on the Jerusalem journey. Another companion, Demas, probably a Macedonian from Thessalonica, would have a regrettable future.

There was also a runaway slave in the household.

Paul one day found himself confronted by the lost property of one of his close friends. The slave, Onesimus, whose name means "Useful," had run away from Colossae in Asia, where he was owned by no less than Philemon, the mainspring of the Colossian church. Like many escaped slaves, Onesimus had drifted to Rome, for in Ephesus or other great cities of Asia he might easily be recognized and hauled back to expect the usual, fearful fate of runaways. Whether Onesimus, in distress or debt, had sought out Paul or had been discovered by one of the companions, Paul "brought him to birth in my imprisonment." He worked as Paul's servant and greatly endeared himself, so that Paul described him as "my very heart." More than that, he became part of the missionary team, "a faithful and beloved brother."

Then Epaphras, the original missionary to Colossae, which Paul had never reached, arrived in Rome. He made Paul happy with excellent news of the Colossians' faith in Christ and love for their fellow Christians. But a heresy was troubling and puzzling them. Epaphras, who felt intense desire that they should become mature and "fully assured in the will of God," discussed the heresy with Paul at length. A great man of prayer, Epaphras wrestled in spirit and stirred others to pray for Colossae. Paul spoke of him as "my fellow prisoner," and whether sharing voluntarily or under some sort of similar custody, Epaphras could not return to Asia. Paul determined to write to the Colossians and send the letter by Tychicus. This would deal specially with the Colossian problem; but Paul would send another, more general letter that Tychicus should deliver to the Ephesians for circulation among other churches in Asia, including cities Paul had not visited.

Colossians and the other letter, known as Ephesians, emerged similar in content yet distinctive in style. Thoughts much in Paul's mind are found in both, sometimes in identical phrases so that it is even possible that he composed the letters together, dictating part of one, then part of the other. Or he may have written one and then adapted it for the other. To Colossae, with a particular church in mind, he included personal messages, while his message to the Ephesians is more formal yet gives intimate autobiographical comments, especially when his mind was with those who had never seen him.

Drawn out of the very depths of Paul's spiritual experiences, containing analogies between Christ's love for the church and a man's love for his wife, Ephesians has proved a mine for Christian mystics that no generation has exhausted. Both letters, in striking sentences—consistent with his earliest writing yet with fresh touches as he worked over the themes from different angles—emphasize God's love and its purpose. To the Ephesians: "He destined us in love to be His sons through Jesus Christ according to the purpose of His will, to the praise of His glorious grace which He freely bestowed on us in the Beloved. In Him we have redemption through His blood, the forgiveness of our trespasses, according to the riches of His grace which He lavished upon us.... God, who is rich in mercy, out of the great love with which He made us alive together with Christ; by grace you have been saved." He repeated it. "By grace you have been saved through faith; and this is not your own doing, it is the gift of God—not because of works, lest any man should boast. For we are His workmanship, created in Christ Jesus for good works, which God prepared beforehand, that we should walk in them."

To the Colossians, he poured out the same theme but directed his teaching to answer their special problem. Heretics in Colossae were saying that they could not know God through Jesus Christ alone but must recast and expand the message in the light of contemporary thought; they wanted to change the very image of God as Christ had revealed Him; to hammer out fresh terms to express His reality; to reach Him by means more reasonable to those among whom they lived. Their theories were peculiarly similar in essence, though not in detail, to the theological ferments of the later twentieth and twenty-first centuries.

Paul directed the Colossian Christians firmly back. "As therefore you received Christ Jesus the Lord, so live in Him, rooted and built up in Him and established in the faith, just as you were taught, abounding in thanksgiving. See to it that no one makes a prey of you by philosophy and empty deceit, according to human tradition … and not according to Christ." Paul was in no doubt whatsoever: "*Christ* is the visible likeness of the invisible God. God created the whole universe through Him and for Him. He existed before all things, and in union with Him all things have their proper place. He is the head of His body, the church; He is the source of the body's life; He is the firstborn Son who was raised from death, in order that He alone might have the first place in all things."

The only knowledge of God, the only road to God, whether on earth or in remotest space, is through Jesus: "In Him all the fullness of God was pleased to dwell, and through Him to reconcile all things to Himself, whether on earth or in heaven, making peace through the blood of the cross."

On this foundation Paul built exhortation and encouragement, urging the Ephesians: "Walk in love as Christ loved us and gave Himself up for us," and the Colossians: "If you have been raised with Christ, seek the things that are above…. You have put on the new nature, which is being renewed in knowledge after the image of its Creator…. Put on, as God's chosen ones, compassion, kindness, lowliness, meekness, and patience." Both letters contain advice and direction grounded in clear spiritual teaching: how a church should be guided and grow; how its different members, including masters and slaves, husbands and wives, fathers and children, should best please God.

When Paul closed his letter to the Colossians, he sent personal messages for particular people and news of friends in Rome. The letter to Ephesus, being for general circulation, could not close like that. To end it, he hit a stroke of genius, which may have been actually suggested by one of his guards, and certainly was provoked by his interest in the soldiers. He could often watch them performing drills on the fields outside the walls near the camp of the Praetorian Guard and in his traveling days had grown familiar with their service equipment.

So now, checking with his soldier of the day, Paul created one of his famous passages, the Christian's Armor, which will enable him to stand his ground when the fight is hottest, deflect the arrows tipped with burning tow, and advance wielding a trusty weapon. He went on to describe the belt round the loins; the iron breastplate; the sandals; the shield and helmet and sword.

"Take unto you the whole armor of God, that ye may be able to stand in the evil day, and having done all, to stand. Stand therefore, having your loins girt about with truth, and having on the breastplate of righteousness: and your feet shod with the preparation of the Gospel of peace; above all, taking the shield of faith, wherewith ye shall be able to quench all the fiery darts of the wicked. And take the helmet of salvation, and the sword of the Spirit which is the Word of God, praying always with all prayer and supplication in the Spirit, and watching thereunto with all perseverance and supplication for all saints."

THIRTY-FIVE

THE YEARS OF FREEDOM

A third letter remained before Tychicus could leave for Asia: a note for Onesimus to hand to his master. Paul knew that he must return Onesimus to Philemon, and Onesimus knew what could happen to a recovered slave.

The only one of all Paul's epistles to be concerned solely with a personal matter, it shows him in a most engaging light, and without it any estimate of his character lacks balance. Paul, who has just been consciously the authoritative voice of "the mystery of Christ revealed to His holy apostles and prophets by the Spirit," now showed the tactful, diffident, kindly side of himself, even the humorous: He made puns on the name Onesimus meaning "useful" or "beneficent."

By implication, the letter to Philemon displays Paul's total rejection of slavery as a state compatible with the gospel in a Christian society. Paul was no Spartacus calling slaves to revolt: a sudden end of slavery would reduce the Roman Empire to chaos, and he was realistic enough to recognize that to agitate for abolition in his lifetime would be senseless, merely provoking the crushing of Christians as a menace to law and order. But he had taught consistently that "in Christ there is neither slave nor free," since all are equal in the sight of their Master, Christ. Both the letters to the Ephesians and Colossians (Onesimus and Philemon being surely much in mind as he wrote) emphasize the new relationship between slave and free in which each must look on the other as a brother. And now he was sending back to Philemon not a piece of lost property but a brother Christian, an honored fellow worker.

Philemon had the legal right to butcher Onesimus, to whip or brand him, or put him to hard labor for life. Paul wished to save Philemon from doing wrong. And though Paul may not have expected this personal letter to circulate, its influence and that of his other passages about slavery eventually made the institution so distasteful, as Christianity permeated society, that it withered, slowly enough, and died out in the Christian world, though many Christians were sold into slavery by their Muslim conquerors. It died out, only to be revived in the New World by Spanish and Portuguese Roman Catholics—despite condemnation by both the pope and English Protestants, with all the distress and problems that followed.

The incompatibility of slavery with the gospel is only implied. The letter itself is a window right into the hired house of Rome in AD 62. Tychicus was absent when it was penned, and the penman probably was Timothy. Epaphras, Mark, Aristarchus, Demas, and Luke were sitting around (with the inevitable soldier) when Paul began to dictate for Philemon and his family, opening as in the other two letters with warm gratitude and assurance of prayer. "I have derived much joy and comfort from your love, my brother, because the hearts of the saints have been refreshed through you.

"Accordingly, though I am bold enough in Christ to command you to do what is required, yet for love's sake I prefer to appeal to you—I, Paul, an ambassador and now a prisoner also for Christ Jesus, I appeal to you for my child, Onesimus, whose father I have become in my imprisonment." Here Paul made his little play on words: "Formerly he was *useless* to you, but now he is indeed *useful* to you and to me. I am sending him back to you, sending my heart. I would have been glad to keep him with me, in order that he might serve me on your behalf during my imprisonment for the Gospel, but I preferred to do nothing without your consent in order that your goodness might not be by compulsion but of your own free will.

"Perhaps this is why he was parted from you for a while, that you might have him back forever, no longer as a slave but *more than a slave: as a beloved brother*, especially to me but how much more to you, both in the flesh and in the Lord. So if you consider me your partner, receive him *as you would receive me*. If he has wronged you at all, or owes you anything, charge that to my account."

Paul seized the pen and scrawled, "I, Paul, write this in my own hand; I will repay it." He handed back the papyrus and added, "to say nothing of you owing me even your own self! Yes, brother, I want some benefit from you in the Lord. Refresh my heart in Christ.

"Confident of your obedience, I write to you, knowing you will do even more than I say."

Paul sniffed the air of freedom himself. The final words of the letter before farewells to Philemon were confident. He would see Colossae at last: "At the same time, prepare a guest room for me, for I am hoping through your prayers to be granted to you." And he added a note to both the other letters about his coming trial: "Pray for me," he asked the Ephesians, "that the right words may be given me, that I may open my mouth boldly to make known the secret of the Gospel for which I am an ambassador in chains: that I may declare it boldly, as I ought to speak."

His plan was to turn his trial into a testimony, whether or not Caesar presided. For the first seven years of the reign when he was still under twenty-five, Nero deputed the presidency of trials to the Praetorian prefect, the bluff, straightforward Burrus or the hated Tigellinus, who succeeded him. Yet in AD 62, he had begun to amuse himself by presiding, and thus, in the splendid star-domed justice hall of the palace on the Palatine, he may have heard Paul's reasoning of "righteousness, temperance, and judgment to come." The red-haired Nero's descent into extravagance and lust was gathering pace. He divorced the daughter of Claudius Caesar to marry Poppaea, the Jewish proselyte and previously wife of a close friend, and she encouraged Nero in vice and despotism and had Paul's trial delayed much longer; her influence most likely would have overridden justice to secure his execution.

Instead, whatever their personal reactions to Paul's plain-speaking, the distinguished consuls and senators who sat as assessors apparently gave a majority of votes in his favor, and Nero—who often ignored opinion anyway—acquitted him.[29] The effect of the verdict was to substantiate Gallio's earlier decision: Christianity was ruled in no way an illegal cult. The gospel could be preached freely throughout the Roman world, little more than thirty years since the crucifixion of Christ.

No one then realized how utterly hollow this tolerance would prove.

Paul's fetters were struck off. He left the Palatine palace a free man. The rest of his life, probably about five years, is known only hazily, if we discount legends and late traditions. The evidence is fragmentary; three letters survive, but the provenance of two of them—the place of origin and the sequence in which they were written—is uncertain, and information about his personal movements slight.

He may have gone to Spain as he had planned when writing Romans. Clement of Rome, in his letter to the Corinthians thirty years later, stated that Paul "reached the farthest bounds of the West." Clement must have known Paul, but the phrase is vague: It could mean he evangelized as far as Cádiz, the "Gate of the West," and looked out across the Atlantic. Or that he evangelized the Celts: Christianity penetrated very early deep into Gaul up the valley of the Rhône, but no local tradition mentions Paul, nor can a shred of reliable evidence support the romance of Paul landing in Britain.

The belief that he went to Spain was held firmly by several of the Early Fathers, although again there is no local tradition. Since he had intended to evangelize Spain like Galatia, Greece, and the province of Asia, his time there could have stretched nearly to two years. Then he was back in the eastern Mediterranean: with Titus in Crete; with Timothy in Ephesus (despite Paul's earlier conviction that he would never see the elders again); and surely, if at all possible, he found his way at last up the Meander and Lycus valleys to enjoy Philemon's guest room at Colossae, served by a delighted Onesimus. In his letters to Timothy and Titus, Paul mentioned being at Miletus and revealed his plans to spend a winter in Nicopolis in the Epirus of western

Greece. The picture at this point is of constant movement rather than settled work, though slower, as if bones were old and rheumatism and arthritis were catching up; and he was slower too in his style of writing.

The sense of urgency was undiminished. For his work was being attacked on all sides.

In the year 64, the favorable legal decision handed down at Paul's trial was turned into a mockery by the whim of Nero after the Fire of Rome, when he deflected the wrath of the populace from his own head by accusing the Christians of arson. In the famous words of Tacitus, then a child of ten and writing fifty years later: "A vast multitude were not only put to death, but put to death with insult, in that they were either dressed up in the skins of beasts to perish by the worrying of dogs, or else put on crosses to be set on fire, and when the daylight failed, to be burned for use as lights by night. Nero had thrown open his gardens for that spectacle, and was giving a circus exhibition, mingling with the people in a jockey's dress, or driving in a chariot." His excesses produced commiseration with the Christians despite the unpopularity they had earned for rejecting the gods, because people recognized that they were not suffering for the good of the state so much as "to satisfy the cruelty of an individual."

Praetorian soldiers who had learned to love Paul were among those ordered to torture his friends. Former guards who were now Christians were themselves dying in agony. And the way Christians died was in itself a testimony: "In the midst of the flame and the rack," wrote Seneca, "I have seen men not only not groan, that is little: not only not complain, that is little: not only not answer back, that too is little; but I have seen them smile, and smile with a good heart."

Survivors of the persecution took refuge in the catacombs, the warren caves and burial places deep under the outskirts of Rome. In eastern Europe, Paul too may have had to "go underground" for his travels and preaching, as the new imperial policy gained momentum in the provinces. The horrors of 64 certainly give point to his words written to Timothy at this time: "I urge that petitions, prayers, intercessions, and thanksgivings be offered for all men: for sovereigns and all in high office, that we may lead a tranquil and quiet life in full observance of religion and high standards of morality."

Several of his converts or trusted elders made shipwreck of their faith. The unsettled times—persecution in Rome, Judea seething with rumors of messiahs, and with unrest about to explode in the Great Rebellion of AD 66—led to a ferment of ideas old and new. Leaving for Macedonia, Paul urged Timothy at Ephesus to "insist that certain people stop teaching strange doctrines and taking notice of endless genealogies; these things are only likely to raise irrelevant doubts instead of furthering the designs of God which are revealed in faith." To Titus in Crete, Paul wrote of "many insubordinate men, empty talkers and deceivers, especially the Circumcision party; they must be silenced, since they are upsetting whole families, teaching for base gain what they have no right to teach." Paul emphasized this, in a spark of the old fire, by a choice quote from the Cretan poet Epimenides of Knossos: "One of their own countrymen said, 'Cretans are always liars, vicious brutes, lazy gluttons'—and he told the truth!"

Paul had to warn Timothy against ascetics who disapproved of marriage and against conceited controversialists "with a craze for questioning everything and arguing about words," which all led to jealousy, contention, and mistrust. He had to denounce those who sought to make money by Christian service and coined his memorable phrase "the love of money is the root of all evils." "It is through this craving," he added, "that some have wandered away from the faith and pierced their hearts with many pangs. But as for you, man of God," lest Timothy himself should waver, "shun all this. Aim at righteousness, godliness, faith, love, steadfastness, gentleness. Fight the good fight of faith; take hold of the eternal life to which you were called when you made the good confession in the presence of many witnesses."

Paul heartened and guided Timothy. Titus needed advice, but Timothy, the same timid and delicate yet sometimes self-willed Timothy, still very much a young man in Paul's eyes, needed encouragement and care, even in matters of health: "Do not drink water only, but take a little wine to help your digestion, since you are sick so often." "Let no one despise your youth," Paul urged, "but set the believers an example in speech and conduct, in love, in faith, in purity. Till I come, attend to the public reading of Scripture, to preaching, to teaching."

Paul was "constantly travelling." Timothy and Titus stayed longer at one place, but they too were in frequent movement, at Paul's behest, strengthening the sorely tried Christians, rebutting falsehoods, restoring the lapsed. Paul did not resent the fact that—far from enjoying a tranquil old age, venerated, uncontradicted, honored—he must battle to the last, for he had expected this trouble. "The Spirit says expressly," he warned, "that in after times some will desert from the faith and give their minds to subversive doctrines.... Timothy," he begged, "keep safe that which has been entrusted to you. Turn a deaf ear to empty and wordy chatter, and the contradictions of so-called knowledge, for many who lay claim to it have shot wide of the faith."

It was essential to build up healthy, expanding churches under local leadership, for "God our Savior desires all men to be saved and to come to the knowledge of the truth." The two letters of this period, the First Epistle to Timothy and the Epistle to Titus, quickly became classics of pastoral wisdom wherever Christianity spread. Timothy in Asia and Titus in Crete were shown how to select and train elders; instructed about church discipline and worship; advised what to do about widows and others in distress or need, how young men and slaves and all other believers should behave so that Christians, however traduced or abused by Nero or their neighbors, might "add luster to the doctrine of God our Savior. For," Paul reminded Titus, "the grace of God has dawned upon the world with healing for all mankind." The aged Paul was more than ever sure of "the glorious Gospel of the blessed God with which I have been entrusted. I thank Him," he wrote to Timothy, "who has given me strength for this, Christ Jesus our Lord, because He judged me faithful by appointing me to His service, though I formerly blasphemed and persecuted and insulted Him. But I received mercy because I acted ignorantly in unbelief, and the grace of our Lord overflowed for me with the faith and love that are in Christ Jesus.

"This saying is sure and worthy of full acceptance, that Christ Jesus came into the world to save sinners. And I am the foremost of sinners! But I received mercy for this reason, that in me, as the foremost, Jesus Christ might display His perfect patience for an example to those who were to believe in Him for eternal life.

"To the King of ages, immortal, invisible, the only God, be honor and glory for ever and ever."

THIRTY-SIX

NO KIND OF DEATH

Paul was arrested for the last time probably in the summer of AD 66. It may have been in northwest Asia Minor or eastern Macedonia, for he had left his belongings at Troas: his winter sheepskin cloak, perhaps a present from Philemon in the choice wool of Colossae; his papyrus rolls, which would have been handwritten notes of the sayings of the Lord Jesus and possibly copies of his own epistles and Luke's writings; and the vellum parchments, most likely the Law and the Prophets, which he had treasured since his earliest days.

The immediate cause of arrest may be inferred from Paul's statement soon afterward: "Alexander the coppersmith did me great harm." True to his teaching in Romans, "Never avenge yourselves," Paul quoted a psalm: "The Lord will repay him for what he has done." But he warned Timothy against the man because "he strongly opposed our message." To add to Paul's distress, "all who are in Asia deserted me, including Phygelus and Hermogenes." Paul presumably was writing hyperbole rather than a statistical statement, for the context suggests abandonment at the idea of danger, such as Jesus suffered in the Garden of Gethsemane, rather than deliberate and widespread rejection of his teachings.

Opposed, arrested, deserted, Paul would have been hurried by the Via Egnatia and the Adriatic to Rome, and flung into jail. Or he may have returned to Rome before arrest, since he mentioned leaving Trophimus at Miletus and Erastus at Corinth as if they had been together on the journey westward. If so, intending a brief visit to encourage the decimated community in Rome, he joined the underground existence of Christians who went about their normal affairs in daytime but gathered for preaching and prayer in the catacombs at night. The walls have several mural portraits of Paul: a long face and nose, unruffled yet with an eager expression, the beard white and the head nearly bald. They date from the next century, too late for the artists to have seen Paul themselves; but in childhood they could easily have heard old men describe him from their own childhood memories.

Paul was once more seized, shackled, and this time placed in rigorous confinement in Rome, not as an honorable citizen on remand but "chained like a criminal. But the Word of God is not chained," he could add. He was among the felons in the Mamertine or an equally obnoxious dungeon, reached only by rope or ladder let through a hole in the floor above. His weary body must lie on rough stones. The air was foul, sanitation almost nonexistent.

They put him on trial as one of those who had caused the Great Fire. If convicted, he would die as he might have died in Ephesus, as many Roman Christians had already died: driven into the arena to be torn to pieces by lions. The trial of a citizen could not be summary: Paul must appear before Caesar in the great basilica in the Forum, where, besides the senators and consuls on the bench and the depraved Nero, whom all Rome now hated, a large crowd of spectators packed the galleries. Paul confidently expected Christians to testify on his behalf. He looked in vain. The Terror had driven them away. "At my first defense," he wrote to Timothy, "no one took my part; all deserted me. May it not be charged against them! But the Lord stood by me and gave me strength to proclaim the Word fully, that all the Gentiles might hear it. So I was rescued from the lion's mouth." Once again he had turned a court hearing into a proclamation of the gospel, and his voice had carried to the farthest gallery.

He was acquitted of arson but remanded again, to be punished for the less dishonorable offense of propagating a forbidden cult; a capital charge because it implied treason against the divine emperor. Back in prison, possibly no longer the Mamertine, he was lonely. One trusted friend had deserted, and Paul's zeal for the gospel did not let him keep others in Rome who might visit and comfort: "Demas, in love with this present world, has deserted me and gone to Thessalonica; Crescens has gone to Galatia (or Gaul), Titus to Dalmatia. Luke alone is with me."

Then an Asian Christian, who being of some substance in the eyes of the authorities stood to lose much by associating with a criminal, came to Italy. Onesiphorus of Ephesus "was not ashamed of my chains, but when he arrived in Rome he searched for me eagerly and found me" and cheered Paul many times.

Paul was now able to write to Timothy, perhaps by the pen of Luke and the hand of Onesiphorus, urging him to "do your best to come to me before winter" and to find Mark and bring him, "for he can help me in the work," which continued regardless of prison walls. Above all he urged Timothy, "Do not be ashamed of testifying to our Lord, nor of me His prisoner; but take your share of suffering for the Gospel in the power of God, who saved us and called us with a holy calling, not in virtue of our works but in virtue of His own purpose and the grace which he gave us in Christ Jesus ages ago, and now has manifested through the appearance of our Savior Christ Jesus, who abolished death and brought life and immortality to light through the Gospel. For this Gospel I was appointed a preacher, and apostle, and teacher, and therefore I suffer as I do.

"But I am not ashamed. For I know whom I have believed! And I am sure that He is able to guard until that Day what has been entrusted to me."

He recalled their service and sufferings together in those far-off days in Galatia on the first missionary journey and encouraged Timothy: "You then, my son, be strong in the grace that is in Christ Jesus, and what you have heard from me before many witnesses entrust to faithful men who shall be able to teach others also.... Preach the Word, be urgent in season and out of season, convince, rebuke, and exhort, be unfailing in patience and teaching." Undeflected by those who seek teachers "to suit their own likings," Timothy must "always be steady, endure suffering, do the work of an evangelist, fulfill your ministry."

Paul was not depressed or dismayed at the surrounding stress. Though Christianity might seem in process of extinction by fire and sword, or of being wrested into a different gospel, he could affirm with utmost confidence that "the foundation of God stands sure." The fearful war that had broken out in Judea might be the first portent of the Lord's return to earth; if so, it would mean that all Israel would recognize the Lord Jesus at last and be gathered in. If the Lord delayed, the gospel would continue to be preached.

The Lord did delay, and Paul's work stood the test of time. Corinth, though always with its difficulties, became an important center, and Ephesus, which the Revelation of St. John commended (with reservations) nearly thirty years later, a great bishopric. When the Roman Empire at last gave Christianity complete toleration in AD 313, not one of Paul's churches had disappeared. Yet always, as he had warned, the gold of faith was flawed by dross, and in Asia Minor disputes and political ambitions led to such weakening of what now boasted itself a Christian empire, that fourteen hundred years after Paul, Islam triumphed.

If many of his churches fell to conquerors who denied the divinity of Christ, Paul's writings have survived every attempt to discredit or dismember them. The great thinker, Christ's interpreter, towers above men who would rewrite him or who charge him with twisting and debasing his Master's words and meaning. Paul had expected such activities: "They will turn away from listening to the truth and wander into myths." His own call, in the Second Epistle to Timothy, remains in all its simplicity: "Remember Jesus Christ, risen from the dead, born of David's line. This is the theme of my Gospel."

"As for me, I am now ready to be offered, and the time of my departure is at hand. I have fought a good fight. I have finished my course, I have kept the faith. Henceforth there is laid up for me a crown of righteousness, which the Lord, the righteous judge, shall give me at that Day: and not to me only but unto all them that love His appearing."

Of Paul's final trial, nothing is known beyond a tradition that he was condemned by resolution of the senate on the charge of treason against the divine emperor. How long Simon Peter and Paul were in prison together before being executed the same day, as an early and strong belief asserts, cannot be fixed: possibly as much as nine months. The date honored in the city of their martyrdom is June 29, 67: Peter nailed to a cross as a public spectacle at Nero's Circus on the Vatican, head downward at his own request; and Paul, as a Roman citizen, beheaded in a less public place.

The ancient tradition of Paul's execution site is almost certainly authentic, but the details cannot be confirmed. Whereas Christ's Via Dolorosa may be followed step by step, Paul's remains vague. He would have it so. And because Christ had walked that earlier road, Paul's was no Via Dolorosa, for they were walking it together: "Thanks be to God, who in Christ always leads us in triumph." "For to me to live is Christ and to die is gain."

They marched him out through the walls past the pyramid of Cestius, which still stands, on to the Ostian Way toward the sea. Crowds journeying to or from Ostia would recognize an execution squad by the lictors with their fasces of rods and ax, and the executioner carrying a sword, which in Nero's reign had replaced the ax; by the escort, and by the manacled criminal, walking stiffly and bandy-legged, ragged and filthy from his prison: but not ashamed or degraded. He was going to a feast, to a triumph, to the crowning day to which he had pressed forward. He who had talked often of God's promise of eternal life in Jesus could not fear; he believed as he had spoken: "All God's promises find their 'yes' in Him." No executioner was going to lose him the conscious presence of Jesus; he was not changing his company, only the place where he enjoyed it. Better still, he would see Jesus. Those glimpses—on the Damascus Road, in Jerusalem, at Corinth, on that sinking ship; now he was going to see Him face-to-face, to know even as he had been known.

They marched Paul to the third milestone on the Ostian Way, to a little pinewood in a glade, probably a place of tombs, known then as Aquae Salviae, or Healing Waters, and now as Tre Fontane where an abbey stands in his honor. He is believed to have been put overnight in a tiny cell, for this was a common place of execution. If Luke was allowed to stay by his window, if

Timothy or Mark had reached Rome in time, the sounds of the night vigil would not be of weeping but singing: "as sorrowful yet always rejoicing; as dying and, behold, we live."

At first light, the soldiers took Paul to the pillar. The executioner stood ready, stark naked. Soldiers stripped Paul to the waist and tied him, kneeling upright, to the low pillar, which left his neck free. Some accounts say the lictors beat him with rods; a beating had been the usual prelude to beheading, though in recent years it had not always been inflicted. If they must administer this last, senseless dose of pain to a body so soon to die, "Who shall separate us from the love of Christ? Shall tribulation ... or sword?

"I reckon that the sufferings of this present time are not worthy to be compared with"—the flash of a sword—"the glory."

NOTES

Note: For the reader's convenience dates are given in a modern form.

1. Compare Mark 7:14–23 with Romans 14:14 and Galatians 5:19–22.

2. Compare Matthew 5:14–16 and Luke 8:16 with Philippians 2:16.

3. Following Sir William Ramsay, as against many scholars, I place the vision in the temple that Paul referred to in Acts 22 ("Make haste and get quickly out of Jerusalem") at a later date. See chapter 8.

4. See chapter 19.

5. Acts 22.

6. The *Authorized (King James) Version* translates Luke's term for *Deputy*, the title in use in 1611 for the governor of England's sole major colony, Ireland.

7. In English miles. The Roman mile was slightly shorter. Sir William Ramsay's estimate for a first-century foot traveler's day is between sixteen and twenty Roman miles.

8. Assuming, with the backing of an impressive array of scholars, that Paul wrote to Christians in southern Galatia and not, as Lightfoot taught, to the actual Gallic tribe of Galatians around the capital Ancyra (Ankara) in the north, whose name the Romans took for the whole province. It is not certain that Paul ever visited them. Biographically, the southern Galatian destination of the letter makes complete sense.

9. The Greek text of Acts has Zeus and Hermes, as in the *Revised Standard Version*. The *Authorized Version* followed the curious Elizabethan habit of translating Greek divinities by their Latin equivalents, to which the *New English Bible* rather oddly reverted, possibly because the Baucis story is best known from Ovid. In any case, the Lycaonians must have used Anatolian equivalents, or Paul and Barnabas would have gotten wind of it sooner.

10. Luke's statement "they went *down* to Attalia, and from there they sailed to Antioch" is another instance of his extraordinary precision of terms, as any visitor to the delightful resort of Antalya may confirm.

11. Scholars who accept southern Galatia as the epistle's destination are not unanimous in dating it from Antioch and thus as the earliest of all Paul's writings. Evidence for the early date was strongly argued by Ramsay, and the discussion is well summarized in Kirsopp Lake's *The Earlier Epistles of St. Paul* (London: Rivingtons, 1911), pages 253–323. As a biographer, I found that as soon as I rejected my previous ideas and accepted the early date, Paul's life fell into shape.

12. The words *of Jesus*, missing from the *King James Version*, were in the Western Text (then known as *Codex Bezae*) and are found in the best of the ancient manuscripts discovered since 1611. See, for example, the *Revised Standard Version* and the *New English Bible*.

13. Richard Wurmbrand, *In God's Underground*, ed. Charles Foley (London: W.H. Allen, and Co., Ltd., 1968), 194–95. (Published in the United States as *Christ in the Communist Prisons*, 1968.)

14. The Western Text says the jailer first secured the prisoners before leading Paul and Silas out. Luke was tantalizingly silent about their subsequent fate.

15. First Thessalonians 5:2 following Luke 12:39–40; 1 Thessalonians 4:15–16 following Luke 21:27. Also, compare 1 Thessalonians 5:3, 6–7 with Luke 21:34.

16. Many scholars, ancient and modern, have held that they went by land. Luke's meaning is not clear.

17. The question whether Paul addressed the Areopagites on this little hill (the Areopagus itself), where they met for formal trials, or in the Royal Portico of the marketplace below, where they conducted day-by-day business, has been much discussed. Most modern scholars tend to favor the marketplace. My choosing the hill may be a case of a biographer's dramatic sense getting the better of his scholarship.

The *Authorized Version* translation of Areopagus (Ares' Hill) into "Mars' Hill" is another instance of converting Greek into Latin gods, Ares being the god of war.

18. The sermon in the synagogue is taken from Romans 10:5–15. Paul's diction in chapters 9 and 10 of the Epistle to the Romans, which he composed in Corinth a few years later, was held by Professor C. H. Dodd to be very similar to his style of synagogue preaching.

19. I find myself convinced by A. N. Sherwin-White, in his *Roman Society and Roman Law in the New Testament* (Grand Rapids, MI: Baker, 1963), that Sosthenes suffered as a Christian from Jews and not as an (unconverted) Jew from a Greek rabble. (The word *Greeks* in the *Authorized Version* is not in the best manuscripts.)

If the Greeks had assaulted someone in full sight of Gallio, he would have been bound to punish a breach of the peace. If the Jews exercised their domestic jurisdiction by punishing one of their number, the only irregularity was that they punished in public instead of private. However, this theory (which was ridiculed by Ramsay) does not entirely fit the implication of Luke's account, in which he seemed to invite a reader's reaction of "Serves Sosthenes right for trying to ruin Paul."

20. The classic statement of the Ephesus theory is *St. Paul's Ephesians Ministry* (1929) by Professor G. S. Duncan of St. Andrews. However, he overstated his case and tried to squeeze *all* the prison epistles, including sections of the pastorals, into the Ephesus years.

21. Or they may have been administrators of the temple dedicated to the honor of the emperor (not the Temple of Artemis). The evidence is inconclusive.

22. Modeled closely on Tyndale's work of the 1550s. For *agapē*, the *King James Version* changed Tyndale's *love* to *charity*, a word of wider meaning then, describing any loving action that did not depend on the love being returned, not only "alms" or "charity" in the modern sense.

23. Jewish days were reckoned from 6:00 p.m. to 6:00 p.m. The first day of the week thus began on Saturday evening.

24. The modern traveler approaching ruined Assos by Paul's route sees the remains of a Byzantine fortress on the rock.

25. Sir William Ramsay was able to date the voyage very exactly in *St. Paul the Traveller*.

26. The final paragraph is from the *New English Bible*. For the rest of the speech, I worked directly from the Greek, as no version quite conveys the unpolished spontaneity of Paul's words.

27. Adramyttium itself, now Edremit in Turkey, sticks in my memory because as we drove through, a pony carrying a small boy shied at some cattle and bolted. The boy's fur cap flew off. I picked it up, and we drove slowly after them. The pony collided with a cow, the boy was thrown and winded, but made me a charming if painful bow when I restored his cap.

28. See *The Voyage and Shipwreck of St. Paul* by James Smith of Jordanhill, 1848 (4th edition, with revisions, 1880).

29. But the evidence is scanty, and many scholars hold that Paul was convicted and executed in AD 62. The balance of probability, however, leans toward acquittal.